LEAD
TOEFL iBT
LISTENING

LEAD
TOEFL iBT
LISTENING

초판1쇄   2021년 4월 01일

지 은 이   DAVID CHIN
번   역   김슬기 박현욱 김은영
디 자 인   최주호(PETER CHOI)
펴 낸 이   박영은
펴 낸 곳   리드에듀북스
등록번호   395-91-01356
전   화   070-4512-5236
팩   스   0504-489-4844
이 메 일   leadedubooks@naver.com
홈페이지   https://leadedubooks.modoo.at
저작권자 DAVID CHIN, 리드에듀북스

Photo Credit ⓒShutterstock.com

ISBN   979-11-973714-2-4 13740

이 책의 저작권은 저자와 출판사에 있습니다.
저작권자와 출판사의 허락없이 책의 일부 또는 전재 및 복제, 발췌하는 것을 금합니다.

낙장 및 파본은 구매처에서 교환해 드립니다.

값 25,900 원

PREFACE

　토플을 공부하는 학생들의 대부분은 교재의 선택권이 한정되어 있습니다. 점수 향상을 위해서는 다양한 지문을 읽고 수많은 문제를 풀어보아야 하지만, 선택권이 많지 않은 학생들은 불가피하게 비슷한 지문과 문제를 반복해서 풀 수밖에 없는 상황에 놓여 있습니다. 리드 토플은 이러한 상황이 개선되기를 바라는 학생들의 요구를 반영하여 만들어진 책입니다.

　저자인 저는 미국에서 초등, 중등, 고등 교육부터 대학 교육까지 받은 네이티브로서 영어-한국어 이중 언어 구사자입니다. 한국으로 귀국한 뒤 영어교육의 메카인 목동과 대치동에서 토플만을 전문적으로 강의하면서 다양한 강의 자료와 교수법을 직접 연구하고 개발하였으며 수업에 실제로 적용하였습니다. 그러한 과정에서 시중에는 존재하지 않는 새로운 교재 출간의 필요성을 느끼고 리드토플을 집필하였습니다.

　이 책은 기초를 다질 수 있는 연습 문제를 비롯하여, 높은 난이도의 실전 문제까지 세심한 주의를 기울여 설계된 문제들이 실려있습니다. 끊임없는 교재 개발과 연구를 바탕으로 한, 제가 가진 토플에 관한 모든 지식과 노하우가 담긴 책입니다.

　토플을 처음 접하는 학생, 혹은 영어 실력이 중급 수준인 학생들은 실전 문제집을 공부하는 것을 부담스럽게 느끼고 어려워합니다. 문제를 해결하는 스킬을 세심하게 알려주는 본 교재의 컨텐츠 디자인을 따라가면서 다양한 연습문제와 실전문제를 차근차근 풀어 나아간다면 자연스럽게 점수가 향상되는 경험을 하게 될 것입니다.

　앞으로도 풍성한 구성과 질 좋은 컨텐츠를 담아 지속적으로 출간될 리드 토플 교재가 여러분들의 토플 실력 향상에 커다란 밑거름이 되기를 소망합니다.

DAVID CHIN

How to Use This Book

This book has been made to help new test takers understand the different question types first, then apply the step-by-step methods to solve the practice questions in each chapter. After understanding and practicing the six different question types, test takers will then solve actual tests to further improve their skills and scores.

The listening section of the TOEFL test requires excellent notetaking. Test takers should practice taking perfect notes by listening to the same conversation or lecture at least two or three times and filling in any details they might have missed in the first listening. If the speed of the conversation or lecture is too fast, test takers can always practice taking notes by decreasing the speed of the listening in their media player. Practice makes perfect.

Although some will argue that background knowledge is important when solving the TOEFL listening, they are mistaken in believing that they can apply that knowledge in solving the questions. In reality, background knowledge tends to hurt scores because students will answer the questions without considering the listening. REMEMBER, test takers are to answer the questions based on what they heard from the conversation or lecture. The only time background knowledge can be useful is when test takers can listen to the lecture with interest, since they already know the subject.

Like any standardized test, it is best to achieve a top score by studying for the test within a minimal amount of time. Otherwise, the test taker will tire themselves out and eventually give up on their prospective score.
The following chart is a tentative study plan for those who wish to achieve a high score on the TOEFL listening section.

LEAD TOEFL series all follow a 3 week study plan, so it is recommended that test takers use LEAD TOEFL Reading, Speaking, and Writing simultaneously while studying for the Listening section.
The schedule has been balanced with the intention that test takers study for all four sections on a daily basis.

3 Week Study Plan

	Day 1	Day 2	Day 3	Day 4	Day 5
Week 1	Chapter 1 + Practice perfect notes	Chapter 2 + Practice perfect notes	Chapter 3 + Practice perfect notes	Chapter 4 + Practice perfect notes	Chapter 5 + Practice perfect notes
	Day 6	**Day 7**	**Day 8**	**Day 9**	**Day 10**
Week 2	Chapter 6 + Practice perfect notes	AT1 – Part 1 + Practice perfect notes	AT1 – Part 2 + Practice perfect notes	AT2 – Part 1 + Practice perfect notes	AT2 – Part 2 + Practice perfect notes
	Day 11	**Day 12**	**Day 13**	**Day 14**	**Day 15**
Week 3	AT3 – Part 1 + Practice perfect notes	AT3 – Part 2 + Practice perfect notes	AT4 – Part 1 + Practice perfect notes	AT4 – Part 2 + Practice perfect notes	AT5 + Practice perfect notes
Official TOEFL Test					

During the perfect notes practice, test takers are recommended to use different colored pens to take notes, so that they can visually see how much detail they are missing. The first listening can be done in black ink, and the second listening can be written in red. Hopefully there won't be too much red ink on the notes.

Remember that most listeners will understand the main idea of the conversation or lecture. It's the detail questions that test takers will get wrong because they failed to write down detailed notes. By practicing perfect notes, test takers will be able to answer all of the questions on the listening section.

About the TOEFL iBT

TOEFL (Test of English as a Foreign Language) iBT (Internet-Based Test) is an internet exam for students who speak English as a second language. The test is designed to assess a student's reading, listening, speaking, and writing abilities and how well they understand each section. Thus, the TOEFL test is divided into four sections: Reading, Listening, Speaking, and Writing.

Subject	Content	Time	Score
Reading	3~4 reading passages 10 questions per passage	54~72 minutes	0~30
Listening	Conversation: 2~3 with 5 questions per conversation Lecture: 3~4 with 6 questions per lecture	41~57 minutes	0~30
Break time: 10 minutes			
Speaking	1 independent 3 integrated	17 minutes	0~30
Writing	1 integrated 1 independent	50 minutes	0~30
		3 hours~3 hours 30 minutes	0~120

About the TOEFL Listening Section

Format:

The listening section of the TOEFL test normally contains two parts. If you happen to stumble upon the listening dummy, you will be given three parts. Each part can have either one conversation and one lecture or one conversation and two lectures. In total, the two part listening section will contain two conversations and three lectures, while the three part listening section will have three conversations and four lectures.

Times:

The time it takes to solve the listening section will range between 41-57 minutes. The length of each conversation is roughly 3 minutes, while the length of each lecture can be around 6 minutes.

Questions:

Each conversation will have five questions, while the lecture will contain six questions.

Although some conversations will be based on everyday topics that occur in the university, others will revolve around an academic discussion, almost similar to that of a lecture. Also, the lecture based questions tend to be more detailed than before.

The conversation or lecture will only be played once, so it is highly advised that test takers take diligent notes and refer to them when answering questions.

Table of Contents

Chapter 1 – Main idea question   11

Chapter 2 – Supporting details question   21

Chapter 3 – Connecting contents question   31

Chapter 4 – Function question   41

Chapter 5 – Attitude question   51

Chapter 6 – Inference question   61

Actual Test 1   71

Actual Test 2   93

Actual Test 3   115

Actual Test 4   137

Actual Test 5   159

Answers and Script

CHAPTER
01

Main Idea

Main Idea

This is almost always the first question that will be asked after listening to a conversation or a lecture. The main idea of the conversation or lecture will always be stated in the first part of the listening. In the conversation, the purpose of the student's visit or why the professor called the student will be announced in the first 30 seconds into the conversation. In the lecture, the main idea of the lesson will be stated in the first 60 seconds into the lecture.

How to identify main idea questions:

What is the main topic of the lecture / conversation?

What does the professor / speaker mainly discuss about?

What is the main idea of the discussion / talk?

What is the talk / lecture about?

Why does the student go to see the professor?

Why did the professor call the student?

What problem does the man/woman have?

How to solve step-by-step:

1) Since the main idea is always stated in the beginning of the conversation or lecture, focus your attention in the first 30 to 60 seconds of the listening.

2) If you happen to miss the first part of the lecture or conversation, look at your notes and determine what the main idea is by associating the explanations and examples.

3) Remember, the main idea is something that is general. The main idea should not be something specific.

4) The main idea should also contain the keyword that was repeated throughout the conversation or lecture.

Additional note:

Main idea signal phrases:

The flow of a conversation will look like this:

> Simple introduction or greetings → A question or a problem given by the student or professor → A response or solution given by the student or professor

A question can be asked in the following ways:
How can I help?
What can I do for you (name)?
What do you need?
Did you want to talk about something?

A problem can be stated in the following ways:
The problem is…
I came to talk about…
I wanted to ask you about…
I did not understand…

The flow of a lecture will look like this:

> Quick review of the lesson discussed in the previous class → Introduction of the day's topic → Specific examples and details

The main idea of the lecture can be introduced in the following ways:
Today, let's talk about…
Right now, I'm going to discuss…
We'll continue from what we talked about in the last class…

If you hear any of the phrases in the conversation or lecture, the main idea is about to come out, so pay careful attention!

Practice A:

Listen to part of a conversation between a student and a professor.

(CH1-1.mp3)

Why did the student visit the professor?

    A) To confirm how long the steam engine has been used for.

    B) To talk about an individual for his research paper.

    C) To request assistance in choosing a topic for his research paper.

    D) To request an extension for his research paper.

> M: Good morning Mrs. Wood.
>
> W: Good morning David. What brings you to my office?
>
> M: Well, I was researching about mass transit, you know, for my research paper in your class. I know that Boston had the first subway system and New York soon followed after. But… I read an even earlier attempt by Alfred Beech? My research is a bit scattered… can we talk about it? It will help my research.
>
> W: Ah, Alfred Beech. He was actually an inventor as well as a publisher for a tech magazine. He actually saw subways as a solution to urban congestion. But at the time, there was no way to put a train underneath the ground.
>
> M: But steam engines have been used for years, haven't they?

Answer: B. The first signal phrase was *"…what brings you to my office?"* This should alert the test taker that the student is about to give his reason for his visit. The next signal phrase was *"…can we talk about it?"* This phrase was followed after the student states that his research on Alfred Beech is scattered. So the student came to talk about an individual, named Alfred Beech, with his professor.

A is not the answer because there was no signal phrase that mentions that this is the main idea. Also, discussing about the steam engine seems like a minor detail, compared to the bigger topic of Alfred Beech. C is not the answer because the student already chose a topic for his research paper, mass transit. D is not the answer since extending his research paper was not even discussed.

Practice B:

Listen to part of a lecture in a literature class.

(CH1-2.mp3)

What is the main topic of the lecture?

    A) How America changed socially in the 1830's.

    B) The differences between American and European literature.

    C) Description of some prominent romantic authors.

    D) How nature influenced American romantic authors.

> Good morning everyone! Let's get right down to business. On our last class we discussed about an important literary movement called American Romanticism. For the next few weeks, we will be focusing our attention on specific authors of that movement, the romantic authors. However, before we start discussing about these authors, I would like to talk about their views on nature and how it influenced their writings.
>
> So let's begin. American Romanticism started in the late 1830's. There were several social changes that were occurring at that time. First, the country was expanding at a fast rate because Americans were moving towards the West. Second, factories were appearing at an alarming rate in the Northeast. And finally, towns were changed into urban cities.

Answer: D. The signal phrase was *"...before we start discussing about these authors, I would like to talk about their views on nature and how it influenced their writings."* This should alert the test taker that the professor is about to give the main idea of the lecture, which is NOT a discussion about romantic authors, but how nature influenced their writings.

A is not the answer because although the professor does talk about some social changes that were occurring in America, he pointed out that he would like to talk about nature and its influence in the authors. B is not the answer because the lecture did not even mention European literature. C is not the answer because although the professor mentions he will be discussing about the romantic authors in the following weeks, he mentions that he will first discuss what influenced them.

Vocabulary:

announce	v.	make a public and typically formal declaration about a fact, occurrence, or intention.	*report, declare*
identify	v.	establish or indicate who or what (someone or something) is.	*recognize, spot, pinpoint*
focus	n.	the center of interest or activity.	*center, focal point*
associating	v.	connect (someone or something) with something else in one's mind.	*link, connect, couple*
confirm	v.	establish the truth or correctness of (something previously believed, suspected, or feared to be the case).	*affirm, verify, corroborate*
assistance	n.	the action of helping someone with a job or task.	*help, aid, support*
extension	n.	a part that is added to something to enlarge or prolong it; a continuation.	*addition, augmentation*
transit	n.	the carrying of people, goods, or materials from one place to another.	*transport, movement*
attempt	v.	make an effort to achieve or complete (something, typically a difficult task or action).	*strive, venture, endeavor*
scattered	adj.	occurring or found at intervals or various locations rather than all together.	
congestion	n.	the state of being congested.	*crowding, blockage, stoppage*

alert	adj.	quick to notice any unusual and potentially dangerous or difficult circumstances; vigilant.	*aware, watchful, attentive*
prominent	adj.	important; famous.	*important, well known, distinguished*
romantic	adj.	of, characterized by, or suggestive of an idealized view of reality.	*lovely, beautiful, charming*
social	adj.	relating to society or its organization.	*community, group*
alarming	adj.	worrying or disturbing.	
urban	adj.	in, relating to, or characteristic of a town or city.	*town, city*

Additional Vocabulary:

```
_____
_____
_____
_____
_____
_____
_____
_____
_____
```

CHAPTER 02

Supporting Details

Supporting Details

Supporting detail questions are very specific. If you wrote down the information in your notes or happen to remember it, then you will get the point. This question type appears the most in any listening, usually 2~3 questions for each conversation or lecture. Sometimes, test takers are asked to choose TWO answers, so make sure to read the answer choices carefully before submitting the answers.

In the case of a conversation, the supporting detail questions revolve around the details in the solutions discussed between the student and the professor or employee. In the case of a lecture, the supporting detail questions are about the main idea in the form of an example or a description.

Point to remember: answers must be chosen based on the content from the conversation or lecture. You are NOT to use your own knowledge learned from schools or academies to solve these questions.

How to identify supporting details questions:

What does the professor / school employee offer to do…?

What are the characteristics of…?

According to the lecturer, what is…?

What does the speaker say about…?

How to solve step-by-step:

1) Remember that the supporting details are always about the main idea.
2) Take quick and detailed notes, especially when it is giving a solution or describing something.
3) The answer choices are always paraphrased, so look for synonyms and similar descriptions that were mentioned from the conversation or lecture.
4) Remember to choose the answer based on what came out in the conversation or lecture! Do not use your own background information to solve the problem.

Additional note:

The flow of a conversation will look like this:

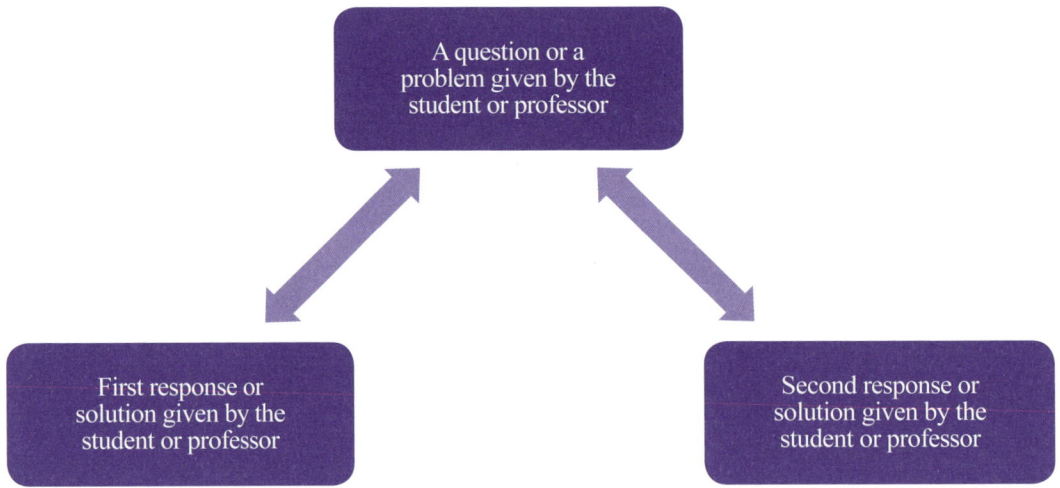

Focus your notes on the response or solution. The supporting detail question will ask about a small detail from the response or solution.

The supporting detail question may not necessarily focus on the response or solution, so be sure to take continuous notes until the conversation is finished.

The flow of a lecture will look like this:

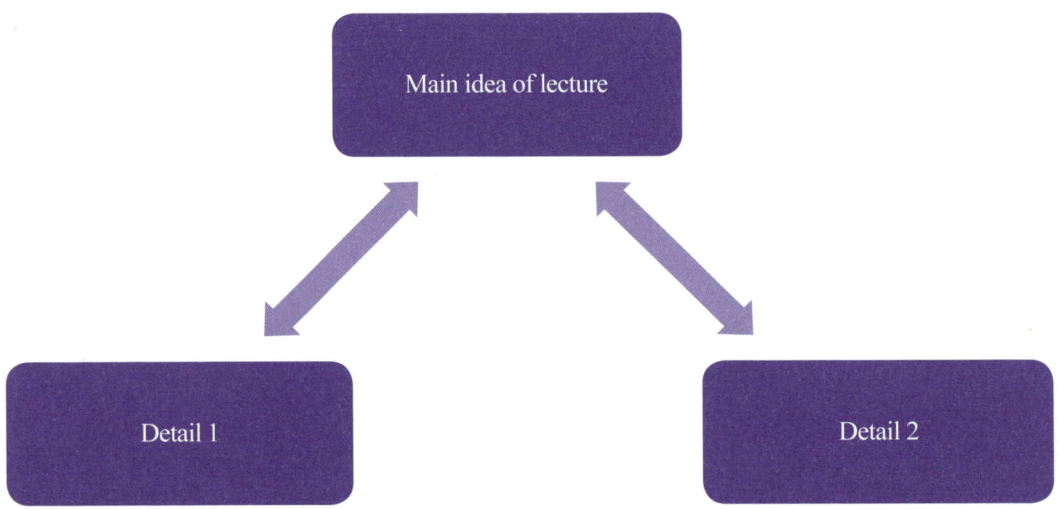

The majority of your notes will be centered on the details of the lecture. Pay careful attention to transition words like "In fact" and "However".

Practice A:

Listen to part of a conversation between a student and a professor.

(CH2-1.mp3)

What was an innovative method Beech used to promote underground tunnels?

    A) He improved upon a device which allowed him to dig underground.

    B) He improved the steam engine to create minimal soot.

    C) He made a shield to protect workers from collapsing rocks.

    D) He made a below-ground tube to move passengers.

> W: Although steam engines had been in use for many years, it created too much soot for underground tunnels. Also, constant ventilation proved that the steam engine was not a practical choice. And you have to remember, in 1866, gasoline and electric motors were not yet available, so a novel method had to be applied for a transport to move in an underground tunnel. Alfred Beech came up with some innovative methods to overcome this situation. First, he built an above-ground tube which transported passengers from one end of a building to the other. He also designed a drill, strong enough to tunnel underground. In order to compensate for the structural support within the tunnel, Beech made a drill inside a shield. So how it worked was a drill would move forward, while the workers stayed inside the shield, and provided structural support for the tunnel by laying bricks.

Answer: A. This part of the discussion focuses on a problem underground tunnels posed and how Alfred Beech was able to overcome them. So, your notetaking should have been focusing on the problem and the solutions, or the innovations that Beech provided. It says in the discussion, *"He also designed a drill, strong enough to tunnel underground."* Answer choice A states *"He improved upon a device…"* The device is referring to the drill.

B is not the answer because the steam engine made too much soot and it does not mention that he improved the engine. C is not the answer because although a shield was mentioned, its purpose was to provide structural support within the tunnel, not protect the workers. D is not the answer because the tube was above-ground, not below-ground.

Practice B:

Listen to part of a lecture in a literature class.

(CH2-2.mp3)

How did America's wilderness affect romantic authors?

    A) They came to be more dependent on European styles of writing.

    B) Their poems became more rigid and relied on set traditional forms.

    C) Their writings became more natural.

    D) They gave up writing and became lumberjacks.

> What set America apart from Europe was America's endless terrain of wild land, untouched by mankind and urbanization. In Europe, the land had been altered by human civilization for more than a thousand years. So because America had its land, which seemed limitless, it singled out America as a nation. And this actually helped the romantics in forming their ideals. Romantic authors became more independent. They had their own stories to tell and wanted to show America to the rest of the world. These authors especially focused on the natural world America had to offer. And the influence that America's wilderness had on these authors were shown in their writings. Some of the romantic poets departed from the traditional European forms, with its fixed length and rhyme patterns. They believed that their poems should be more organic, and so their writings changed and became more life-like.

Answer: C. It says in the lecture, *"They believed that their poems should be more organic, so their writings changed and became more life-like."* The keywords here are organic and life-like, and natural happens to be a synonym to these words.

A is not the answer because it says that romantic authors *"...became more independent."* It also states that some of the romantic poets *"...departed from the traditional European forms..."* B is not the answer because romantic authors departed from traditional forms. D is not the answer because it does not mention that romantic authors gave up writing and lumberjacks were not even mentioned.

Vocabulary:

submit	v.	present (a proposal, application, or other document) to a person or body for consideration or judgment.	*present, offer*
revolve	v.	move in a circle on a central axis.	*rotate, spin, whirl*
promote	v.	further the progress of (something, especially a cause, venture, or aim); support or actively encourage.	*encourage, assist, aid*
innovative	adj.	(of a product, idea, etc.) featuring new methods; advanced and original.	*new, novel, original*
minimal	adj.	of a minimum amount, quantity, or degree; negligible.	*minimum, least, slightest*
soot	n.	a black powdery or flaky substance consisting largely of amorphous carbon, produced by the incomplete burning of organic matter.	
shield	v.	protect (someone or something) from a danger, risk, or unpleasant experience.	*protect, cover*
collapse	v.	(of a structure) fall down or in; give way.	*cave in, fall down*
ventilation	n.	the provision of fresh air to a room, building, etc.	
practical	adj.	of or concerned with the actual doing or use of something rather than with theory and ideas.	*pragmatic, applied, real*
novel	adj.	new or unusual in an interesting way.	*new, original*

overcome	v.	succeed in dealing with (a problem or difficulty).	*prevail over*
compensate	v.	give (someone) something, typically money, in recognition of loss, suffering, or injury incurred; recompense.	*repay, reimburse*
rigid	adj.	unable to bend or be forced out of shape; not flexible.	*stiff, hard, firm*
traditional	adj.	existing in or as part of a tradition; long-established.	*conventional, established*
lumberjack	n.	a person who fells trees, cuts them into logs, or transports them to a sawmill.	
single out	v.	to treat or to speak about (someone or something in a group) in a way that is different from the way one treats or speaks about others	
ideal	adj.	satisfying one's conception of what is perfect; most suitable.	*perfect, complete*
depart	v.	leave, especially in order to start a journey.	*leave, go*
organic	adj.	relating to or derived from living matter.	*natural, living*

CHAPTER 03

Connecting Contents

Connecting Contents

Connecting contents questions require test takers to look at the overall organization of the conversation or lecture. The question will ask how the lecture is organized or what the student or professor meant when they said a particular word or phrase.

The organization of the lecture might follow a list of ideas, give a chronological succession of events, or provide several examples to a topic. In the conversation, you should be able to guess why the student or the professor said a particular word or phrase based on what was said before. Sometimes in the lecture, the question might ask why the professor mentioned a particular keyword, which would require you to look at your notes and see what the professor said before and after the keyword.

Usually there is only one connecting contents question per conversation or lecture. Sometimes, there may be none.

How to identify connecting contents questions:

Why does the professor mention…?

How is the lecture/discussion organized?

How to solve step-by-step:

1) Instead of focusing on small details, you should be focusing on the overall content.
2) Look at your notes and see how the ideas are connected. Do they follow a chronological order or is it a list of examples?
3) If something is mentioned in the listening which seems completely irrelevant to the main topic, you have to understand the connection.

Additional note:

In a connecting contents question, conversations tend to be easier to solve because the student or the professor approaches the other with a specific request or a problem. As long as you understand the situation, it should not be difficult to connect the dots in the dialogue.

Scenarios:

Student goes to see the professor

- Student did not understand the lecture or part of a lecture.
- Student did not understand the assignment or project assigned.
- Student is requesting for something from the professor.

Professor calls the student

- Professor is concerned with the student's grade.
- Professor is asking for an update on the student's assignment.
- Professor wants to discuss the student's major or career path.

Student goes to see a university employee

- Student goes to see the dormitory official, university librarian, or administration employee to discuss a matter.

Lectures tend to focus on why the professor mentioned the specific keyword or phrase. In this case, do not focus on the details of the keyword or phrase, but focus on what was said before and after.

Your notetaking should be comprehensive as you try to understand and connect the content with the overall topic.

Practice A:

Listen to part of a conversation between a student and a professor.

(CH3-1.mp3)

Why does the professor mention William Tweed?

    A) To mention that he was the head politician in New York City.

    B) To show an obstacle Beech had to confront.

    C) To compare him with Beech in terms of influence.

    D) To describe how he came to power.

> W: At the time, New York City was ruled by the democratic authoritarian, William Tweed. He was an immoral politician and held onto power by giving favors to his friends and allies. One of his many illegal activities involved collecting a tribute from existing railroads. So a privately funded subway, like something Beech was about to build, would undermine his profits.
>
> M: I remember reading about him in the books. So how did Beech work around him?
>
> W: Well Beech was very sneaky. He sent a proposal for a mail transport system, while hiding a building permit amongst the paperwork. This allowed him to build his subway secretly without Tweed knowing what was going on.
>
> M: But that's what confuses me. I mean, New York City is a metropolitan city. People are constantly going around the city. How was he able to keep it a secret?
>
> W: No one knows for sure. Maybe Beech bribed some of the workers. Nevertheless, he was able to complete his project without detection in three months.

Answer: B. In the discussion, it says that William Tweed was ruling New York City and he held power by giving favors. It also mentions that a private subway would cut his profits. So here, the professor is talking about an obstacle to building the subway. The student questions how Beech was able to work around him, and the professor goes on to explain how Beech cleverly hid a building permit amongst the paperwork for a proposal. So when we connect the content, Tweed was someone Beech had to go around in order to build his subway.

A is not the answer because although Tweed was the head politician in New York City, it is not the reason why the professor mentions him. C is not the answer because Tweed and Beech are not being compared in terms of influence. D is not the answer because although it does mention that he stayed in power because of giving favors to his friends, it is not why the professor decides to talk about him.

Practice B:

Listen to part of a lecture in a literature class.

(CH3-2.mp3)

Why does the professor mention metaphor?

    A) To describe the definition of something that is misunderstood.

    B) To emphasize that romantic authors used it a lot in their writings.

    C) To compare it with another technique romantic authors used.

    D) To help explain the relationship between nature and the romantic writers.

> Professor: Romantic writers saw nature as a great instructor. For these writers, nature was the origin of specific value, like beauty, independence, and truth. Let me see if I can make this more clear… Can anyone remember what a metaphor is?
>
> Student: Isn't a metaphor a technique where two different things are compared without using the words "like" or "as"?
>
> Professor: So close. Metaphor is an implied comparison between two different things. Take the popular phrase, "All the world's a stage." Here, the world is being compared to a theatrical stage. Basically, romantic writers saw nature as a metaphor for human experience. In other words, in order to understand how one should live, a person had to understand nature first.

Answer: D. The professor starts by saying that *"…nature was the origin of specific value…"* for romantic authors. Then he tries to make it easier to understand and mentions "metaphor". So if we connect the content, metaphor is used to help explain what nature was for these romantic writers.

A is not the answer because although the professor corrects the student's definition of metaphor, it is not the reason why the professor said it in the first place. B is not the answer because it does not mention that romantic writers used metaphors in their writings. C is not the answer because metaphor is not being compared with another technique.

Vocabulary:

chronological	adj.	(of a record of events) starting with the earliest and following the order in which they occurred.	*consecutive, ordered*
succession	n.	a number of people or things sharing a specified characteristic and following one after the other.	*sequence, series, chain*
comprehensive	adj.	complete; including all or nearly all elements or aspects of something.	*inclusive, complete, full*
obstacle	n.	a thing that blocks one's way or prevents or hinders progress.	*barrier, hurdle, bar*
confront	v.	meet (someone) face to face with hostile or argumentative intent.	*challenge, oppose, resist*
authoritarian	adj.	favoring or enforcing strict obedience to authority, especially that of the government, at the expense of personal freedom.	*autocratic, dictatorial*
immoral	adj.	not conforming to accepted standards of morality.	*unethical, wrongful, wicked*
favor	n.	approval, support, or liking for someone or something.	*approval, goodwill*
allies	n.	a person or organization that cooperates with or helps another in a particular activity.	*associate, partner, supporter*

illegal	adj.	contrary to or forbidden by law, especially criminal law.	*illicit, unlawful*
tribute	n.	an act, statement, or gift that is intended to show gratitude, respect, or admiration.	*praise, acclaim*
fund	v.	provide with money for a particular purpose.	*finance, sponsor*
sneaky	adj.	furtive; sly.	*clever, devious*
metropolitan	adj.	relating to or denoting a metropolis, often inclusive of its surrounding areas.	
bribe	v.	persuade (someone) to act in one's favor, typically illegally or dishonestly, by a gift of money or other inducement.	*buy off, pay off*
detection	n.	the action or process of identifying the presence of something concealed.	*observation, noting, spotting*
clever	adj.	quick to understand, learn, and devise or apply ideas; intelligent.	*bright, smart, talented*
origin	n.	the point or place where something begins, arises, or is derived.	*start, genesis*

CHAPTER 04

Function

Function

A function question verifies whether you understood what the speaker is trying to say. Function questions will appear once in each conversation or lecture and is likely to replay a small part of the listening to help answer the question.

In regards to a conversation, a function question will ask what the purpose of the comment is, or if there is a hidden meaning. If the question seems to ask for an alternative meaning, it is important to understand what was said before and after.

In regards to a lecture, a student and a professor will exchange comments back and forth. In the midst of the discussion, the professor will try to grab the students' attention or recall what he or she said. This is when a function question is likely to appear.

How to identify function questions:

Why does the student / professor say this?

What does the speaker mean by saying this?

What does the professor mean by this?

How to solve step-by-step:

1) Colloquial expressions will be used, so become familiar with them.

   Stop pulling my leg → Stop lying to me

   He is a stuck up → He is conceited

   I am getting heavy eyed → I am getting sleepy

2) Instead of listening to the part that is replayed, look at your notes and see what was mentioned before and after. Then try to understand the phrase in the context.

3) It is important to understand the tone, volume, and speed the phrase was said. The factors listed describe the function of the phrase.

Additional note:

In the conversation or lecture, a function question will involve a phrase that was said by the speaker or the professor. In order to understand the function of the phrase, look at how the phrase was introduced. Usually, the expression's function lies in the tone of the speaker or what was said before and after the expression.

When notetaking, instead of focusing on the small details, focus on the big details and the flow of the conversation or lecture. When you hear a change in tone, or a colloquial expression being used, pay careful attention and take good notes.

A speaker's tone can tell a great deal on the function of the expression. Tone can determine if the speaker is complaining about a subject or is satisfied with the matter. It can also tell if the speaker is pessimistic or optimistic.

Whenever the question replays a specific part of the conversation or lecture, think of it as a second chance to write your notes. Quickly find the part where the replay is and fill in additional details to make your notes more complete. When the question replays the smaller part of the replay, really focus on that part and see how it relates to what was said before and after.

Practice A:

Listen to part of a conversation between a student and a professor.

(CH4-1.mp3)

Listen to part of the conversation. Then answer the question.

Why does the professor say this?

A) Beech's idea would have become the standard if it had occurred in better timing.

B) Beech's idea would have never succeeded no matter when it occurred.

C) Timing is not as important as the idea itself.

D) Timing is a factor one should consider when inventing something.

> W: Although people were fascinated by Beech's novel transport, politicians were not on his side. Even though Beech received the approval for an entire subway line from the state legislature, it was vetoed by the governor, who happened to be pressured by the infamous Tweed. For two long years, Beech was unable to extend his underground subway. Eventually, a new governor came to power and approved Beech's innovation.
>
> M: *What confuses me is, how Beech's idea never became the standard. Wasn't he the first person to actually realize an underground subway?*
>
> W: **Unfortunately, it was all bad timing.** After the new governor approved Beech's request, a stock market crash soon followed. Investors withdrew their support and public funding became unavailable. So there were no subways for the next 25 years. Sadly, Beech died during that time, so no one was there to push his idea. Also, gas and electric powered engines had improved in transportation.

Answer: A. The student comments, *"Wasn't he the first person to actually realize an underground subway?"* The professor responds by saying, ***"Unfortunately, it was all bad timing."*** So the function of the saying is to respond why Beech's idea never became the standard. It was due to the stock market that crashed right after and the improvement in gas and electric powered engines. So, Beech's idea would have become the standard had it occurred in better timing.

B is not the answer because it says that Beech's idea would have never succeeded. But "never" is such a strong word, so we cannot choose this. C is not the answer because the listening mentions that it was bad timing, in other words, timing was important for Beech's idea to become the standard. It is not comparing timing and idea. D is not the answer because the listening is discussing about why Beech's idea didn't become the standard. It is not talking about the factors that are needed in inventing something.

Practice B:

Listen to part of a lecture in a literature class.

(CH4-2.mp3)

Listen again to part of the lecture. Then answer the question.

What does the professor mean when he says this?

    A) The professor has had enough answering the student's questions.

    B) The professor wants the student to review the question first before asking.

    C) The professor wants to check if it is raining outside.

    D) The professor has another matter to attend and cannot answer the question.

Professor: Romantic authors were cynical of urban life. Its lifestyle offered chaos and materialism, as well as degrading human values. When the romantic authors turned to nature, they were not trying to escape from these negative aspects of urban life, but trying to learn from their experiences. They felt it necessary to absorb the values nature had to offer in order to preserve their own identities. And by spreading these values in their writings, they hoped to redeem the spirit of the nation that was falling into urban lifestyles.

Student: Ah, now I understand professor. Thanks for explaining that to me. I actually have another question that troubled me in class.

Professor: ***Ah… let's take a rain check on that.*** I have to go to a faculty meeting right now. How about seeing me after class next time?

Student: That sound's good. Thank you professor.

Answer: D. When the student states that she has another question to ask, the professor responds by saying a famous colloquial expression. *"Let's take a rain check on that"* means let's do that at a later time. The professor also asks the student to see him after class next time, which means he will answer her question then.

A is not the answer because the professor is not impatient with the student and is not refusing to answer any more of her questions. B is not the answer because nowhere in the listening does it hint that the student should be reviewing the question before asking. C is not the answer because it is not related to the discussion at all.

Vocabulary:

verify	v.	make sure or demonstrate that (something) is true, accurate, or justified.	
alternative	adj.	(of one or more things) available as another possibility.	*another, substitute*
pessimistic	adj.	tending to see the worst aspect of things or believe that the worst will happen.	*negative, cynical*
optimistic	adj.	hopeful and confident about the future.	*cheerful, positive*
veto	n.	a constitutional right to reject a decision or proposal made by a law-making body.	*rejection, denial*
infamous	adj.	well known for some bad quality or deed.	*notorious, disreputable*
realize	v.	cause (something desired or anticipated) to happen.	*fulfill, accomplish*
withdraw	v.	leave or cause to leave a place or situation.	*leave, evacuate*
cynical	adj.	believing that people are motivated by self-interest; distrustful of human sincerity or integrity.	*skeptical, doubtful*
chaos	n.	complete disorder and confusion.	*disorder, disarray*
materialism	n.	a tendency to consider material possessions and physical comfort as more important than spiritual values.	
degrade	v.	lower the quality of; cause to deteriorate.	*degenerate, corrupt*

preserve	v.	maintain (something) in its original or existing state.	*conserve, maintain*
redeem	v.	compensate for the faults or bad aspects of (something).	*save, justify*
faculty	n.	the teaching staff of a university or college, or of one of its departments or divisions, viewed as a body.	

Additional Vocabulary:

ns

CHAPTER
05

Attitude

Attitude

Attitude questions focus on your ability to understand the attitudes or opinions of the speakers. It may ask how the speaker feels about a particular subject, whether the speaker likes or dislikes something, or why the speaker is experiencing a specific emotion. It will also ask you to identify the speaker's opinion on various topics.

These questions appear at least once in both conversations and lectures.

How to identify attitude questions:

What is the professor's attitude toward…?

What is the professor's opinion of…?

How does the woman seem to feel about…?

How to solve step-by-step:

1) Carefully listen to the tone of the speaker. The tone can describe the person as optimistic or pessimistic.
2) When the professor mentions their personal opinion on a subject, pay close attention. Throughout the lecture, the professor will only state facts. But in the middle, the professor will mention their personal preferences. Learn to separate the facts and the opinions.
3) Learn to read between the lines. The literal meaning of the phrases may not be their actual meanings.
4) Focus on what was said before and after. Understand the context in order to understand the attitude.

Additional note:

In order to understand the attitude of the speaker, the best strategy is to understand the tone or the context of where it was said.

Instead of taking notes on the specific phrase, be sure to focus on what was said before and after. Sometimes, just focusing on the phrase may be ambiguous. You need to understand what was said before to understand the attitude of the phrase.

In the lecture, whenever the professor uses the phrase "In my opinion", "I think" or "Personally", the professor is about to give their opinion on the subject, so pay careful attention.

Listen to a change in tone of the speaker. The tone can describe if the speaker is negative, positive, sarcastic, angry, and more.

Example: Positive and cheerful
    Professor: We are going to have a pop quiz today!
    Student: That's great! (excited and happy)

Example: Negative and sarcastic
    Professor: We are going to have a pop quiz today!
    Student: That's great….. (disappointed and sad)

Practice A:

Listen to part of a conversation between a student and a residential advisor

(CH5-1.mp3)

What is the student's attitude towards her math exam?

A) The student is not confident she did well on it.

B) The student is sure she aced the exam.

C) The student does not seem to care for the exam.

D) The student did not even know she had an exam.

RA: Hey Rebecca! How did you do on your math exam today? You were worried about it yesterday, but I hope you did ok.

Student: Oh that? Haha… well I did write down the answers to all the questions. But did I get them correct? Hahaha….

RA: I'm sure you did fine. You did study for it diligently for the past several days.

Student: Thanks. Hopefully I get some good news. I'm actually here to see you on a different matter. Do you have some time?

RA: Of course. How can I help you?

Answer: A. When the RA asks the student how she did, the student responds by saying, *"Oh that? Haha... well I did write down the answer to all the questions. But did I get them correct? Hahaha...."* The tone shows that she is not confident with her score. She did manage to write down all the answers, but she is not sure if she got them all correct. Her laughter is also nervous and trails off.

B is not the answer because her tone does not show that sort of confidence. C is not the answer because the student seems to care since she did study for the exam for the past several days. D is not the answer since she studied for the exam.

Practice B

Listen to part of a lecture in a health class

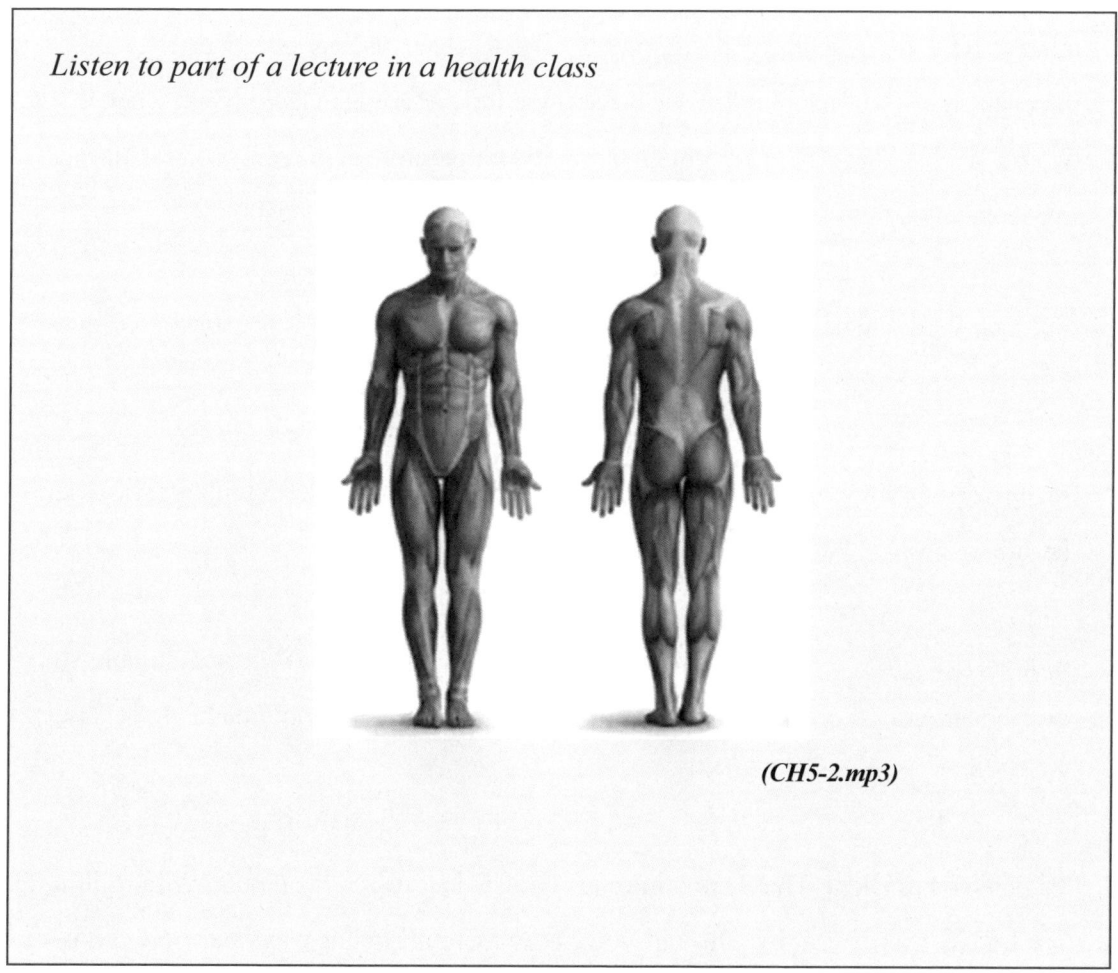

(CH5-2.mp3)

What is the professor's attitude toward the human body?

    A) The professor thinks it's overly complex.

    B) The professor thinks it has too many limitations.

    C) The professor thinks it's a wonder how it works.

    D) The professor thinks it is still evolving.

Professor: It is important to understand how our body maintains itself physically in a variety of unhealthy environments. Today, let's discuss our body's cooling mechanisms. The first thing I'm sure everyone is aware of is that we sweat when it's warm. We sweat in order to maintain our body temperature at the right point. But can someone explain to me how sweating works to accomplish that task?

Student: Well… when the sweat evaporates from our skin, it cools the surface, which regulates our body temperature.

Professor: Very good. And can you think of a situation when sweat will not cool the body?

Student: Hmm… if the humidity is too high, then our sweat will not be able to evaporate. Also, if our body is dehydrated, then our body will not be able to release sweat.

Professor: Excellent. There are numerous cases when the environment will prohibit our bodies from sweating. But did you know there are other ways our body cools itself? Let me tell you, it's just fascinating how our body works.

Answer: C. After the student responds to situations when the human body will not sweat, the professor praises the student and introduces other ways the human body cools itself. But before he goes on, he comments *"it's just fascinating how our body works."* This is not factual, but an opinion given by the professor regarding how the human body works.

A, B, and D are not the answers because the professor nor the student mentions anything about the complexity of the human body, limitations the human body has, nor the evolution the human body is going through.

Vocabulary:

literal	adj.	taking words in their usual or most basic sense without metaphor or allegory.	*bare, simple, straightforward*
ambiguous	adj.	unclear or inexact because a choice between alternatives has not been made.	*ambivalent, arguable*
sarcastic	adj.	marked by or given to using irony in order to mock or convey contempt.	*sardonic, satirical*
aced	v.	get an A or its equivalent in (a test or exam).	
diligent	adj.	having or showing care and conscientiousness in one's work or duties.	*industrious, hard working*
mechanism	n.	a natural or established process by which something takes place or is brought about.	*process, system, operation*
regulate	v.	control or maintain the rate or speed of (a machine or process) so that it operates properly.	*control, adjust, manage*
humidity	n.	a quantity representing the amount of water vapor in the atmosphere or in a gas.	
evaporate	v.	turn from liquid into vapor.	
dehydrate	v.	cause (a person or their body) to lose a large amount of water.	
prohibit	v.	formally forbid (something) by law, rule, or other authority.	*forbid, ban, veto*
fascinating	adj.	extremely interesting.	*engrossing, captivating*

Chapter notes:

CHAPTER
06
Inference

Inference

In inference questions, you are to answer questions that are implied from the conversation or lecture, or infer information based on what you heard. Remember that in inference questions, answers are not directly stated in the listening. Sometimes, part of the conversation or lecture will be replayed, or you may need to arrive at a conclusion based on what you heard.

There is usually one inference question per conversation or lecture.

How to identify inference questions:

What can be inferred about …?

What does the professor imply about…?

What can be concluded about…?

What will the student/professor do next?

What does the speaker imply when he/she says this?

How to solve step-by-step:

1) Try to understand the implied meaning in the statements. Do not literally take in whatever the speaker said. Learn to read between the lines.
2) Listen closely at the end of the talk. Here, the professor or speaker will mention what they will do next.
3) For replay questions, listen to what was said before and after. The context is very important when making inferences.
4) Even though answers are inferred and are not directly stated, the keywords should have been mentioned in the listening. Delete answer choices with keywords that did not appear in the listening.

Additional note:

There is a clear difference between guessing and inferring. Guessing does not take the content or context into account, while inferring does. Inferring is making smart guesses by associating ideas and logically connecting them to infer what the speaker means or infer what might happen next.

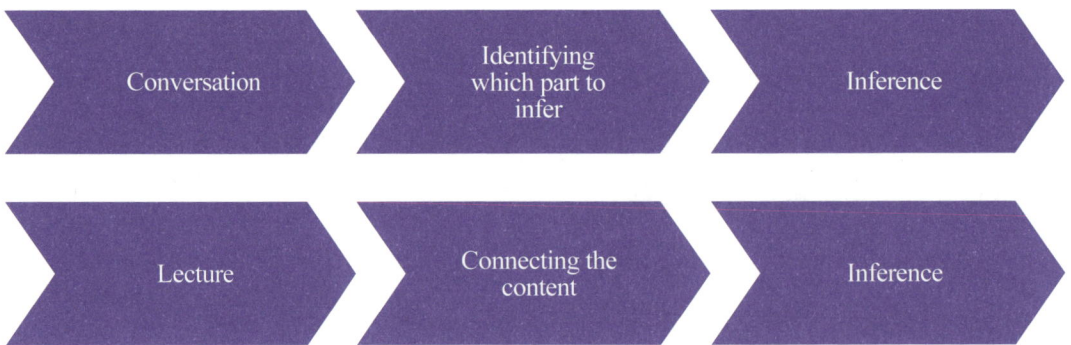

In a lecture, inference questions will be about the main idea. Sometimes, the inference questions may revolve around the details. In a conversation, inference questions will be based on problems and solutions.

When listening to a conversation or lecture, the speakers may provide hints on what they will do next after the conversation or lecture ends. The conversation may finish with the student hinting at going to the library to redo his paper, or the professor attending a meeting he is already late for. The lecture may suddenly stop with the professor leading onto the next topic, or she may finish the class altogether.

When making inference answers, remember that they do not require background knowledge nor comprehensive understanding of the topic. Just understanding the gist of the listening and avoiding keywords that were not mentioned in the listening will provide you with the correct answer.

Practice A:

Listen to part of a conversation between a student and a residential advisor

(CH6-1.mp3)

What will the student do next?

A) Ask her sister to stay at a hotel.

B) Ask the RA what kind of conventions the school holds.

C) Ask her roommate if her sister can stay overnight.

D) Ask the RA for restaurant recommendations.

> RA: Oh! I almost forgot! You have to get your roommate's permission before you let your sister stay in your room. Since you do share a room with her, it's important that your roommate agrees to inviting a guest. After all, having someone over can be inconvenient for some people. If your roommate happens to be studying for her exams or writing an overdue essay, it would be better for your sister to stay somewhere else.
>
> Student: I don't think my roommate will object. She is the friendliest person that I know. But just to be safe, I'll head over and ask her now.
>
> RA: Great! And if your sister needs a different place to stay overnight, I can recommend some great hotels nearby campus that can accommodate her. Our school hosts a lot of conventions, so hotels have made great strides in improving their services.

Answer: C. After the RA mentions that the student should check with her roommate before inviting her sister, the student responds by saying, *"...I'll head over and ask her now."* So the student will go ask her roommate if her sister can stay over.

A is not the answer because her roommate has not yet confirmed if her sister can stay over or not. B is not the answer because although the RA mentions that the school holds lots of conventions, this conversation is not revolving around what sort of conventions are held at the school. D is not the answer because restaurants were not even mentioned in the dialogue.

Practice B

Listen to part of a lecture in a health class

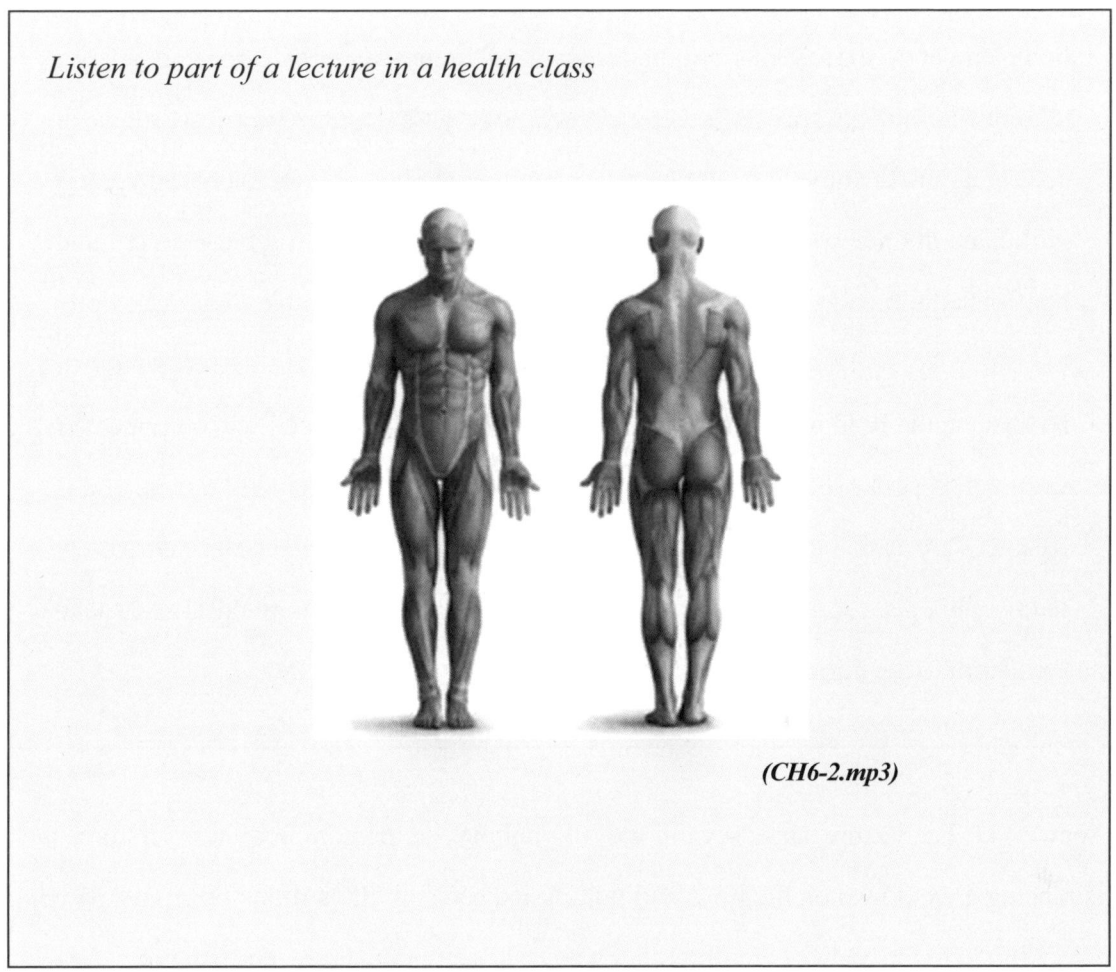

(CH6-2.mp3)

Which of the following should be administered to someone having a heat stroke?

    A) Cover them in a blanket.

    B) Give them a hot cup of soup or drink.

    C) Give them medication to combat the fever.

    D) Massage the arms and legs to move colder blood to the body's core.

> Professor: In the case of a heat stroke, a person can recover from it as long as the core body temperature does not stay high for too long. Your body has an amazing defense system that quickly tries to lower the core body temperature. The heart rate will accelerate faster to move cooler blood throughout the body. Also, the blood vessels will dilate in order to move heat out of the body, which will turn your skin red and hot. It is important to point out that the brain is the most vulnerable part of the body to heat stroke, so it's important to cool the person's head first. The body loses most of its heat via the head pretty quick, so cooling the head and the neck will help recover from a heat stroke. Placing a wet towel on the head can help lower the heat, and if ice packs are available, placing them in the armpits and groin will cool the core body temperature faster. Of course, while performing these procedures, dial 911 and move the victim to the hospital for additional treatment.

Answer: D. The lecture states several ways to help lower the core body temperature, such as placing a wet towel on the head and putting ice packs in the armpits or groins. Moving colder blood to the body's core is another way of lowering the body temperature.

A and B are not the answers because covering someone with a blanket or serving them a hot soup or drink will only increase the core body temperature. C is not the answer because we don't know if the medication will help drop the body temperature, and it does not mention giving medicine in the lecture.

Vocabulary:

imply	v.	strongly suggest the truth or existence of (something not expressly stated).	*hinted, suggested*
revolve	v.	treat as the most important point or element.	*focused on*
convention	n.	a way in which something is usually done, especially within a particular area or activity.	*custom, tradition*
inconvenient	adj.	causing trouble, difficulties, or discomfort.	*awkward, difficult*
overdue	adj.	not having arrived, happened, or been done by the expected time.	*late*
object	v.	say something to express one's disapproval of or disagreement with something.	
accommodate	v.	(of physical space, especially a building) provide lodging or sufficient space for.	*house, board*
host	v.	act as host at (an event) or for (a television or radio program).	
stride	n.	a step or stage in progress toward an aim.	*progress, advance*
combat	v.	fighting between armed forces.	*battle, conflict*
accelerate	v.	increase in amount or extent.	*hurry up*
dilate	v.	make or become wider, larger, or more open.	*enlarge, widen*
vulnerable	adj.	susceptible to physical or emotional attack or harm.	*endangered, unsafe*
via	prep.	by means of.	

Chapter notes:

Actual Test
01

Listening Section Directions

This section of the TOEFL test measures your ability to comprehend conversations and lectures in the English language.

The listening section is divided into two or three separately timed parts. Each part will contain 1 conversation and 1 or 2 lectures. You will only hear the conversation or lecture one time.

After each listening, questions related to the conversation or lecture will follow. The questions will ask about the main idea and supporting details. Some questions might ask for the speaker's purpose or attitude. You are to answer the questions based on what is stated or implied by the speakers.

Taking notes is recommended. It will help you answer the questions. Your notes will not be scored.

If the volume of the conversation or lecture is too loud or too soft, click on the **VOLUME ICON** at the top of the screen.

In some questions, you will see a headphone icon. This indicates that you will listen to part of the conversation or lecture.

Some of the questions have special directions, such as placing the answers in order or checking the answers in the correct space. The directions to these questions will appear in a gray box on the screen.

A clock at the top of the screen will show you how much time is remaining. The clock will not count down while you are listening. The timer will only start ticking while you are answering the questions.

Part 1 - Conversation

(AT1-1.mp3)

1) What problem does the student have?

   A) The construction noise is disturbing her studies in the study lounge.

   B) Her group is required to choose a new midterm project.

   C) The building's renovations affect where she wants to paint her mural.

   D) She needs help with her group assignment.

2) **Listen again to part of the conversation. Then answer the question.**

   (AT1-2.mp3)

   What is the student's opinion about the building renovations?

   A) She is upset about the renovations.

   B) She is surprised there will be renovations.

   C) She does not seem to care about the renovations.

   D) She is annoyed that the extent of the renovations were not stated.

3) What is the group planning to paint a mural of?

   A) A window

   B) A hallway

   C) A portrait

   D) A wall

4) What is the correct definition of Trompe-l'oeil technique?

   A) It is a two dimensional rendition of a three dimensional art.

   B) It is an art form with its origin in France.

   C) It is a technique that was made in the past few centuries.

   D) It creates an optical illusion of a realistic scene on a medium.

5) Why does the professor mention a door in a hallway?

   A) To correct the student's idea.

   B) To give an example of Trompe-l'oeil technique.

   C) To list a renovation being made in the building.

   D) To recommend painting the mural there.

6) What does the professor suggest at the end of their conversation?

   A) The students should ignore the renovations and continue with their project on the wall.

   B) The students should paint their mural on a sheet of wood.

   C) The students should wait until after their vacation to do their project.

   D) The students should practice Trompe-l'oeil art.

Part 1 - Lecture

(AT1-3.mp3)

7) What is the lecture's main idea?

A) A comparison of two bird species.
B) The possible cause of Australia's mass extinction.
C) Scientific methods of analyzing rocks and lakebed.
D) The various scientific hypothesis for mass extinction.

8) **Listen again to part of the lecture. Then answer the question.**

(AT1-4.mp3)

Why does the professor say this?

A) To introduce another hypothesis.
B) To check if the students are being attentive.
C) To show that scientists have no idea how the mass extinction happened.
D) To confirm if the students understood the previous examples.

9) What kind of knowledge does the professor say that primitive Australians had?

A) How to hunt large mammals.
B) How to start fires.
C) How to make tools and weapons.
D) How to capture eggs.

10) According to the professor, what could have naturally started the fire?

   A) Sudden changes in temperature.
   B) Lightning strike.
   C) A lake drying up.
   D) Limited vegetation.

11) How do scientists know what sort of plant existed 50,000 years ago?
   Choose 2 answers.

   A) By analyzing bird egg shells.
   B) By taking samples of water.
   C) From the remains found in soil underneath lakebeds.
   D) From primitive weapons and tools.

12) What is the professor's opinion of Emu?

   A) He believes it was able to endure the warmer climates.
   B) He thinks that because it could fly, it escaped the fires.
   C) He believes that its ability to adapt allowed it to survive.
   D) He sees no difference between it and other birds.

Part 2 - Conversation

(AT1-5.mp3)

1) Why does the student visit the office?

   A) To ask about graduation requirements.

   B) To register for a physical education class.

   C) To inquire about his transfer credits.

   D) To meet with the dean.

2) What is the student majoring in?

   A) Mechanics.

   B) Electrical Engineering.

   C) Physical Education.

   D) Philosophy

3) What was the reason the woman gives to explain why the registrar could not transfer the student's other classes?

   A) They forgot to file them in the computer system.

   B) His classes were denied by the university.

   C) The staff does not have enough knowledge to access the transfer classes.

   D) The student did not satisfy the course requirements.

4) **Listen again to part of the conversation. Then answer the question.**

(AT1-6.mp3)

What is the woman trying to find out when she asks this?

A) The location of the offices.

B) If the student had already visited the offices.

C) How far the offices are from the current location.

D) Whether or not she needs to give the location of the offices.

5) What does the registrar recommend the student do? *Choose 2 answers.*

A) Apply to register early.

B) Fill out the transfer credit form.

C) Submit an appeal to overturn the disapproval of the credit transfer.

D) Prepare his former transcripts and syllabi.

Part 2 - Lecture

(AT1-7.mp3)

6) What is the main idea of the lecture?

   A) Ways that a company can maintain their positive image.

   B) Steps that a company should take before starting a building project.

   C) How human resources are important to a business.

   D) Market strategies for products and services.

7) According to the professor, how does a company maintain its positive image?

   A) By focusing on profit.

   B) By being attentive to one's resources.

   C) By hiring successful public relations employees.

   D) By starting an effective advertising campaigns.

8) **Listen again to part of the lecture. Then answer the question.**

(AT1-8.mp3)

Why does the professor say this?

   A) To emphasize that the school's mistake was illogical and could have been avoided.

   B) To doubt the purpose of the school's building project.

   C) To point out how students should critically consider about public relations.

   D) To move onto the next example.

9) What new facilities were mentioned that the school was building?

   A) A community center.

   B) A fitness center.

   C) A theater.

   D) A lecture hall.

10) What can be inferred about the school's neighbors?

   A) They were previously disturbed by the school.

   B) They wish to have regular community meetings concerning the school.

   C) They thought the local authorities would be of no use.

   D) They were not aware of the benefits the building project would bring them.

11) What is the professor's opinion about the school's construction project?

   A) He was annoyed because the noise interrupted his lectures.

   B) He thought it was a good chance for him to teach about public relations.

   C) He believes he could have done a better job advertising it.

   D) He was shocked to find out that the school was building new facilities.

Part 2 - Lecture

(AT1-9.mp3)

12) What is the main idea of the lecture?

   A) Possible uses for the Moon's water.

   B) The SPA Basin and going back to the Moon.

   C) SPA Basin's origin.

   D) The discoveries made by the Clemente Missions.

13) Why does the professor mention the tiny craters found in the SPA Basin?

   A) To emphasize its size.

   B) To show evidence of its age.

   C) To show the location of the Moon's ice water.

   D) To describe how it was formed.

14) **Listen again to part of the lecture. Then answer the question.**

(AT1-10.mp3)

   Why does the professor say this?

   A) He agrees with the student's interest.

   B) He thinks that the student's inquiry is humorous.

   C) He wants the students to care about the topic.

   D) He is caught off guard by the student's question.

15) Why does the professor support another lunar mission?

Choose 2 answers.

A) To retrieve Moon dust samples.

B) To learn more about the water found on the Moon.

C) To travel deeper into space.

D) To take more photos.

16) What does the professor imply about Moon dust?

A) It is the only practical way to study the Moon.

B) It was the reason for the first lunar missions.

C) It is hard to get a hold of.

D) It is only available at certain times of the year.

17) According to the lecture, the professor talks about the Moon water and some of its potential for scientists.

Click in the correct box for each phrase.

Potential uses of Moon water	Yes	No
Oxygen for astronauts		
An energy source for electricity		
Irrigation for Moon colony crops		
Hydrogen to fuel rockets		

Vocabulary:

proposal	n.	a plan or suggestion, especially a formal or written one, put forward for consideration or discussion by others.	plan, program, scheme
renovation	n.	the action of renovating a building.	restoration, refurbishment
recall	v.	bring (a fact, event, or situation) back into one's mind; remember.	remember, recollect
mural	n.	a painting or other work of art executed directly on a wall.	
proceed	v.	begin or continue a course of action.	begin, move
ironic	adj.	happening in the opposite way to what is expected, and typically causing wry amusement because of this.	paradoxical, incongruous
elevate	v.	raise or lift (something) up to a higher position.	raise, hoist, upraise
illusion	n.	a thing that is or is likely to be wrongly perceived or interpreted by the senses.	mirage, hallucination
virtuoso	n.	a person highly skilled in music or another artistic pursuit.	genius, expert
extent	n.	the area covered by something.	expanse, range, scope
optical	adj.	relating to sight, especially in relation to the physical action of light.	
roughly	adv.	approximately	about, around

perish	v.	suffer complete ruin or destruction.	*fall, expire*
suspect	v.	have an idea or impression of the existence, presence, or truth of (something) without certain proof.	*feel, fancy*
susceptible	adj.	likely or liable to be influenced or harmed by a particular thing.	*vulnerable to*
excessive	adj.	more than is necessary, normal, or desirable; immoderate.	*immoderate, unrestrained*
master	v.	acquire complete knowledge or skill in (an accomplishment, technique, or art).	*know inside out*
aforementioned	adj.	denoting a thing or person previously mentioned.	
rampant	adj.	(especially of something unwelcome or unpleasant) flourishing or spreading unchecked.	*uncontrolled, unrestrained*
spontaneous	adj.	performed or occurring as a result of a sudden inner impulse or inclination and without premeditation or external stimulus.	*unprompted, unforced*
scarce	adj.	(especially of food, money, or some other resource) insufficient for the demand.	*scant, meager, sparse*
investigate	v.	carry out a systematic or formal inquiry to discover and examine the facts of (an incident, allegation, etc.) so as to establish the truth.	*probe, explore*
conclude	v.	bring (something) to an end.	*finish, end*
restrict	v.	put a limit on; keep under control.	*limit, regulate*

attentive	adj.	paying close attention to something.	*alert, awake, perceptive*
endure	v.	suffer (something painful or difficult) patiently.	*undergo, experience*
frustration	n.	the feeling of being upset or annoyed, especially because of inability to change or achieve something.	*annoyance, vexation*
comprehend	v.	grasp mentally; understand.	*understand, apprehend*
scenario	n.	a postulated sequence or development of events.	
credential	n.	a qualification, achievement, personal quality, or aspect of a person's background, typically when used to indicate that they are suitable for something.	
holistic	adj.	characterized by comprehension of the parts of something as intimately interconnected and explicable only by reference to the whole.	
well-rounded	adj.	pleasingly varied or balanced.	
compulsory	adj.	required by law or a rule; obligatory.	*obligatory, requisite*
deny	v.	state that one refuses to admit the truth or existence of.	*contradict, repudiate*
appeal	v.	be attractive or interesting.	*attract, interest*
overturn	v.	abolish, invalidate, or reverse (a previous system, decision, situation, etc.).	*cancel, reverse, repeal*
perspective	n.	a particular attitude toward or way of regarding something; a point of view.	*outlook, view, position*

consistent	adj.	acting or done in the same way over time, especially so as to be fair or accurate.	*steady, constant*
impression	n.	an idea, feeling, or opinion about something or someone, especially one formed without conscious thought or on the basis of little evidence.	*feeling, sense*
asset	n.	a useful or valuable thing, person, or quality.	*advantage, strength*
liability	n.	the state of being responsible for something, especially by law.	*accountability, responsibility*
ripple effect	n.	the continuing and spreading results of an event or action.	
overlook	v.	ignore or disregard (something, especially a fault or offense).	*neglect, ignore*
enrage	v.	make very angry.	*infuriate, inflame*
halt	v.	bring or come to an abrupt stop.	*stop, come to rest*
predicament	n.	a difficult, unpleasant, or embarrassing situation.	*mess, difficulty*
imperative	adj.	of vital importance; crucial.	*vital, crucial*
celestial	adj.	positioned in or relating to the sky, or outer space as observed in astronomy.	*heavenly, astronomical*
topography	n.	a detailed description or representation on a map of the natural and artificial features of an area.	
projectile	n.	an object propelled through the air, especially one thrown as a weapon.	
simulation	n.	imitation of a situation or process.	

extract	v.	remove or take out, especially by effort or force.	*pull out, withdraw*
convert	v.	cause to change in form, character, or function.	*transform, transfigure*
endeavor	n.	an attempt to achieve a goal.	*attempt, effort*
fortune	n.	a large amount of money or assets.	*wealth, riches*
inquiry	n.	an act of asking for information.	*question, investigation*
irrigation	n.	the supply of water to land or crops to help growth, typically by means of channels.	

Additional Vocabulary:

Actual Test 02

Listening Section Directions

This section of the TOEFL test measures your ability to comprehend conversations and lectures in the English language.

The listening section is divided into two or three separately timed parts. Each part will contain 1 conversation and 1 or 2 lectures. You will only hear the conversation or lecture one time.

After each listening, questions related to the conversation or lecture will follow. The questions will ask about the main idea and supporting details. Some questions might ask for the speaker's purpose or attitude. You are to answer the questions based on what is stated or implied by the speakers.

Taking notes is recommended. It will help you answer the questions. Your notes will not be scored.

If the volume of the conversation or lecture is too loud or too soft, click on the **VOLUME ICON** at the top of the screen.

In some questions, you will see a headphone icon. This indicates that you will listen to part of the conversation or lecture.

Some of the questions have special directions, such as placing the answers in order or checking the answers in the correct space. The directions to these questions will appear in a gray box on the screen.

A clock at the top of the screen will show you how much time is remaining. The clock will not count down while you are listening. The timer will only start ticking while you are answering the questions.

Part 1 - Conversation

(AT2-1.mp3)

1) Why did the professor want to see the student?

   A) To check how she is doing with her project.

   B) To see if she is able to help with his research project.

   C) To give advice on her future career opportunities.

   D) To discuss her previous work with translating articles.

2) How is the professor funding the translation work?

   A) He took out a personal loan for the money.

   B) The university department provided the money.

   C) The school gave him a grant.

   D) The government gave him assistance.

3) What benefits does the professor mention to persuade the student to help him?
   Choose 2 answers.

   A) The work could assist her in getting a research job next semester.

   B) She can create her own work schedule.

   C) The work pays better than her other part time job.

   D) The project will give her translation experience.

4) **Listen to part of the conversation. Then answer the question.**

(AT2-2.mp3)

What does the professor imply when he says this?

A) He thinks he has pressured the student.

B) The student should quit her other job so she can make more time.

C) Other students' assistance will decrease the workload.

D) The student should not underestimate the importance of the project.

5) How many articles does the student agree to translate for the professor?

A) None.

B) Only one.

C) One per week.

D) One every two weeks.

Part 1 - Lecture

(AT2-3.mp3)

6) Why does the professor mention the habitat of the Diana monkeys?

   A) To explain why there are variations in the alarm calls.

   B) To compare with the predator's habitat.

   C) To point out the geographical advantage.

   D) To explain why altruistic behavior is needed.

7) According to the professor, what are some of the reactions the Diana monkeys make to the alarm calls? *Choose 2 answers.*

   A) Standing on two legs and looking down.

   B) Concealing themselves in a bush.

   C) Holding onto another Diana monkey.

   D) Diving into the closest river.

8) Why does the professor mention altruistic behavior?

   A) To describe the newly discovered behavior of the Diana monkey.

   B) To show the advantages of the behavior.

   C) To compare two different views concerning alarm calls.

   D) To point out the Diana monkey's stand in life.

9) What can be inferred about young Diana monkeys?

   A) They are willing to be the sacrificial monkeys.

   B) They are often confused with which alarm calls they should make.

   C) They take a longer time to develop their alarm calls.

   D) They have strong emotional relationships with their mother.

10) What is the professor's opinion toward the Diana monkeys?

   A) He is doubtful of their communication methods.

   B) He mocks their level of intelligence.

   C) He thinks they are worth studying.

   D) He believes they are the most evolved apes.

11) In the lecture, the professor explains several different alarm calls made by the Diana monkey. Indicate which alarm is related to the predator.

Click in the correct box for each phrase.

	Leopard	Eagle	Snake
A) Tonal alarm			
B) Low-pitch grunt			
C) High-pitch chutter			
D) Short alarm			

Part 2 - Conversation

(AT2-4.mp3)

1) What is the conversation mainly about?

   A) Being advised on how to decorate a room.

   B) Looking for a roommate.

   C) Getting a room at the school dormitory.

   D) Making a reservation with a moving company.

2) Why does the student want to move out of his current living arrangements?

   A) He has trouble paying the rent.

   B) He wants to make friends.

   C) He is against the studio's strict rules.

   D) His rental term has ended.

3) According to the conversation, what are the university's policies concerning dormitory use? *Choose 2 answers.*

   A) Students are only allowed to move in and out of the dorm during the weekdays.

   B) The room should be in its original condition when the student vacates.

   C) Moving should only be done by moving companies.

   D) Students need to reimburse the school if the built-in furniture gets damaged.

4) **Listen to part of the conversation. Then answer the question.**

(AT2-5.mp3)

What does the student mean when he says this:

A) The student does not have any specific plans.

B) The student is worried that the wall is not hard enough.

C) The student plans to completely cover the wall.

D) The student has not decided when to move in.

5) According to the conversation, what will the student probably do next?

A) He will fill out the paperwork to move in to the dormitory.

B) He will put his name in the dormitory's waiting list.

C) He will go shopping for decorations.

D) He will make an appointment with a moving company.

Part 2 - Lecture

(AT2-6.mp3)

6) What is the main idea of the lecture?

   A) The reasons behind Roman sculptures.

   B) The primary examples of Greek and Roman sculptures.

   C) What kind of influence the Greeks had on Roman sculptures.

   D) Greek and Roman sculptures' differences.

7) How does the professor organize her lecture?

   A) By comparing the sculpture's subjects and how they are portrayed.

   B) By first discussing the sculpting techniques of the Greeks then the Romans.

   C) By mentioning the origins of Roman sculpture and giving examples of it.

   D) By going over Greek mythology and how they were portrayed in the sculptures.

8) What purpose did Roman sculptures serve?

   A) Retelling the stories from Roman mythology.

   B) Glorifying Roman individuals.

   C) Representing the ideal beauty of the human body.

   D) Decorating the interiors of buildings.

9) Why do many of the Roman sculptures have less captivating characteristics?

   A) The artists were making a stand not to follow Greek influences.

   B) The artists used over-exaggerations to show ideals.

   C) The sculptures showed realistic images of their subjects.

   D) Amateur sculptors had made them.

10) **Listen again to part of the lecture. Then answer the question.**

   (AT2-7.mp3)

   What does the professor mean when she says this:

   A) Roman sculptors often made mistakes, so they had to go back and fix them.

   B) Roman sculptors made some effort to improve the image of their subjects.

   C) Roman sculptors were not happy with how their sculptures turned out.

   D) Roman sculptors carefully choose the subjects of their sculptures.

11) What part of the modern Zeus sculpture did not match with the subject?

   A) Stomach and wrinkles.

   B) Bolt of lightning

   C) Position on top of the mountain.

   D) Sculpted by an amateur.

Part 2 - Lecture

(AT2-8.mp3)

12) What is the main idea of the lecture? *Choose 2 answers.*

   A) The ecological importance of keystone species.

   B) The harms and benefits caused by keystone species.

   C) The different categories of keystone species.

   D) How to save endangered keystone species.

13) Why does the professor talk about keystones used in architecture?

   A) To emphasize the connection between two different fields.

   B) To show the similarity in its role and in ecology.

   C) To understand biology from a different perspective.

   D) To show the importance of studying different subjects.

14) According to the professor, which of the following are true about keystone species? *Choose 3 answers.*

   A) Their absence may lead to a collapse of an ecosystem.

   B) They may prevent certain organisms from crowding out.

   C) They have a minor effect on other species because their numbers are so low.

   D) Most of them are carnivores and few are plants.

   E) They can reconstruct or maintain the physical environment.

15) Why are the elephants' feeding habits important in the African savannahs?

A) It maintains the grass that feeds different grazing animals.

B) It helps expand the population of trees that shelter small mammals.

C) It disperses the tree's seeds and promotes plant diversity.

D) It decreases the number of dominant predators.

16) What is the professor's opinion of saving the environment by focusing on the keystone species?

A) The overall influence is still doubtful.

B) It is of great importance and urgency.

C) The time it takes is too long to have any effect.

D) It neglects the need to protect other endangered species.

17) What will the professor do next?

A) Finish the class.

B) Assign the class homework.

C) Continue talking about keystone species.

D) Talk about his experience working as a conservationist.

Vocabulary:

obligation	n.	an act or course of action to which a person is morally or legally bound; a duty or commitment.	*duty, commitment*
retrieve	v.	get or bring (something) back; regain possession of.	*recover, reclaim*
compensate	v.	give (someone) something, typically money, in recognition of loss, suffering, or injury incurred; recompense.	*repay, reimburse*
tedious	adj.	too long, slow, or dull; tiresome or monotonous.	*boring, dull*
monotonous	adj.	dull, tedious, and repetitious; lacking in variety and interest.	*tedious, uninteresting*
fulfilling	adj.	making someone satisfied or happy because of fully developing their character or abilities.	
eager	adj.	(of a person) wanting to do or have something very much.	*anxious, longing, yearning*
bolster	v.	support or strengthen; prop up.	*strengthen, boost*
tempting	v.	entice or attempt to entice (someone) to do or acquire something that they find attractive but know to be wrong or not beneficial.	*entice, persuade, convince*
bar	n.	a barrier or restriction to an action or advance.	*check, obstacle*
commitment	n.	the state or quality of being dedicated to a cause, activity, etc.	*dedication, devotion*

relay	v.	receive and pass on (information or a message).	*transfer, pass on*
elicit	v.	evoke or draw out (a response, answer, or fact) from someone in reaction to one's own actions or questions.	*extract, evoke*
aerial	adj.	existing, happening, or operating in the air.	
asset	n.	a useful or valuable thing, person, or quality.	*benefit, advantage*
altruistic	adj.	showing a disinterested and selfless concern for the well-being of others; unselfish.	*selfless, considerate*
instinctual	adj.	relating to or denoting an innate, typically fixed pattern of behavior; based on instinct.	
reserved	adj.	slow to reveal emotion or opinions.	*restrained, private*
hectic	adj.	full of incessant or frantic activity.	*frantic, restless*
clueless	adj.	having no knowledge, understanding, or ability.	*oblivious, ignorant*
decent	adj.	conforming with generally accepted standards of respectable or moral behavior.	*proper, appropriate*
firm	adj.	solidly in place and stable.	*secure, steady, fixed*
term	n.	a fixed or limited period for which something, e.g., office, imprisonment, or investment, lasts or is intended to last.	*period, time*
vacate	v.	leave (a place that one previously occupied).	*leave, evacuate*
imitate	v.	copy or simulate.	*mirror, echo*

proportion	n.	the relationship of one thing to another in terms of quantity, size, or number; ratio.	*ratio, distribution*
contribute	v.	give (something, especially money) in order to help achieve or provide something.	*donate, give*
in spite of		without being affected by the particular factor mentioned.	
stark	adj.	severe or bare in appearance or outline.	*sharp, crisp*
aesthetic	adj.	concerned with beauty or the appreciation of beauty.	*beautiful, elegant*
commission	n.	an order for something, especially a work of art, to be produced.	
reputation	n.	the beliefs or opinions that are generally held about someone or something.	*stature, status*
counterpart	n.	a person or thing holding a position or performing a function that corresponds to that of another person or thing in another place.	*equivalent, equal*
idealize	v.	regard or represent as perfect or better than in reality.	*romanticize*
exaggerate	v.	represent (something) as being larger, better, or worse than it really is.	*overstate, overemphasize*
gloss over	v.	try to conceal or disguise something unfavorable by treating it briefly or representing it misleadingly.	*conceal, disguise*
critic	n.	a person who expresses an unfavorable opinion of something.	*detractor, attacker*

bulge	n.	a rounded swelling or protuberance that distorts a flat surface.	*swelling, bump*
topple	v.	overbalance or become unsteady and fall slowly.	*tumble, overturn*
dominate	v.	have a commanding influence on; exercise control over.	*control, influence*
misplace	v.	put in the wrong place and lose temporarily because of this; mislay.	*lose, miss*
permit	v.	give authorization or consent to (someone) to do something.	*allow, sanction*
mutual	adj.	(of a feeling or action) experienced or done by each of two or more parties toward the other or others.	*reciprocal, required*
disperse	v.	distribute or spread over a wide area.	*scatter, disseminate*
feces	n.	waste matter discharged from the bowels after food has been digested; excrement.	*dung, manure*
refrain	v.	stop oneself from doing something.	*abstain, forgo*
flourish	v.	(of a person, animal, or other living organism) grow or develop in a healthy or vigorous way, especially as the result of a particularly favorable environment.	*thrive, prosper*
cease	v.	bring or come to an end.	*halt, stop*
promote	v.	further the progress of (something, especially a cause, venture, or aim); support or actively encourage.	*advance, further*

endangered	adj.	(of a species) seriously at risk of extinction.	
absence	n.	the state of being away from a place or person.	*nonappearance*
shelter	v.	protect or shield from something harmful, especially bad weather.	*protect, shield*
doubtful	adj.	feeling uncertain about something.	*hesitant, wavering*

Additional Vocabulary:

Actual Test
03

Listening Section Directions

This section of the TOEFL test measures your ability to comprehend conversations and lectures in the English language.

The listening section is divided into two or three separately timed parts. Each part will contain 1 conversation and 1 or 2 lectures. You will only hear the conversation or lecture one time.

After each listening, questions related to the conversation or lecture will follow. The questions will ask about the main idea and supporting details. Some questions might ask for the speaker's purpose or attitude. You are to answer the questions based on what is stated or implied by the speakers.

Taking notes is recommended. It will help you answer the questions. Your notes will not be scored.

If the volume of the conversation or lecture is too loud or too soft, click on the **VOLUME ICON** at the top of the screen.

In some questions, you will see a headphone icon. This indicates that you will listen to part of the conversation or lecture.

Some of the questions have special directions, such as placing the answers in order or checking the answers in the correct space. The directions to these questions will appear in a gray box on the screen.

A clock at the top of the screen will show you how much time is remaining. The clock will not count down while you are listening. The timer will only start ticking while you are answering the questions.

Part 1 - Conversation

(AT3-1.mp3)

1) Why does the student go to see the professor?

   A) To tell him that she is registered to take his class next semester.

   B) To talk about taking his class next semester without getting credits.

   C) To inquire when he will be teaching his economics class.

   D) To get advice on what classes to take next semester.

2) Why does the student wish to audit the class, instead of taking it for a grade?

   A) She does not have the finance to pay for it.

   B) She is afraid she will fail in the class.

   C) She has already registered the maximum number of classes.

   D) She needs the information for her research paper.

3) What is the professor's opinion of paying for audited classes?

   A) He feels it is unfair for students having financial difficulty.

   B) He is angry at the university for charging students.

   C) He believes it should be accepted only because it says so in the policy.

   D) He feels it is necessary because professors are doing a service.

4) **Listen again to part of the conversation. Then answer the question.**

(AT3-2.mp3)

What does the professor imply?

A) The class is already full.

B) The student is horrible at economics.

C) The professor is doubtful that the student will be able to audit.

D) The professor does not seem to care for the student.

5) What will the student do?

A) Take the class when she needs a grade.

B) Register to audit the class.

C) Talk to the school administrator about paying for the audit class.

D) Continue talking to the professor about next semester.

Part 1 - Lecture

(AT3-3.mp3)

6) What is the main idea of the lecture?

   A) The application of low pressure in desalination.

   B) The use of heat exchange technology.

   C) Desalination techniques that help conserve energy.

   D) Desalination's influence on the environment.

7) What is the professor's opinion on desalinization?

   A) She thinks that it is not that reliable.

   B) She is hesitant that it will have a positive effect on nature.

   C) She believes it can be more efficient.

   D) She feels that it is needed now more than ever.

8) How does the professor introduce the desalinization process?

   A) By comparing it with the previous desalinization process.

   B) By naming the countries it is most used.

   C) By mentioning the natural occurrence it is based on.

   D) By pointing out the flaws of traditional desalinization methods.

9) What makes flash generators practical for desalinization?

   A) They rapidly cool the vapor to fresh water.

   B) They remove more salt from the ocean water.

   C) They preheat the ocean water so that it boils faster.

   D) They decrease water's boiling point.

10) What does the professor say about heat exchange technology and flash generators?

   A) They are often used together.

   B) They still need to be perfected.

   C) They require more energy than traditional methods.

   D) They create environmental problems.

11) **Listen again to part of the lecture. Then answer the question.**

   (AT3-4.mp3)

   What does the professor mean when she says this?

   A) Heat exchange greatly benefits the environment.

   B) Heat exchange provides a solution to more than one problem.

   C) Heat exchange works twice as fast compared to other methods.

   D) Heat exchange depends on two energy sources.

Part 2 - Conversation

(AT3-5.mp3)

1) What is the main topic of the conversation?

   A) Getting an approval on shooting a film about global warming.

   B) How to alert the people about the negative effects of global warming.

   C) What the best way is to make a film on how birds are affected by global warming.

   D) The best ways to interview people in an information film.

2) What is the professor's opinion towards film production?

   A) With careful planning, it is not difficult.

   B) Film majors are the only ones who can direct it.

   C) It should not start filming until everything is organized.

   D) It is difficult and a challenging task.

3) What can be inferred about the student's movie?

   A) He still needs to find more information on the topic.

   B) He has already come up with good questions to ask.

   C) He is having trouble finding people to interview.

   D) He plans to include the pros and cons of global warming.

4) What are some things to consider when deciding whether or not to film the same interview several times? *Choose 2 answers.*

   A) The size of the interview set.

   B) The quality of the sound.

   C) If the interview will be cut into parts.

   D) The number of people being interviewed.

5) In the conversation, the professor and student talk about the different aspects of the student's movie. Indicate whether the following were mentioned.

   Click in the correct box for each phrase.

	Included	Not included
A) How to prepare the equipment.		
B) Where to find reference materials.		
C) Where to effectively insert the interviews.		
D) When to use several camera.		

Part 2 - Lecture

(AT3-6.mp3)

6) What is the main idea of the lecture?

   A) The variable characteristics of different kinds of matter.

   B) The properties of two different types of mixtures.

   C) The advantages of certain kinds of mixtures.

   D) The study of modern chemistry.

7) According to the lecture, which of the following is true about homogeneous mixtures?

   A) They can be made up of more than one phase.

   B) Filtration can separate the materials inside them.

   C) They are mostly liquid solutions.

   D) The compositions are spread out evenly.

8) Which of the following is true of air?

   A) It is always homogeneous.

   B) It can become heterogeneous.

   C) It is homogeneous when smoggy.

   D) Pure air is heterogeneous.

9) Why does the professor mention tea?

   A) To give an example of a heterogeneous mixture.

   B) To show how changes in composition can influence mixtures.

   C) To explain how something heterogeneous can turn homogeneous.

   D) To point out that homogeneous mixtures cannot be filtered.

10) How does the professor organize the lecture?

    A) By chronologically discussing the historical discoveries.

    B) By listing their natural and artificial combinations.

    C) By providing definitions and explaining their properties.

    D) By ranking them according to the number of phases they have.

11) In the lecture, the professor talks about different types of mixtures.

   Click in the correct box for each phrase.

	Homogeneous	Heterogeneous
A) Salt water		
B) Sandy water		
C) Sand		
D) Tea		
E) Smoke		

Part 2 - Lecture

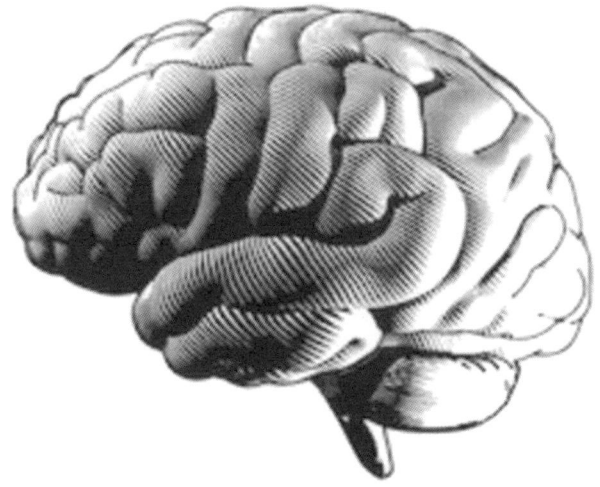

(AT3-7.mp3)

12) What is the main idea of the lecture?

A) How neurotransmission works.

B) The history of glial cell research.

C) Glial cells and the different roles they play in the brain.

D) Comparing and contrasting glial cells and neurons.

13) Which of the following is true of neurons? *Choose 2 answers.*

A) They control our voluntary and involuntary movements.

B) They transmit electrical signals to each other.

C) They act as connective tissue in the brain.

D) They are referred to as synapses.

14) What does the professor imply about the early understanding of glial cells neuroscientists had?

A) They thought that glial cells were influential in only certain parts of the brain.

B) They incorrectly believed that glial cells contained neurotransmitters.

C) They thought that the role glial cells had were miniscule.

D) They overcame difficulties finding glial cells despite poor equipment.

15) What is a difference between glial cells and neurons?

   A) Glial cells outnumber neurons.

   B) Only neurons can make neurotransmitters.

   C) Glial cells can reproduce.

   D) Neurons glue the glial cells together.

16) How does the professor organize her lecture on glial cell functions?

   A) Discoveries made in chronological order.

   B) From simple to complex.

   C) The order in which they happen in the brain.

   D) According to biological importance.

17) How does the professor feel toward research in glial cells?

   A) She believes that it is less important than neuron research.

   B) She confirms it will continue to be the forefront in brain study.

   C) She questions if more important finds will be made.

   D) She is disturbed that scientists have made so many mistakes.

Vocabulary:

spare	n.	an item kept in case another item of the same type is lost, broken, or worn out.	
scale	n.	an instrument for weighing, originally a simple balance (a pair of scales) but now usually a device with an electronic or other internal weighing mechanism.	*balance*
keen	adj.	having or showing great perception or insight.	*acute, astute*
audit	v.	attend (a class) informally, not for academic credit.	
exception	n.	a person or thing that is excluded from a general statement or does not follow a rule.	
reputation	n.	the beliefs or opinions that are generally held about someone or something.	*stature, status*
refund	v.	pay back (money), typically to a customer who is not satisfied with goods or services bought.	*repay, restore*
upset	v.	make (someone) unhappy, disappointed, or worried.	*distress, disturb*
finite	adj.	having limits or bounds.	*limited, restricted*
incorporate	v.	take in or contain (something) as part of a whole; include.	*include, assimilate*
condense	v.	change or cause to change from a gas or vapor to a liquid.	*precipitate, liquefy*
principle	n.	a fundamental source or basis of something.	

integrate	v.	combine (one thing) with another so that they become a whole.	*merge, blend*
direct	v.	control the operations of; manage or govern.	*manage, control*
hesitant	adj.	tentative, unsure, or slow in acting or speaking.	*uncertain, unsure*
flaw	n.	a mark, fault, or other imperfection that mars a substance or object.	*defect, blemish*
provoke	v.	stimulate or give rise to (a reaction or emotion, typically a strong or unwelcome one) in someone.	*arouse, evoke*
insight	n.	the capacity to gain an accurate and deep intuitive understanding of a person or thing.	*intuition, perception*
conduct	v.	organize and carry out.	*oversee, control*
pursue	v.	follow (someone or something) in order to catch or attack them.	*follow, chase*
uniform	adj.	remaining the same in all cases and at all times; unchanging in form or character.	*constant, unvarying*
phase	n.	a distinct and homogeneous form of matter (i.e. a particular solid, liquid, or gas) separated by its surface from other forms.	
component	n.	a part or element of a larger whole, especially a part of a machine or vehicle.	*component, element*
alternate	v.	occur in turn repeatedly.	
constituent	adj.	being a part of a whole.	*component, integral*

filter	n.	a porous device for removing impurities or solid particles from a liquid or gas passed through it.	*strainer, sieve*
variable	adj.	not consistent or having a fixed pattern; liable to change.	*changeable, varying*
compose	v.	(of elements) constitute or make up (a whole).	*constitute, comprise*
pinch	n.	an amount of an ingredient that can be held between fingers and thumb.	*bit, dash*
fundamental	adj.	forming a necessary base or core; of central importance.	*foundational, rudimentary*
process	n.	a series of actions or steps taken in order to achieve a particular end.	*procedure, operation*
conscious	adj.	aware of and responding to one's surroundings; awake.	*aware, alert*
systematic	adj.	done or acting according to a fixed plan or system; methodical.	*methodical, organized*
appropriate	adj.	suitable or proper in the circumstances.	*proper, relevant*
sole	adj.	one and only.	*only, unique*
frequency	n.	the rate at which something occurs or is repeated over a particular period of time or in a given sample.	*prevalence*
critical	adj.	having a decisive or crucial importance in the success, failure, or existence of something.	*crucial, vital*

insulator	n.	a substance which does not readily allow the passage of heat or sound.	
shift	v.	move or cause to move from one place to another, especially over a small distance.	*move, transfer*
heighten	v.	make or become more intense.	*intensify, enhance*
transmit	v.	cause (something) to pass on from one place or person to another.	*transfer, impart*
miniscule	adj.	extremely small; tiny.	*minute, micro*

Additional Vocabulary:

Chapter notes:

Actual Test
04

Listening Section Directions

This section of the TOEFL test measures your ability to comprehend conversations and lectures in the English language.

The listening section is divided into two or three separately timed parts. Each part will contain 1 conversation and 1 or 2 lectures. You will only hear the conversation or lecture one time.

After each listening, questions related to the conversation or lecture will follow. The questions will ask about the main idea and supporting details. Some questions might ask for the speaker's purpose or attitude. You are to answer the questions based on what is stated or implied by the speakers.

Taking notes is recommended. It will help you answer the questions. Your notes will not be scored.

If the volume of the conversation or lecture is too loud or too soft, click on the **VOLUME ICON** at the top of the screen.

In some questions, you will see a headphone icon. This indicates that you will listen to part of the conversation or lecture.

Some of the questions have special directions, such as placing the answers in order or checking the answers in the correct space. The directions to these questions will appear in a gray box on the screen.

A clock at the top of the screen will show you how much time is remaining. The clock will not count down while you are listening. The timer will only start ticking while you are answering the questions.

Part 1 - Conversation

(AT4-1.mp3)

1) Why does the student go to the housing office?

   A) To request a switch to a new dorm room.
   B) To comply with the housing office's investigation.
   C) To request the removal of some of his dorm mates.
   D) To file a complaint about his dorm life.

2) Why does the RA permit misbehavior in the dormitory?

   A) He holds no authority of stopping it.
   B) He believes it is not bothering anyone.
   C) He is friends with those that are causing the misbehaviors.
   D) He is afraid of the trouble makers.

3) How does the employee plan to deal with the situation?

   A) By immediately firing the RA.
   B) By reviewing the rules for the dormitory.
   C) By promising an investigation into the problem.
   D) By offering to refund part of the student's dorm payment.

4) What will the student do next?

A) Fill out the paperwork to change his room.

B) Talk to the RA to bring order in the dormitory.

C) Notify the campus security of the RA's actions.

D) Wait for the RA to be investigated.

5) **Listen to part of the conversation. Then answer the question.**

(AT4-2.mp3)

What does the employee mean when she says this:

A) She suspects there were other similar instances.

B) She is not satisfied with one misbehavior.

C) She wants the student to elaborate on the situation.

D) She is sorry that the student had to endure the situation.

Part 1 - Lecture

(AT4-3.mp3)

6) What is the main idea of the lecture?

   A) Mistakes that new businesses make.

   B) How to differentiate a new business.

   C) Strategies for various types of new businesses.

   D) Methods of advertising to potential customers.

7) According to the lecture, what does a financial incentive do?

   A) It persuades consumers to purchase high-priced goods.

   B) It attracts consumers by charging less than the competition.

   C) If offers a service that the competition does not offer.

   D) It maintains a competitive edge over the consumers.

8) **Listen again to part of the discussion. Then answer the question.**

(AT4-4.mp3)

   Why does the professor say this:

   A) To point out the effectiveness of special deals and promotions.

   B) To differentiate product cost and quality.

   C) To show the reasons to shop at different stores.

   D) To mention a problem in the point of view of the consumer.

9) According to the lecture, what is an important part of any business strategy?

   A) Offering prices that can compete with the competition.

   B) Maintaining uniqueness until a profit is made.

   C) Keeping policies if they make the business stand out.

   D) Giving customers security in shopping with the business.

10) What does the professor imply about consumers?

   A) They prefer special deals and promotions over unique products.

   B) They stay loyal to a company regardless of price change.

   C) They don't buy the products based on quality.

   D) They are likely to shop at long lasting stores than new ones.

11) How is the lecture organized?

   A) By categorizing the types of business.

   B) By describing a theory and mentioning the flaws in it.

   C) By providing definitions of terms with examples.

   D) By comparing and contrasting the strategies.

Part 2 - Conversation

(AT4-5.mp3)

1) Why does the student go to see the professor?

   A) To give an excuse why she couldn't be at the last lecture.

   B) To request an extra ticket for her classmate.

   C) To seek permission to skip a play.

   D) To ask for more information about a play.

2) According to the conversation, the woman is worried about

   A) Getting a ride to the art theater.

   B) Understanding the foreign play.

   C) Purchasing the tickets for the play.

   D) Being able to read the supertitles.

3) What can be inferred about the upcoming test?

   A) The test will be in French.

   B) The date of the test is on the syllabus.

   C) The test will occur two weeks after the play.

   D) The questions will be about a Chinese film.

4) **Listen again to part of the conversation. Then answer the question.**

(AT4-6.mp3)

Why does the professor say this?

A) To ask the student to wait as he looks for another syllabus.

B) To inform the student an important date on the syllabus.

C) To point out that the student has the last copy.

D) To discourage the student from misplacing the syllabus again.

5) What will the professor ask the students to do on the test?

A) Explain the history of tragic plays.

B) Translate sections of the play's dialogue.

C) Identify who said the phrases from the play.

D) Describe the set and structure of the performance.

Part 2 - Lecture

(AT4-7.mp3)

6) What is the main idea of the lecture?

   A) Comparing physical and historical geology.

   B) Conflicting theories regarding Earth's geologic history.

   C) How Hutton contributed to Earth's geologic history.

   D) Why people from long ago had difficulty determining the age of Earth.

7) Why does the professor talk about human bias in scale?

   A) To demonstrate how humans can influence the geologic processes.

   B) To show the quick development of human understanding.

   C) To compare the life spans of modern humans with those long ago.

   D) To point out why people were unable to comprehend Earth's long history.

8) According to the lecture, why was the catastrophism theory popular for a long time?

   A) With the number of marine fossils, it was easy to prove.

   B) Earthquake and volcano records supported it.

   C) It described why common geological processes occurred.

   D) It was consistent with the estimation of the Earth's age at the time.

9) What can be inferred about uniformitarianism?

   A) It was influenced by the theories the Greek philosophers made.

   B) It was made during the same time as the catastrophism theory.

   C) It assumes that our planet is billions of years old.

   D) It goes against the idea that volcanoes affected our planet.

10) **Listen to part of the discussion. Then answer the question.**

(AT4-8.mp3)

Why does the student say this?

   A) To show that catastrophic events happen even today.

   B) To encourage the class to observe their surroundings for geological events.

   C) To point out that volcanoes and earthquakes do not occur every day.

   D) To argue that catastrophism is mainly responsible for the change in landscape.

11) Indicate whether each statement describes catastrophism or uniformitarianism.

Click in the correct box for each phrase.

	Catastrophism	Uniformitarianism
A) Assumption that Earth is billions of years old.		
B) Estimation that Earth is not as old as human's recorded history.		
C) Greek philosophers influenced the creation of this theory.		
D) Created by geologist James Hutton.		

Part 2 - Lecture

(AT4-9.mp3)

12) What is the main idea of the lecture?

   A) The dangers associated with animal play.
   B) Several explanations for an animal's playful behavior.
   C) How playing varies between different species.
   D) Comparison between human and animal behaviors.

13) According to the professor, what do people say against the preparation theory?

   A) Animals can get injured during play.
   B) Playful behavior does not develop hunting skills.
   C) Different animals show the same behavior.
   D) The behavior shown by juveniles is not the same as adults.

14) What does the professor think about the surplus energy theory?

   A) He finds it promising so it should be explored more.
   B) He believes it does not completely explain playful behavior.
   C) He is upset that many do not support it.
   D) He thinks it should be incorporated in the flexibility theory.

15) According to the lecture, prohibiting a young animal from playing will

   A) Decrease the animal's physical strength.

   B) Hinder brain development.

   C) Enhance its ability to solve problems.

   D) Impair its ability to interact with others.

16) **Listen to part of the lecture. Then answer the question.**

(AT4-10.mp3)

Why does the professor say this:

   A) To express how normal the behavior is.

   B) To point out the unlikelihood of the event.

   C) To encourage students to question their observations.

   D) To state that the observation is not trustworthy.

17) The professor talks about three theories about why animals engage in play behavior. Indicate the correct theory for each answer choice.

Click in the correct box for each phrase.

	Preparation Theory	Surplus Energy Theory	Flexibility Theory
A) To pass boredom.			
B) Learn important skills.			
C) Develops brain growth.			
D) Suggested by a Greek philosopher.			

Vocabulary:

presume	v.	suppose that something is the case on the basis of probability.	*assume, suppose*
rowdy	adj.	noisy and disorderly.	*unruly, disorderly*
ruckus	n.	a disturbance or commotion.	
violation	n.	the action of violating someone or something.	*breach, infringement*
regulation	n.	a rule or directive made and maintained by an authority.	*rule, order, act*
investigate	v.	carry out a systematic or formal inquiry to discover and examine the facts of (an incident, allegation, etc.) so as to establish the truth.	*probe, explore*
harass	v.	subject to aggressive pressure or intimidation.	*pester, badger*
authority	n.	the power or right to give orders, make decisions, and enforce obedience.	*power, jurisdiction*
suspect	v.	have an idea or impression of the existence, presence, or truth of (something) without certain proof.	*feel, have suspicion*
elaborate	adj.	involving many carefully arranged parts or details; detailed and complicated in design and planning.	*detailed, intricate*
distinguish	v.	recognize or treat (someone or something) as different.	*discriminate, discern*
premium	n.	a sum added to an ordinary price or charge.	*subcharge*

perception	n.	a way of regarding, understanding, or interpreting something; a mental impression.	*insight*
incentive	n.	a thing that motivates or encourages one to do something.	*motivation, stimulus*
imperative	adj.	of vital importance; crucial.	*crucial, vital*
potential	adj.	having or showing the capacity to become or develop into something in the future.	*possible, prospective*
loyal	adj.	giving or showing firm and constant support or allegiance to a person or institution.	*faithful, true*
mandatory	adj.	required by law or rules; compulsory.	*binding, compulsory*
overlap	v.	extend over so as to cover partly.	
project	v.	present or promote (a particular view or image).	*convey, present*
aspect	n.	a particular part or feature of something.	*feature, characteristic*
motive	n.	a reason for doing something, especially one that is hidden or not obvious.	*reason, rationale*
misplace	v.	put in the wrong place and lose temporarily because of this; mislay.	*lose, mislay*
geosphere	n.	any of the almost spherical concentric regions of matter that make up the earth and its atmosphere, as the lithosphere and hydrosphere.	
assume	v.	suppose to be the case, without proof.	*presume, suppose*

belief	n.	an acceptance that a statement is true or that something exists.	*opinion, attitude*
unearth	v.	find (something) in the ground by digging.	*excavate, mine*
contradict	v.	deny the truth of (a statement) by asserting the opposite.	*deny, refute*
contribute	v.	help to cause or bring about.	*give, donate*
span	n.	the full extent of something from end to end; the amount of space that something covers.	*stretch, reach*
resemble	v.	have qualities or features, especially those of appearance, in common with (someone or something); look or seem like.	*look alike*
mirror	v.	correspond to.	*match, imitate*
forage	v.	(of a person or animal) search widely for food or provisions.	*search, hunt*
maturity	n.	the state, fact, or period of being mature.	*adulthood*
coincide	v.	occur at or during the same time.	*concur, match*
neglect	v.	fail to care for properly.	*abandon*
juvenile	adj.	of, for, or relating to young people.	*young, adolescent*
motivation	n.	the reason or reasons one has for acting or behaving in a particular way.	*incentive, stimulus*
aside	adv.	to one side; out of the way.	*apart, alongside*
promising	adj.	showing signs of future success.	*favorable, encouraging*

hinder	v.	create difficulties for (someone or something), resulting in delay or obstruction.	*hamper, obstruct*
enhance	v.	intensify, increase, or further improve the quality, value, or extent of.	*magnify, amplify*
impair	v.	weaken or damage something (especially a human faculty or function).	*damage, weaken*
surplus	n.	an amount of something left over when requirements have been met; an excess of production or supply over demand.	*excess, overabundance*

Additional Vocabulary:

Chapter notes:

Actual Test
05

Listening Section Directions

This section of the TOEFL test measures your ability to comprehend conversations and lectures in the English language.

The listening section is divided into two or three separately timed parts. Each part will contain 1 conversation and 1 or 2 lectures. You will only hear the conversation or lecture one time.

After each listening, questions related to the conversation or lecture will follow. The questions will ask about the main idea and supporting details. Some questions might ask for the speaker's purpose or attitude. You are to answer the questions based on what is stated or implied by the speakers.

Taking notes is recommended. It will help you answer the questions. Your notes will not be scored.

If the volume of the conversation or lecture is too loud or too soft, click on the **VOLUME ICON** at the top of the screen.

In some questions, you will see a headphone icon. This indicates that you will listen to part of the conversation or lecture.

Some of the questions have special directions, such as placing the answers in order or checking the answers in the correct space. The directions to these questions will appear in a gray box on the screen.

A clock at the top of the screen will show you how much time is remaining. The clock will not count down while you are listening. The timer will only start ticking while you are answering the questions.

Part 1 - Conversation

(AT5-1.mp3)

1) Why does the student visit the residential office?

   A) To lower his bills.
   B) To renew his parking permit.
   C) To file a complaint against his roommates.
   D) To get permission to live with his family.

2) How does the student feel about living on campus?

   A) He is upset by the high costs.
   B) He finds that it helps him to focus in school.
   C) He is uncomfortable being surrounded by so many people.
   D) He is bothered by his roommates causing so much trouble.

3) What problem will the student encounter if he decides to move?

   A) He will have to pay a more expensive rent.
   B) He will not be able to drive his car to school.
   C) He will live far from a bus stop.
   D) He will have difficulty making friends on campus.

4) Why is the student excited about the free bus pass?

   A) His commute to school will decrease.

   B) He will save money on spending gas.

   C) He will not have to drive his parent's car.

   D) He will not have to look for parking spaces.

5) **Listen again to the conversation. Then answer the question.**

   (AT5-2.mp3)

   Why does the employee say this:

   A) To determine the whereabouts of the office.

   B) To assist the student find the city hall.

   C) To see if the student needs directions.

   D) To show where the student can get his student ID.

Part 1 - Lecture

(AT5-3.mp3)

6) What is the main idea of the lecture?

   A) Different ways to fly.

   B) A new inspiration for aircraft engineers.

   C) Comparing bat and bird anatomy.

   D) How vortexes affect flight.

7) How does the professor feel about engineers using bats as templates for aircraft?

   A) She thinks positively about their results.

   B) She argues that it will be pointless.

   C) She believes that we have minimal understanding of bats.

   D) She prefers birds to be the models of airplanes.

8) When compared to bird wings, the wings of bats

   A) Are more rigid.

   B) Are not identical to human hands.

   C) Show more independent joints.

   D) Are lined with feathers.

9) What did researchers find out from putting a bat inside a wind tunnel?

   A) Fog hindered the animal's ability to fly.
   B) Bats used up more energy compared to flying against the wind.
   C) The bat's wings showed that it could handle strong wind.
   D) The bat created two vortexes from its wings.

10) Why does the professor talk about pregnant bats?

   A) To show how long a bat's pregnancy is.
   B) To emphasize how much weight the bats could support while flying.
   C) To point out that bats are mammals.
   D) To illustrate a bat's reproductive rate.

11) **Listen again to part of the lecture. Then answer the question.**

(AT5-4.mp3)

Why does the professor say this:

   A) To show satisfaction with modern onboard technology.
   B) To emphasize the effects of atmospheric conditions.
   C) To point out how much help sensor technology will provide.
   D) To push students to become pilots.

Part 2 - Conversation

(AT5-5.mp3)

1) Why does the student visit the professor?

　　A) To turn in a research paper.

　　B) To check if she is qualified for a scholarship.

　　C) To be excused from giving a presentation.

　　D) To confirm the requirements for a research paper.

2) According to the conversation, why won't the presentation be graded?

　　A) It's almost the end of the school term.

　　B) It has nothing to do with the actual subject of the course.

　　C) It does not take much time to complete.

　　D) It is for those who need extra credit.

3) What suggestion does the professor provide for the student's problem with the presentation?

　　A) Go over her class notes.

　　B) Receive help from a student tutor.

　　C) Have a classmate help her.

　　D) Participate in the review session.

4) **Listen again to part of the conversation. Then answer the question.**

(AT5-6.mp3)

What does the student imply when she says this:

A) She is not sure what to do for her project.

B) She will skip going to the tutoring service.

C) She questions if others will understand her project.

D) She has not yet chosen a topic for her presentation.

5) According to the conversation, the history scholarship cannot be given if

A) The student only has a minor in history.

B) The student did not complete enough credits.

C) The student is majoring in a non-history major.

D) The student has no recommendation.

Part 2 - Lecture

(AT5-7.mp3)

6) What is the main idea of the discussion?

   A) The history of music.

   B) Rhythms in early music.

   C) Various singing techniques.

   D) The fundamental elements in Western music theory.

7) Researchers believe that the prehistoric instrument found in various places were mainly used for

   A) Confusing animals during a hunt.

   B) Holding musical performance.

   C) Communicating with others over long distances.

   D) Celebrating important events.

8) What is the professor's opinion on ancient music?

   A) It may have had other uses including entertainment.

   B) It started in Asia.

   C) It was played with complex sound patterns.

   D) It used objects that did not have acoustic properties.

9) What is so important about the bone flute?

   A) It proved that humans purposely made music during the Stone Age.

   B) It showed when humans first began to play with music.

   C) It served as a model for how the modern flute was designed.

   D) It indicated that humans long ago valued entertainment.

10) **Listen to part of the discussion. Then answer the question.**

(AT5-8.mp3)

What can be inferred about the professor when he says this:

   A) He thinks that rhythm is more important than tonal patterns.

   B) He prefers not to listen to vocal performances.

   C) He believes that rhythm is critical in good music.

   D) He thinks music today is missing the rhythmic patterns of early music.

11) Why does the professor talk about common time?

   A) To compare baroque and early music.

   B) To show how rhythm in music was integrated.

   C) To explain the reason for the popularity of baroque music.

   D) To describe the insignificance of it in music.

Part 2 - Lecture

(AT5-9.mp3)

12) What is the main idea of the lecture?

   A) The root system of plants.

   B) The process of photosynthesis.

   C) The importance of certain chemicals in leaves.

   D) How food is produced in the leaves of plants.

13) According to the lecture, why do leaves turn brown and orange in winter?

   A) Daylight hours shorten.

   B) Chlorophyll breaks down.

   C) Plants start to store energy.

   D) Photosynthesis halts in low temperature.

14) What does the professor think of the theory that anthocyanin wards off herbivores?

   A) She believes it to be misleading.

   B) She thinks it requires more research.

   C) She is sure that it will become popular.

   D) She wants the theory to be included in textbooks.

15) What can be inferred about photosynthesis?

   A) It makes chlorophyll.

   B) It stops harmful oxidation in plant cells.

   C) It makes colorful hues in leaves.

   D) It cannot use certain wavelengths of light.

16) According to the lecture, what is one purpose carotenoids have?

   A) Stop oxidation.

   B) Break apart anthocyanin.

   C) Prevent damage to chlorophyll.

   D) Stimulate reproduction of seeds.

17) Which of the following belongs to the appropriate chemical?

Click in the correct box for each phrase.

	Chlorophyll	Carotenoids	Anthocyanin
A) Yellow color			
B) Green color			
C) Red color			
D) Supplies energy for photosynthesis			

Vocabulary:

dictate	v.	lay down authoritatively; prescribe.	*impose, prescribe*
deed	n.	a legal document that is signed and delivered, especially one regarding the ownership of property or legal rights.	*contract*
renew	v.	extend for a further period the validity of (a license, subscription, or contract).	*extend, prolong*
commute	v.	travel some distance between one's home and place of work on a regular basis.	
fundamental	adj.	forming a necessary base or core; of central importance.	*basic, rudimentary*
derive	v.	obtain something from (a specified source).	*obtain, acquire, procure*
physique	n.	the form, size, and development of a person's body.	*body, build figure*
soar	v.	fly or rise high in the air.	*wing, take flight*
elastic	adj.	able to encompass variety and change; flexible and adaptable.	*flexible, pliant*
elongated	adj.	long in relation to width, especially unusually so.	
generate	v.	cause (something, especially an emotion or situation) to arise or come about.	*give rise to, bring about*
feat	n.	an achievement that requires great courage, skill, or strength.	*achievement, accomplishment*

maneuverable	adj.	(especially of a craft or vessel) able to be maneuvered easily while in motion.	
gestation	n.	the process of carrying or being carried in the womb between conception and birth.	*pregnancy, incubation*
detect	v.	discover or identify the presence or existence of.	*notice, perceive*
inspiration	n.	the process of being mentally stimulated to do or feel something, especially to do something creative.	*motivation, stimulation*
template	n.	something that serves as a model for others to copy.	
hinder	v.	create difficulties for (someone or something), resulting in delay or obstruction.	*impede, obstruct*
assist	v.	help (someone), typically by doing a share of the work.	*help, aid*
qualify	v.	be entitled to a particular benefit or privilege by fulfilling a necessary condition.	*be eligible*
radical	adj.	characterized by independence of or departure from tradition; innovative or unorthodox.	*revolutionary, progressive*
origin	n.	the point or place where something begins, arises, or is derived.	*birth, genesis*
ancestor	n.	a person, typically one more remote than a grandparent, from whom one is descended.	*forefather, predecessor*
steady	adj.	firmly fixed, supported, or balanced; not shaking or moving.	*stable, firm*

acoustic	adj.	relating to sound or the sense of hearing.	
insignificance	n.	the quality of being too small or unimportant to be worth consideration.	
hue	n.	a color or shade.	*color, tint*
expend	v.	spend or use up (a resource such as money, time, or energy).	*spend, disburse*
pigmentation	n.	the natural coloring of animal or plant tissue.	
shade	n.	a color, especially with regard to how light or dark it is or as distinguished from one nearly like it.	*hue, tint*
minimal	adj.	of a minimum amount, quantity, or degree; negligible.	*minimum, least*
ward off		prevent someone or something from harming or affecting one.	*fend off, repel*
reliable	adj.	consistently good in quality or performance; able to be trusted.	*dependable*
barrier	n.	a fence or other obstacle that prevents movement or access.	*barricade, blockade*
halt	v.	bring or come to an abrupt stop.	*stop*

Chapter notes:

Answers and Script

Chapter 01
Q1 Main Idea

Page.12~13

메인 아이디어

이 유형은 거의 항상 대화나 강의를 들은 후에 묻는 첫 번째 질문이다. 대화나 강의의 주요 아이디어는 항상 리스닝의 첫 부분에 언급될 것이다. 대화에서는 학생이 방문한 목적이나 교수가 학생에게 전화를 건 이유가 30초 안에 언급된다. 강의의 주요 아이디어는 강의 시작 60초 안에 언급될 것이다.

단계별 풀이 방법

1) 주요 아이디어는 항상 대화나 강의의 도입부에서 언급되기 때문에, 리스닝의 첫 30초에서 60초 사이에 집중하라.
2) 강의나 대화의 첫 부분을 놓쳤다면, 메모를 보고 설명과 예시를 연결하여 주요 아이디어를 정하라.
3) 주요 아이디어는 일반적이라는 것을 기억하라. 주요 아이디어는 특정한 것이어서는 안 된다.
4) 주요 아이디어는 대화나 강의 내내 반복되었던 키워드를 담고 있어야 한다.

Page.15~16

연습 A

그 학생은 교수를 왜 찾아갔는가?

A) 증기 엔진을 사용한 기간을 확인하기 위해서
B) 연구 논문을 위한 한 개인에 대해 이야기 하기 위해서
C) 연구 논문의 주제 선정을 위한 도움을 요청하기 위해서
D) 연구 논문 제출 기한의 연장을 요청하기 위해서

M: 안녕하세요. Wood교수님.

W: 안녕하세요. 데이비드, 무슨 일로 왔나요?

M: 음, 저는 교수님께서 아시다시피 수업에 제출 할 연구 논문을 위해 대중 교통에 대해 연구하고 있었어요. 저는 보스턴이 최초의 지하철 시스템을 가지고 있었고 곧이어 뉴욕이 그 뒤를 따랐다는 것을 알고 있어요. 하지만…. 알프레드 비치의 좀 더 앞선 시도를 읽었는데요. 제 연구가 좀 산만해졌는데… 그것에 대해 얘기 좀 할 수 있을까요? 제 연구에 도움이 될 거에요.

W: 아, 알프레드 비치. 그는 기술 잡지의 출판자이자 발명가였죠. 그는 실제로 지하철이 도시 혼잡에 대한 해결책이라고 보았어요. 하지만 그 당시에는, 지하에 기차를 놓을 수 있는 방법이 없었죠.

M: 하지만 증기 엔진은 수년 동안 사용되어 왔지 않나요?

정답: B. 첫 번째 신호 문구는 "…무슨 일로 왔나요?"였다. 이것은 수험생에게 학생이 방문 이유를 말하려고 한다는 것을 알려줄 것이다. 다음 신호 문구는 "…그것에 대해 이야기 할 수 있을까요?"였다. 이 구절은 학생들이 알프레드 비치에 대한 그의 연구가 산만해졌다고 말한 후에 뒤따라온 것이다. 그래서 그 학생은 알프레드 비치라는 이름의 한 개인에 대해 그의 교수와 이야기하기 위해 왔다.

A는 이것이 주요 아이디어라고 언급하는 신호 문구가 없었기 때문에 정답이 아니다. 또한, 증기 엔진에 대해 토론하는 것은 알프레드 비치라는 더 큰 주제에 비해 사소한 세부 사항처럼 보인다. 그 학생은 이미 그의 연구 논문 주제로 대중 교통을 선택했기 때문에 C는 정답이 아니다. 연구 논문 기한 연장은 논의조차 되지 않아 답이 될 수 없기에 D는 정답이 아니다.

Page.17~18

연습B

강의의 주요 주제는 무엇인가?

A) 1830년대에 미국이 어떻게 사회적으로 변했는가
B) 미국 및 유럽 문학의 차이
C) 일부 저명한 낭만주의 작가에 대한 설명
D) 자연이 미국 낭만주의 작가들에게 어떤 영향을 주었는가

> 좋은 아침입니다 여러분! 바로 본론으로 들어갑시다. 지난 수업에서 우리는 미국 낭만주의라고 불리는 중요한 문학 운동에 대해 토론했습니다. 다음 몇 주 동안, 우리는 그 운동의 특정한 저자인 낭만주의 작가들에게 집중할 것입니다. 하지만, 우리가 이 작가들에 대해 토론하기 전에, 저는 자연에 대한 그들의 견해와 그것이 그들의 글에 어떤 영향을 미쳤는지에 대해 말하고 싶습니다.
>
> 자, 시작해 보죠. 미국의 낭만주의는 1830년대 말에 시작되었습니다. 그 당시에는 몇 가지 사회적 변화가 일어나고 있었습니다. 첫째, 미국인들이 서부로 이동하고 있었기 때문에 미국은 빠른 속도로 팽창하고 있었습니다. 둘째, 북동부 지역의 공장들이 놀라운 속도로 늘고 있었습니다. 그리고 마침내, 마을은 도시로 바뀌었습니다.

정답: D. 신호 문구는 "...이 작가들에 대해 논의하기 전에, 자연에 대한 그들의 견해와 그것이 그들의 글에 어떤 영향을 주었는지에 대해 이야기하고자 합니다."였다. 이것은 교수가 낭만주의 작가들에 대해 토론하는 것이 아니라 자연이 그들의 글에 어떤 영향을 미쳤는지가 강의의 주요 아이디어라는 것을 수험생들에게 알려주고 있다.

A는 답이 아니다. 왜냐하면 교수가 미국에서 일어나고 있는 몇몇 사회적 변화에 대해 언급하긴 하지만, 교수는 자연과 자연이 저자들에게 미치는 영향에 대해 말하고 싶다고 지적했기 때문이다. 강연에서 유럽 문학에 대한 언급조차 없었기 때문에 B는 정답이 아니다. C역시 정답이 아니다. 왜냐하면 교수가 다음 주에 낭만주의 작가들에 대해 토론할 것이라고 말하기는 하지만, 교수는 먼저 그들에게 영향을 준 것에 대해 토론할 것이라고 언급하기 때문이다.

Chapter02
Supporting Details

Page.22~23

뒷받침 세부 질문

뒷받침하는 세부 질문은 매우 구체적이다. 만약 당신이 노트에 정보를 적었거나 그 정보를 우연히 기억한다면, 당신은 점수를 획득할 것이다. 이 질문 유형은 모든 리스닝 중 가장 많이 나타나며, 일반적으로 각 대화 또는 강의마다 2~3개의 질문으로 이루어져 있다. 때로는 수험생은 2개의 답을 선택하라는 요청을 받기도 하므로, 정답을 제출하기 전 선택 사항을 주의 깊게 읽어야 한다.

대화에 있어, 뒷받침하는 세부 질문은 학생과 교수 또는 직원 간에 논의된 해결책의 세부 사항을 중심으로 이루어진다. 강의의 경우, 뒷받침하는 세부 질문은 예시나 설명의 형태를 취하는 주요 아이디어에 대한 것이다.

기억할 점: 답변은 대화 또는 강의 내용을 기초로 선택해야 한다. 당신은 이 문제들을 해결하기 위해 학교나 학원에서 배운 지식을 사용해서는 안 된다.

문제 풀이 방법

1) 뒷받침하는 세부 내용은 항상 주요 아이디어에 관한 것임을 기억하라.
2) 특히 해결책을 제시하거나 무언가를 기술할 때는 빠르고 상세한 메모를 하라.
3) 선택지는 항상 다른 말로 바꾸어 표현되므로 대화나 강의에서 언급된 동의어 및 유사한 설명을 찾으라.
4) 대화나 강의에서 나온 내용을 기초로 정답을 골라야 함을 기억하라! 자신의 배경 지식을 사용하여 문제를 해결하지 마라.

Page.25~26

연습A

Beech가 지하 터널을 홍보하기 위해 사용한 혁신적인 방법은 무엇이었는가?

A) 지하를 파헤칠 수 있는 장치를 개발했다.
B) 증기 엔진을 개선하여 그을음을 최소화했다.
C) 붕괴되는 암석으로부터 작업자를 보호하기 위해 보호 장치를 만들었다.
D) 승객을 이동시키기 위한 지하철을 만들었다.

여자: 증기 엔진이 수 년 동안 사용되었지만, 그것은 지하 터널에 너무 많은 그을음을 발생시켰습니다. 또한, 끊임없는 환기는 증기 엔진이 실용적인 선택이 아님을 증명했습니다. 1866년에는 아직 휘발유와 전기 모터를 이용할 수 없었기 때문에 지하 터널에서의 이동 수단을 위한 새로운 방법이 적용돼야 했습니다. 알프레드 비치는 이 상황을 극복하기 위한 몇 가지 혁신적인 방법을 고안해냈습니다. 먼저, 그는 건물 한쪽 끝에서 다른 쪽 끝으로 승객들을 실어 나르는 지상철을 만들었습니다. 그는 또한 지하에 터널을 뚫을 수 있는 튼튼한 드릴을 고안했습니다. 터널 내부의 구조적인 지탱을 보완하기 위해, 비치는 보호 장치 안에서 구멍을 뚫었습니다. 그래서 그것이 작동하는 방법은 일꾼들이 보호 장치 안에 머무르는 동안 드릴이 앞으로 전진하고, 벽돌을 쌓아 터널을 구조적으로 지탱해 주는 것입니다.

답변: A. 이 논의의 장면은 지하 터널에서 생길 수 있는 문제점과 알프레드 비치가 이것들을 어떻게 극복할 수 있었는지에 대해 초첨을 맞추고 있다. 따라서 당신의 노트 필기는 문제와 해결책 혹은 비치가 제안한 혁신에 초점을 맞추어야 한다. 논의에서는 "그가 지하 터널을 뚫을 만큼 강한 드릴을 고안했다."고 말하고 있다. 보기 A에서는 "그가 장비를 개선했다…"라고 언급한다. 이 장비는 드릴을 가리킨다.

증기 기관이 너무 많은 그을음을 발생시키고, 그가 엔진을 개선했다고 말하지 않았으므로 B는 답이 아니다. C는 비록 보호 장치가 언급되었지만, 그것의 목적은 터널 안에서 구조적 지지를 위한 것이고 노동자를 보호하기 위한 것이 아니기 때문에 답이 아니다. D는 전철이 지상에 있고, 지하에 있지 않기 때문에 답이 아니다.

Page.27~28

연습B

미국의 황무지가 낭만주의 작가들에게 어떤 영향을 끼쳤는가?

A) 유럽식 글쓰기에 더 의존하게 되었다.
B) 시는 더욱 융통성이 없어지고, 전통적인 형식에 의존하게 되었다.
C) 글이 더 자연스러워졌다.
D) 글쓰기를 포기하고 벌목꾼이 되었다.

> 미국을 유럽과 차별화시킨 것은 인류의 손길이 닿지 않는 끝없는 황무지였다. 유럽 땅은 천년 이상의 기간 동안 인간 문명에 의해 변화되어 왔다. 북미 대륙은 무한해 보이는 땅을 가지고 있었기 때문에, 국가로 선별되었다. 그리고 이것은 낭만주의자들이 그들의 이상을 형성하는데 도움을 주었다. 낭만주의 작가들은 더욱 독립적으로 되어갔다. 그들에게는 그들만이 할 이야기가 있었고 미국을 다른 세계에 보여주고 싶었다. 그 작가들은 특히 미국이 제공해야 할 자연 세계에 초점을 맞췄다. 그리고 미국의 황무지가 이 작가들에게 끼친 영향은 그들의 글에서 드러났다. 낭만적인 시인들 중 일부는 고정된 길이와 운율 패턴을 가진 전통적인 유럽 형식에서 벗어났다. 그들은 자신들의 시가 좀 더 유기적이어야 한다고 믿었고, 그래서 그들의 글은 더 생생하게 바뀌었다.

정답: C "그들은 자신들의 시가 좀 더 유기적이어야 한다고 믿었기 때문에, 그들의 글은 더 생생하게 바뀌었다"라고 강의에서 말하고 있다. 여기서 키워드는 유기적이고 생생한 것이다. 그리고 자연스러운 것은 이 단어들과 동의어가 될 수 있다.

낭만주의 작가들이 "…더 독립적이 되었다"고 쓰여 있기 때문에 A는 정답이 아니다. 또한 낭만적인 시인들 일부가 "… 유럽의 전통 형식에서 벗어났다…"라고 말하고 있다. 낭만주의 작가들이 전통적인 형태에서 벗어났기 때문에 B는 정답이 아니다. 낭만주의 작가들이 글쓰기를 포기했다는 언급이 없고, 벌목꾼들도 언급조차 되지 않았기 때문에 D도 정답이 아니다.

Chapter03
Connecting Contents

Page.32~34

내용 연결

내용 연결 문제에서 수험생들은 대화나 강의의 전반적인 구성을 살펴봐야 한다. 이 문제는 강의가 어떻게 구성되어 있는지, 학생이나 교수가 특정한 단어나 구절을 말할 때 무엇을 의미하는지 질문할 것이다.

강의의 구성은 아이디어의 목록을 따를 수도 있고, 사건들의 연대순을 나열할 수도 있고, 주제에 대한 몇 가지 예시를 제공할 수도 있다. 대화에서 당신은 학생이나 교수가 왜 이전에 말한 것에 근거하여 특정한 단어나 구절을 말했는지 추측할 수 있어야 한다.
때때로 강의에서 왜 교수가 특정한 키워드를 언급했는지 질문할 수 있는데, 이것은 당신이 노트를 보고 그 키워드 앞뒤에 무슨 말을 했는지 살펴 볼 필요가 있을 것이다.

보통 대화나 강의 마다 내용 연결 문제는 하나만 있거나 없을 수도 있다.

문제 해결 단계

1) 사소한 것에 집중하지 않고 전반적인 내용에 집중해야 한다.
2) 노트를 보고 아이디어가 어떻게 연결되는지 확인한다. 그것들이 연대순을 따르는가, 아니면 예시들의 목록인가?
3) 리스닝에서 주요 주제와 전혀 무관하게 보이는 내용이 언급되면, 그 연관성을 이해해야 한다.
내용 연결 문제에서, 대화는 학생이나 교수가 특정한 요구나 문제를 가지고 상대방에게 접근하기 때문에 더 쉽게 풀 수 있는 경향이 있다. 당신이 상황을 이해하는 한, 대화의 요점을 연결시키는 것은 어렵지 않을 것이다.

시나리오:
학생이 교수를 만나러 간다.
　　- 학생은 강의 또는 강의의 일부 내용을 이해하지 못했다.
　　- 학생은 할당된 과제 또는 프로젝트를 이해하지 못했다.
　　- 학생이 교수에게 무언가를 요청하고 있다.
교수가 학생을 부른다.
　　- 교수는 학생의 성적에 관심이 있다.
　　- 교수는 학생의 과제에 대한 새로운 정보를 요청하고 있다.
　　- 교수가 학생의 전공 또는 진로에 대해 논의하고자 한다.
학생이 대학교 직원을 만나러 간다.
　　- 학생은 기숙사 관리인, 대학 사서, 행정 직원을 찾아가 문제에 대해 논의한다.

강의는 교수가 왜 특정한 키워드나 구문을 언급했는지에 초점을 맞추는 경향이 있다. 이 경우 키워드나 구문의 세부 사항에 초점을 두지 말고 앞뒤에 말한 내용에 초점을 맞추어야 한다.

내용을 이해하고 전체 주제와 연결하려면 노트 필기가 포괄적이어야 한다.

ANSWERS AND SCRIPT

Page.35~36

연습A

교수는 왜 윌리엄 트위드를 언급하는가?

A) 그가 뉴욕시의 수석 정치인이었다는 것을 말하기 위해
B) Beech가 직면해야 하는 장애물을 보여주기 위해
C) 영향력 면에서 그를 Beech와 비교하기 위해
D) 그가 어떻게 권력을 잡았는지 묘사하기 위해

W: 그 당시 뉴욕은 민주당의 권력자인 윌리엄 트위드의 지배를 받았어요. 그는 부도덕한 정치인이었고, 그의 친구들과 협력자들에게 호의를 베풀어 권력을 유지했죠. 그의 많은 불법 행위들 중 하나는 현존하는 철도로부터 헌금을 모으는 것이었어요. 그래서 비치가 지으려고 했던 것과 같은 사설 운영 지하철은 그의 이익을 해칠 것이었어요.

M: 책에서 그에 대해 읽은 기억이 나요. 그러면 비치는 어떻게 그의 주변에서 일했나요?

W: 음, 비치는 매우 교활했어요. 그는 서류 작업 중에 건축 허가증을 숨기는 한편 우편물 운송 시스템에 대한 제안서를 보냈어요. 이것은 무슨 일이 일어나고 있는지 트위드가 모르게 그가 몰래 지하철을 만드는 것을 가능하게 했어요.

M: 하지만 그 점이 저를 혼란스럽게 해요. 제 말은, 뉴욕은 대도시예요. 사람들이 끊임없이 그 도시를 돌아다녀요. 어떻게 그걸 비밀로 할 수 있었을까요?

W: 아무도 확실히 몰라요. 아마 비치가 직원들 중 몇 명에게 뇌물을 준 것 같아요. 그럼에도 불구하고, 그는 3개월 만에 들키지 않고 프로젝트를 완성할 수 있었어요.

정답: B. 이 논의에서, 윌리엄 트위드는 뉴욕시를 통치하고 있었고 그는 호의를 베풀어 권력을 장악했다고 말한다. 또한 사설 지하철이 그의 이익을 감소시킬 것이라고 언급한다. 그래서 여기서, 교수가 지하철 건설의 장애물에 대해 이야기 하고 있다. 학생은 어떻게 비치가 그의 주변에서 일할 수 있었는지에 대해 의문을 제기하고, 교수는 비치가 어떻게 제안을 위한 서류 작업 중에 건축 허가증을 교묘하게 숨겼는지에 대해 설명한다. 그래서 우리가 그 내용을 연결했을 때 트위드는 비치가 지하철을 만들기 위해 함께해야 했던 사람이었다.

비록 트위드가 뉴욕시의 수석 정치인이었지만, 교수가 그를 언급하는 이유는 아니기 때문에 A는 정답이 아니다. 트위드와 비치는 영향력 면에서 비교되지 않기 때문에 C는 정답이 아니다. D가 정답이 아닌 이유는 그가 친구들에게 호의를 베풀어 권력을 유지했지만, 그것이 교수가 그에 대해 이야기하기로 결정한 이유는 아니기 때문이다.

Page.37~38

연습B

교수는 왜 은유를 언급하는가?

A) 오해의 소지가 있는 것에 대한 정의를 기술하기 위해
B) 낭만주의 작가들이 글에서 은유를 많이 사용했다는 것을 강조하기 위해
C) 낭만주의 저자가 사용하는 다른 기법과 비교하기 위해
D) 자연과 낭만주의 작가 사이의 관계를 설명하는 것을 돕기 위해

> 교수: 낭만주의 작가들은 자연을 훌륭한 지도자로 여겼습니다. 이러한 작가들에게 자연은 아름다움, 독립, 진실과 같은 특정한 가치의 원천이었죠. 제가 이걸 좀 더 명확하게 할 수 있는지 봅시다. 은유가 무엇인지 기억하는 사람 있나요?
>
> 학생: 은유는 "~같은" 또는 "~처럼" 같은 단어를 사용하지 않고 서로 다른 두 가지를 비교하는 기술 아닌가요?
>
> 교수: 거의 맞았어요. 은유는 서로 다른 두 가지를 암시적으로 비교하는 거예요. "모든 세상은 무대이다"라는 유명한 구절을 보세요. 여기서 세계는 연극 무대와 비교되고 있죠. 기본적으로, 낭만주의 작가들은 자연을 인간의 경험에 대한 은유라고 봤어요. 다시 말해서, 사람이 어떻게 살아야 하는지를 이해하기 위해 사람은 자연을 먼저 이해해야 했어요.

정답: D. 그 교수는 낭만주의 작가들에게 "자연은 특정한 가치의 원천이었다"고 말하며 시작한다. 그리고 나서 그는 이해를 쉽게 할 수 있도록 "은유"를 언급한다. 그래서 우리가 그 내용을 연결한다면, 은유는 낭만주의 작가들에게 자연이 무엇이었는지를 설명하는 데 사용 된다.

A는 답이 아니다. 왜냐하면 교수가 은유에 대한 학생의 정의를 바로 잡기는 하지만, 처음에 교수가 그것을 말한 이유는 아니기 때문이다. 낭만주의 작가들이 그들의 글에서 은유법을 사용했다는 것을 언급하지 않기 때문에 B는 정답이 아니다. 은유가 다른 기술과 비교되고 있지 않기 때문에 C는 정답이 아니다.

Chapter04
Function

Page.42~44

기능

기능 문제는 화자가 말하려고 하는 것을 이해했는지를 확인한다. 기능 문제는 각 대화 또는 강의에 한 번 나타나며, 리스닝의 일부를 재생하여 질문에 답변하는 데 도움이 될 수 있다.

대화와 관련하여, 기능 질문은 코멘트의 목적이 무엇인지 또는 숨겨진 의미가 있는지 묻는다. 이 질문이 다른 의미를 묻는 것처럼 보인다면, 이전과 후에 언급된 말을 이해하는 것이 중요하다.

강의와 관련하여, 학생과 교수가 앞뒤로 의견을 교환할 것이다. 토론이 진행되는 동안, 교수는 학생들의 관심을 끌거나 자신이 한 말을 기억해 내려고 노력할 것이다. 이 때가 기능 질문이 나타날 가능성이 있는 경우이다.

단계별 해결 방법:

1) 구어체 표현이 사용될 것이므로, 이에 친숙해져야 한다.
   - 내 다리를 잡아당기지 마 → 거짓말 하지 마
   - 그는 거만해 → 그는 자만해
   - 나는 눈이 점점 무거워져 → 나는 졸려
2) 재생되는 부분을 듣는 대신 노트를 보고 이전과 이후에 언급된 내용을 확인한다. 그런 다음 문맥의 문구를 이해하려고 노력하라.
3) 문구의 어조, 볼륨, 속도를 이해하는 것이 중요하다. 나열된 요인들은 구문의 기능을 설명한다.

대화나 강의에서 기능 문제는 발표자나 교수에 의해 발화된 문구를 포함할 것이다. 구문의 기능을 이해하려면, 구문이 어떻게 도입되었는지 살펴보아야 한다. 보통, 그 표현의 기능은 말하는 사람의 어조 또는 그 표현이 사용된 전후에 언급된 것에 있다.

메모할 때는 작은 세부 사항에 초점을 맞추는 대신 대화나 강의의 큰 내용과 흐름에 초점을 맞춰라. 어조의 변화나 구어체 표현이 사용되는 것을 들을 때는, 주의를 기울이고 잘 메모하라.

화자의 어조는 그 표현의 기능에 대해 많은 것을 말해 줄 수 있다. 어조를 통해 화자가 어떤 주제에 대해 불평하고 있는지 또는 그 문제에 대해 만족하고 있는지 결정할 수 있다. 그것은 또한 화자가 비관적인지 아니면 낙관적인지 보여줄 수 있다.

문제가 대화나 강의의 특정 부분을 재생 시킬 때마다, 그것을 메모할 수 있는 두 번째 기회로 생각하라. 다시 듣기가 되는 부분을 빨리 찾고 메모를 더 완성하기 위해 추가 세부 정보를 입력하라. 문제가 다시 듣기의 일부분을 들려주는 경우, 해당 부분에 초점을 맞추고 이전과 이후에 언급된 내용과 어떤 관계가 있는지 확인하라.

ANSWERS AND SCRIPT

Page.45~46

연습A

대화의 일부를 들어라. 그리고 질문에 답하라.

교수는 왜 이런 말을 하는가?
A) 비치의 아이디어는 더 좋은 시기에 등장했더라면 표준이 되었을 것이다.
B) 비치의 아이디어는 언제 등장했더라도 결코 성공하지 못했을 것이다.
C) 타이밍은 아이디어 그 자체 만큼 중요하지 않다.
D) 타이밍은 무언가를 발명할 때 고려해야 할 요소이다.

> W: 사람들은 비치의 새로운 이동 수단에 매료되었지만, 정치인들은 그의 편이 아니었어요. 비치가 주 의회로부터 지하철 노선 전체를 승인 받았음에도 불구하고, 그것은 악명 높은 트위드의 압력을 받은 주지사에 의해 거부당했습니다. 2년 동안, 비치는 지하철을 연장할 수 없었죠. 결국, 새로운 주지사가 권력을 잡았고 비치의 혁신을 승인했습니다.
>
> M: 저를 혼란스럽게 하는 것은, 어떻게 비치의 생각이 기준이 될 수 없었던가 하는 것이었어요. 사실상 그가 지하철을 실현 가능하게 한 첫 번째 사람이 아니었나요?
>
> W: 안타깝게도, 타이밍이 안 좋았어요. 새로운 주지사가 비치의 요청을 승인한 후, 주식 시장 붕괴가 곧 뒤따랐죠. 투자자들은 그들의 지원을 철회했고 공적 자금을 사용할 수 없게 되었죠. 그래서 이후 25년 동안은 지하철이 없었습니다. 슬프게도, 비치는 그 기간에 죽었고, 그래서 아무도 그의 아이디어를 추진하지 않았어요. 또한, 가스와 전기로 작동하는 엔진은 대중교통 부문에서 개선되었죠.

정답: A. 이 학생은 " 사실상 그가 지하철을 실현 가능하게 한 첫 번째 사람이 아니었나요?"라고 말했고, 그 교수는 " 안타깝게도, 타이밍이 안 좋았어요."라고 대답한다. 그래서 이 발언의 기능은 비치의 아이디어가 표준이 되지 않는 이유에 대해 대답하는 것이다. 그것은 직후 폭락한 주식 시장과 가스 및 전기로 움직이는 엔진의 개선 때문이었다. 그래서, 만약 그것이 더 좋은 시기에 일어났다면 비치의 아이디어는 표준이 되었을 것이다.

B는 비치의 아이디어가 결코 성공하지 못했을 것이라고 말하기 때문에 정답이 아니다. "never"는 매우 강한 단어이기 때문에 우리는 이것을 선택할 수 없다. C는 정답이 아니다. 왜냐하면 리스닝에서는 그것이 나쁜 타이밍이었다고 언급하는데, 이는 다시 말하면, 비치의 아이디어가 표준이 되기 위해서는 타이밍이 중요했기 때문이다. 그것은 타이밍과 아이디어를 비교하는 것이 아니다. 리스닝에서 비치의 아이디어가 표준이 되지 않은 이유에 대해 토론하고 있기 때문에 D는 정답이 아니다. 이는 무언가를 발명하는데 필요한 요소들에 대해 이야기하는 것이 아니다.

Page.47~48

연습B

강의의 일부를 다시 들어라. 그리고 질문에 답하라.

교수가 이렇게 말을 한 것은 어떤 의미인가?
A) 교수는 학생의 질문에 충분히 답하였다.
B) 교수는 학생이 질문을 하기 전에 먼저 문제를 복습하기를 바란다.
C) 교수는 밖에 비가 오는지 확인하려고 한다.
D) 교수는 참석해야 할 또 다른 일이 있어 답변할 수 없다.

교수: 낭만주의 작가들은 도시 생활에 대해 냉소적이었습니다. 도시의 생활 방식은 인간의 가치를 떨어뜨릴 뿐만 아니라 혼란과 물질주의를 제공했죠. 낭만주의 작가들이 자연으로 눈을 돌렸을 때, 그들은 도시 생활의 이러한 부정적인 측면을 피하려 하지 않고, 그들의 경험으로부터 배우려고 노력하고 있었습니다. 그들은 자신의 정체성을 보존하기 위해 자연이 제공하는 가치를 받아들일 필요가 있다고 느꼈습니다. 그리고 그들의 글에서 이러한 가치들을 퍼프림으로써, 그들은 도시 생활 방식으로 빠져들어가는 국가의 정신을 되찾기를 희망했습니다.

학생: 아, 이제 교수님 말씀을 이해하겠습니다. 설명해 주셔서 감사합니다. 사실 수업 시간에 저를 괴롭히는 질문이 하나 더 있어요.

교수: 아… 그럼 다음 기회에 하죠. 지금은 교직원 회의에 가야 해요. 다음에 수업 끝나고 보는 게 어때요?

학생: 좋아요. 교수님 감사합니다.

정답: D. 그녀가 또 다른 질문이 있다고 말하자, 그 교수는 유명한 구어체 표현으로 대답한다. "Let's take a rain check on that "은 "그건 나중에 하자"는 뜻이다. 그 교수는 또한 학생에게 다음 수업 후에 만날 것을 요청하는데, 이것은 그가 그녀의 질문에 대답할 것이라는 사실을 의미한다.

A는 답이 아니다. 왜냐하면 교수는 조급해 하지 않으며 그녀의 질문에 더 이상 대답하기를 거부하지 않기 때문이다. B는 답이 아니다. 왜냐하면 리스닝 중 어느 곳에서도 학생이 질문을 하기 전에 문제를 복습해야 한다는 것을 암시하지 않기 때문이다. C는 토론과 전혀 관련이 없기 때문에 정답이 아니다.

Chapter 05
Attitude

Page.52~54

태도

태도 질문은 화자의 태도나 의견을 이해하는 능력에 초점을 맞춘다. 그것은 화자가 어떤 특정한 주제에 대해 어떻게 느끼는지, 말하는 사람이 어떤 것을 좋아하고 싫어하는지, 또는 말하는 사람이 왜 특정한 감정을 경험하는지 질문할 수 있다. 또한 다양한 주제에 대한 화자의 의견을 확인할 것을 요청할 것이다.

이 문제는 대화와 강의에서 최소 한 번씩 나온다.

문제 풀이 순서

1) 말하는 사람의 어조에 주의하라. 어조는 그 사람을 낙관적으로 혹은 비관적으로 묘사할 수 있다.
2) 해당 과목에 대한 교수 개인의 의견을 언급할 때는 주의 깊게 살펴보아야 한다. 그 교수는 강의 내내 사실만을 진술할 것이다. 그러나 중간에 교수는 그들의 개인적 취향에 대해 언급할 것이다. 사실과 의견을 구별하는 법을 배워라.
3) 행간을 읽는 법을 배워라. 구절의 문자 그대로의 의미는 실제의 의미가 아닐 수도 있다.
4) 전후 발언에 집중하라. 태도를 이해하기 위해 맥락을 이해하라.

화자의 태도를 이해하기 위해서, 가장 좋은 전략은 언급된 어조나 문맥을 이해하는 것이다.

문장을 구체적으로 메모하는 대신, 전후에 한 말에 집중하라. 때때로, 문장에만 초점을 맞추는 것은 모호할 수 있다. 그 문장의 태도를 이해하기 위해서는 이전에 말한 것을 이해할 필요가 있다.

강의에서 교수가 (In my opinion / I think / Personally) 이런 표현을 쓸 때마다 그 주제에 대한 의견을 제시하는 것이니 주의 깊게 살펴보라.

연설자의 어조가 바뀌는 것을 들어보라. 그 어조는 화자가 부정적인지, 긍정적인지, 비꼬는지, 화가 났는지 등을 묘사할 수 있다.

예: 긍정적이고 쾌활함
    교수: 우리는 오늘 쪽지 시험을 볼 거야!
    학생: 잘됐네요! (흥분되고 행복함)

예: 부정적이고 비아냥거림
    교수: 우리는 오늘 쪽지 시험을 볼 거야!
    학생: 잘됐네요... (실망하고 슬픔)

ANSWERS AND SCRIPT

Page.55~56

연습 A

수학 시험에 대한 그 학생의 태도는 어떠한가?

A) 학생은 자신이 잘했다고 확신하지 않는다.
B) 학생은 시험을 잘 봤다고 확신한다.
C) 학생은 시험에 관심이 없는 것 같다.
D) 학생은 시험을 봤다는 것도 모른다.

RA: 안녕 레베카! 오늘 수학 시험 어땠어? 어제 걱정했는데, 잘 봤기를 바라.

학생: 아, 그거? 하하… 글쎄, 나는 모든 질문에 대한 답을 적긴 했어. 근데 내가 정답을 맞혔을까? 하하하….

RA: 잘 했을 거야. 지난 며칠 동안 열심히 공부했잖아.

학생: 고마워. 좋은 소식이 있었으면 좋겠네. 실은 다른 일로 너를 만나러 왔어. 혹시 시간 좀 있니?

RA: 물론이지. 무엇을 도와줄까?

답: A. RA가 학생에게 시험을 어떻게 봤냐고 묻자 학생은 이렇게 대답한다. "하하… 글쎄, 모든 질문에 대한 답을 적긴 했어. 근데 내가 정답을 맞혔을까? 하하하…." 이 어조는 그녀가 자신의 점수에 자신이 없다는 것을 보여준다. 그녀는 간신히 모든 답을 적었지만, 정답을 맞혔는지 확신하지 못한다. 그녀의 웃음소리도 긴장되면서 점점 작아진다.

그녀의 어조는 자신감 같은 것이 보이지 않기 때문에 B는 정답이 아니다. C는 답이 아니다. 왜냐하면 그 학생은 지난 며칠 동안 시험공부를 했기 때문에 시험을 신경 쓰는 것처럼 보이기 때문이다. 시험공부를 했기 때문에 D는 답이 아니다.

Page.57~58

연습 B

인체에 대한 교수의 태도는 어떤가?

A) 교수는 인체가 너무 복잡하다고 생각한다.
B) 교수는 인체가 너무 많은 한계를 가지고 있다고 생각한다.
C) 교수는 인체가 어떻게 작동하는지 궁금하게 생각한다.
D) 교수는 인체가 여전히 진화하고 있다고 생각한다.

교수: 우리 몸이 다양한 비정상적인 환경에서 어떻게 물리적으로 자신을 유지하는지 이해하는 것은 중요합니다. 오늘은, 우리 몸의 냉각 메커니즘에 대해 이야기해 봅시다. 첫째로 모든 사람들이 알고 있는 것은 날씨가 따뜻할 때 땀을 흘리는 것입니다. 우리는 적정 지점에서 체온을 유지하기 위해 땀을 흘립니다. 하지만 어떻게 땀이 그 일을 하는 건지 누가 설명해 줄 수 있나요?

학생: 음… 우리 피부에서 땀이 증발하면서, 우리 체온을 조절하는 피부 표면을 식힙니다.

교수: 아주 좋아요. 그리고 땀이 몸을 식히지 못하는 상황에 대해 생각해 볼까요?

학생: 흠… 습도가 너무 높으면, 땀이 증발할 수 없습니다. 또한, 만약 몸이 탈수 상태가 되면, 땀을 흘릴 수 없을 것입니다.

교수: 훌륭합니다. 환경이 우리 몸에 땀을 흘리지 못하게 하는 사례들이 많이 있습니다. 그러나 여러분은 우리 몸이 신체를 스스로 식히는 다른 방법들이 있다는 것을 알고 있었나요? 내가 말하고 싶은 것은, 우리 몸이 작동하는 방법이 정말 놀랍다는 것입니다.

정답: C 학생이 인체가 땀을 흘리지 않는 상황에 대해 대답한 후 교수는 학생을 칭찬하며 인체가 스스로를 식히는 다른 방법을 소개한다. 하지만 그가 계속 말하기 전에, 그는 "우리의 몸이 어떻게 작동하는지가 그저 놀라울 뿐이다."라고 말한다. 이것은 사실이 아니라, 인체가 어떻게 작동하는지에 대한 교수의 의견이다.

A, B, D는 답이 아니다. 왜냐하면 교수 혹은 학생이 인체의 복잡성, 인체가 가진 한계, 그리고 인체가 겪고 있는 진화에 대해 언급하지 않기 때문이다.

Chapter06
Inference

Page.62~64

추론

추론 문제에서는 대화나 강의에서 암시된 질문에 답하거나 들은 내용을 바탕으로 정보를 추론해야 한다. 추론 문제에서 정답은 리스닝에서 직접적으로 언급되지 않는다는 것을 기억하라. 때때로, 대화나 강의의 일부가 다시 재생되거나, 들은 내용을 바탕으로 결론에 도달해야 할 수도 있다.
일반적으로 대화나 강의 당 하나의 추론 문제가 있다.

단계별 해결 방법:

1) 말에 내포된 의미를 이해하도록 노력한다. 화자가 말한 것을 그대로 받아들이지 마라. 행간을 읽는 법을 배워라.
2) 대화의 끝 부분을 잘 들어라. 여기서, 교수나 화자가 다음에 무엇을 할 지 언급할 것이다.
3) 다시 듣기 문제의 경우, 물음에 답하기 위해 앞뒤로 무슨 말을 했는지 들어라. 추론을 할 때 맥락을 파악하는 것은 매우 중요하다.
4) 정답이 암시적으로 드러나고 직접적으로 말하지 않더라도, 리스닝에 키워드가 언급된다. 리스닝에 나오지 않는 키워드를 가진 답안 선택지들을 지워라.

추측과 추론 사이에는 분명한 차이가 있다. 추측은 내용이나 맥락을 고려하지 않지만 추론은 고려한다. 추론이란 아이디어를 연관시키고 논리적으로 연결시켜 화자가 무엇을 의미하는지 혹은 다음에 무슨 일이 일어날 지 추론하는 현명한 추측을 하는 것이다.
강의에서, 추론 문제는 주요 아이디어에 관한 것이 될 것이다. 때때로 추론 문제는 세부 사항들을 중심으로 진행될 수 있다. 대화에서 추론 문제는 문제와 해결 방법에 기초할 것이다.

대화나 강의를 들을 때, 화자들은 대화나 강의가 끝난 후에 무엇을 할 것인지 힌트를 줄 수 있다. 그 대화는 학생이 자신의 논문을 다시 쓰기 위해 도서관에 갈 것을 암시하거나, 교수가 이미 지각한 회의에 참석하는 것으로 끝날 수도 있다. 교수가 다음 주제로 넘어가면서 강의가 갑자기 중단되거나

아예 수업을 마칠 수도 있다.

추론 답변을 할 때, 그들은 배경 지식이나 주제에 대한 포괄적인 이해를 요구하지 않는다는 것을 기억하라. 리스닝의 요지를 이해하고 리스닝에서 언급되지 않은 키워드를 피하기만 하면 정답을 알 수 있다.

Page.65~66

연습A

학생은 다음에 무엇을 할 것인가?

A) 여동생에게 호텔에 묵으라고 한다.
B) 관리인에게 학교가 어떤 대회들을 개최하는지 물어본다.
C) 룸메이트에게 여동생이 하룻밤 묵을 수 있는지 물어본다.
D) 관리인에게 식당을 추천해 달라고 요청한다.

RA: 아! 하마터면 잊을 뻔했네! 당신의 여동생은 방에 들어가기 전에 당신의 룸메이트의 허락을 받아야 해요. 당신은 룸메이트와 방을 같이 쓰기 때문에, 그 룸메이트가 손님을 초대하는 것에 동의하는 것이 중요합니다. 어쨌든, 누군가를 초대하는 것이 어떤 사람들에게는 불편할 수 있습니다. 만약 당신의 룸메이트가 시험 공부를 하거나 기한을 넘긴 에세이를 쓰고 있다면, 당신의 여동생은 다른 곳에 머무는 것이 더 나을 거예요.

학생: 제 룸메이트가 반대할 것 같지는 않아요. 그녀는 내가 아는 사람 중에서 가장 친절한 사람이에요. 하지만 확실하게 하기 위해, 지금 당장 가서 그녀에게 물어봐야겠어요.

RA: 좋아요! 그리고 만약 당신의 여동생이 하룻밤을 묵을 다른 장소가 필요하다면, 저는 그녀를 머무르게 할 수 있는 캠퍼스 근처의 훌륭한 호텔들을 추천할 수 있습니다. 우리 학교는 많은 대회를 개최하고 있어서 호텔들의 서비스가 크게 좋아졌어요.

정답: C. RA가 학생이 여동생을 초대하기 전에 룸메이트와 상의해야 한다고 말하자, 그 학생은 이렇게 대답한다. "지금 당장 가서 물어봐야겠어요." 그래서 그 학생은 그녀의 룸메이트에게 여동생이 머물러도 되는지 물어보러 갈 것이다.

그녀의 룸메이트가 여동생이 머물 수 있는지 없는지 확정하지 않았기 때문에 A는 정답이 아니다. RA가 학교가 많은 대회를 개최한다고 언급했지만, 이 대화는 학교에서 어떤 종류의 대회가 열리는지를 중심으로 돌아가지 않기 때문에 B는 정답이 아니다. 대화에서 레스토랑은 언급되지도 않았기 때문에 D는 답이 아니다.

Page.67~68

연습B

다음 중 열사병에 걸린 사람에게 해야 하는 것은?

A) 담요로 덮는다.
B) 뜨거운 수프나 음료수를 준다.
C) 열을 없앨 수 있는 약을 투여한다.
D) 팔과 다리를 마사지하여 차가운 피를 몸의 중심부로 이동시킨다.

> 교수: 열사병의 경우 체온이 너무 오랫동안 높게 유지되지 않는 한 회복될 수 있습니다. 여러분의 몸은 체온을 빠르게 낮추려고 하는 놀라운 방어 시스템을 가지고 있습니다. 심장박동수는 몸 전체에 걸쳐 더 차가운 피를 이동시키기 위해 더 빠르게 가속될 것입니다. 또한, 혈관은 열을 몸 밖으로 이동시키기 위해 팽창할 것이고, 이것은 여러분의 피부를 붉고 뜨겁게 만들 것입니다. 두뇌가 열사병에 가장 취약한 부위라는 점에 주목해야 하기에, 먼저 머리를 식히는 것이 중요합니다. 인체는 머리를 통해 대부분의 열을 빠르게 잃기 때문에 머리와 목을 식히면 열사병으로부터 회복하는 데 도움이 될 것입니다. 머리에 물수건을 놓으면 열을 내리는 데 도움이 되고, 얼음팩이 있을 경우 겨드랑이와 사타구니에 넣어 두면 체온이 더 빨리 내려갑니다. 물론, 이러한 절차를 수행하는 동안, 911에 전화를 걸어 추가 치료를 위해 환자를 병원으로 옮깁니다.

정답: D. 이 강의는 머리에 물수건을 대고 겨드랑이나 사타구니에 얼음찜질을 하는 등 체온을 낮추는 데 도움이 되는 몇 가지 방법을 설명한다. 더 차가운 피를 몸의 중심부로 옮기는 것은 체온을 낮추는 또 다른 방법이다.

A와 B는 정답이 아니다. 왜냐하면 누군가를 담요로 감싸거나 뜨거운 수프나 음료수를 대접하는 것은 단지 체온을 증가시키기 때문이다. C는 답이 아니다. 왜냐하면 우리는 약이 체온을 떨어뜨리는 데 도움이 될지 모르기 때문이다. 그리고 강의에서 약을 주는 것에 대해 언급하지 않는다.

Actual Test 01

Page.73~78

Part 1 - Conversation

ANSWERS – 1(C) 2(D) 3(A) 4(D) 5(B) 6(B)

S - Hello Professor Johnson!
P - Hello Mindy, do come in. Did you get the email I sent you concerning your midterm group project proposal?
S – Umm… I don't think I did….
P – Oh, then I'm glad you came by. I need to discuss with your group about the renovations that will start in the study lounge in a few days. As I recall, you and your classmates are going to create a mural on the east wall correct? So…. Hmmm… it looks like there might be some problems.
S – Oh no! What kind of problems?
P – Well the school had a faculty meeting a few days ago to discuss the building plans and how the construction may interrupt our classes with construction noise. Well, at the meeting, I found out that the school has decided to take down the east wall and put up a window instead. Therefore, your plans to paint a mural there can be problematic.
S – That is a big problem. Well, should we just give up on our project then?
P – I mentioned to the faculty that you guys were planning on painting a mural on the wall. The faculty agreed that you guys could go ahead and work on your project. Sadly, you'll have to bring it down once the construction crew starts on the wall. So it's up to your discretion whether or not to proceed with the project.
S – **I understand and I think I remember seeing the notice for the building renovations. However, they failed to mention just how much of a renovating they would do and it seems completely understated. Oh well….** I guess it would be a waste of time if my group began working on the mural, only to stop soon after.

S - 안녕하세요 존슨 교수님!
P - 안녕 민디, 어서 오렴. 중간 그룹 프로젝트 제안서와 관련하여 내가 보낸 이메일 받았니?
S - 음… 못 받은 것 같은데요…
P - 아, 그럼 들러 줘서 다행이구나. 며칠 후에 스터디 라운지에서 시작될 보수 공사에 대해 너희 그룹과 상의해야 할 것 같네. 내 기억으로는, 너와 너희 그룹원들이 동쪽 벽에 벽화를 그리는 것이 맞지? 그런데…. 음… 뭔가 문제가 있는 것 같구나.
S - 이런! 어떤 종류의 문제인가요?
P - 음, 며칠 전에 학교에서 교직원 회의를 열어 건축 계획과 공사로 인한 소음으로 수업이 중단될 수 있는 경우에 대해 논의했단다. 회의 중에, 나는 학교가 동쪽 벽을 허물고 대신 창문을 세우기로 결정했다는 것을 알았단다. 그래서, 그곳에 벽화를 그리려는 계획은 문제가 될 수 있단다.
S - 큰 문제네요. 그럼, 저희는 프로젝트를 그냥 포기해야 할까요?
P - 교수진에게 너희가 벽에 벽화를 그릴 계획이라고 말했단다. 교수진들은 너희들이 프로젝트를 계속 진행할 수 있다는 데 동의했단다. 슬프게도, 일단 건설 인부들이 일을 시작하면, 너희들은 그것을 무너뜨려야 할 거란다. 따라서 프로젝트를 진행할지 말지는 너희의 재량에 달려 있단다.
S = 건물 보수 안내문을 본 기억이 있어요. 그러나, 그들은 얼마나 많은 수리를 할 것인지에 대해 언급하지 않았고, 그것은 완전히 축소시킨 것처럼 보이네요. 아, 그래요. 저희 그룹이 곧 관둬야 하는 벽화 작업을 시작한다면, 시간이 아깝겠네요

ANSWERS AND SCRIPT

P – I agree. I think it would be best if your group chooses a different midterm project.
S – Actually, I find this all ironic because our group project was supposed to be centered on a window-themed mural. We thought that the room looked too dark and depressing for a study lounge. So we had decided to draw a mural of a window with a beautiful summertime landscape that would brighten up the room and elevate the study atmosphere. Our only problem was that this idea would not meet the project requirements. Our main issue was that we had trouble connecting it to any of the art topics we discussed in class…
P – Hold on. Have you heard of the art technique Trompe-l'oeil?
S – No, that sounds French though. What style is that?
P – The word is French and ancient Greeks were recorded using this technique. Trompe-l'oeil is the artist using realistic imagery of objects or scenes to create an illusion that is three dimensional, contrast to a two dimensional painting. Let me give you an analogy. Imagine a long hallway. On one of its walls is a Trompe-l'oeil door painted slightly open with a view of a room appearing behind it. Don't you think this virtuoso display makes the corridor look bigger and give it an appearance of a greater depth? I think your group was thinking of Trompe-l'oeil without even knowing it.
S – Yes! That is exactly what we were trying to paint!
P – And lucky for you, we will be discussing about this technique after we return from our vacation, so I see no problem with the project requirements. You guys can even start early! Go ahead and continue with the mural project. However, instead of using a wall, try using a sheet of wood. That way the mural can be placed in different locations when necessary.
S – What a great idea! Thanks Professor Johnson!

P – 동의한단다. 나는 너희 그룹이 다른 중간 프로젝트를 선택하는 것이 가장 좋을 것 같구나.
S – 사실, 저는 이 모든 것이 아이러니하다고 생각해요. 왜냐하면 저희 그룹 프로젝트는 창문을 테마로 한 벽화 위주로 되어 있었기 때문이에요. 저희는 그 방이 스터디 라운지로 쓰이기엔 너무 어둡고 우울해 보인다고 생각하거든요. 그래서 저희는 방을 밝게 만들고 학습 분위기를 좋게 해 줄 수 있는 아름다운 여름 풍경으로 창문의 벽화를 그리기로 결정했었어요. 저희의 유일한 문제점은 이 아이디어가 프로젝트 요건을 충족하지 못한다는 점이었어요. 저희의 주된 문제는 저희가 수업 시간에 논의한 예술 주제와 그것을 연결하는 데 어려움이 있었다는 점인데….
P – 잠깐만, 너희는 Trompe-l'oeil라는 예술 기법에 대해 들어본 적이 있니?
S – 아니요, 프랑스어로 들리는데. 그건 어떤 스타일인가요?
P – 그 단어는 프랑스 단어이며 고대 그리스어는 이 기법을 사용하여 기록되었단다. Trompe-l'oeil는 사물이나 장면의 사실적인 이미지를 사용하여 2차원 그림과 대조적으로 3차원적인 착시를 만들어 내는 예술이지. 비유를 들어 보마. 긴 복도를 상상해 봐라. 그 벽들 중 한 벽에는 Trompe-l'oeil 문이 그려져 있고, 문은 그 뒤에 보이는 경치와 함께 살짝 열려 있다. 이런 높은 수준의 기교를 보여주는 전시는 복도를 더 크고 깊어 보이게 한다고 생각하지 않니? 나는 너희 그룹이 자신도 모르는 사이에 Trompe-l'oeil을 떠올리고 있었다고 생각한단다.
S – 네! 그게 바로 우리가 그리려고 했던 거예요!
P – 그러면 다행스럽게도, 휴가를 마친 후에 함께 이 기법에 대해 논의할 예정이니 프로젝트 요건에 문제가 없다고 본다. 너희는 더 일찍 시작할 수도 있단다! 벽화 프로젝트를 계속 진행하거라. 하지만, 벽을 사용하는 대신 나무 판을 사용해 보길 권한다. 이러한 방식은 필요할 때엔 벽화를 다른 장소에 배치할 수 있기 때문이란다.
S – 정말 좋은 생각이에요! 감사합니다. 존슨 교수님!

1) 학생은 무슨 문제를 겪고 있는가?

    A) 공사 소음 때문에 그녀는 스터디 라운지에서 공부하는 일에 지장이 있다.
    B) 그녀의 그룹은 새로운 중간 프로젝트를 선택해야 한다.
    C) 건물의 보수는 그녀가 벽화를 그리고자 하는 장소에 영향을 미친다.
    D) 그녀는 그룹 과제에서 도움이 필요하다.

2) 대화 내용을 다시 한 번 들어보라. 그리고 질문에 답하라.
   건물 보수 공사에 대한 학생들의 의견은 어떠한가?

    A) 그녀는 보수 공사 때문에 화가 나 있다.
    B) 그녀는 보수 공사가 있을 것이라는 사실에 놀랐다.
    C) 그녀는 보수 공사에 신경 쓰지 않는 것 같다.
    D) 그녀는 보수 공사의 규모가 나와 있지 않은 것에 대해 화가 나 있다.

3) 어느 벽화를 그릴 계획인가?

    A) 창문
    B) 복도
    C) 초상화
    D) 벽

4) Trompe-l'oeil 기법의 올바른 정의는?

    A) 3차원 예술을 2차원적으로 표현한 것이다.
    B) 프랑스에서 유래된 예술 형식이다.
    C) 지난 몇 세기 동안 만들어진 기법이다.
    D) 표현물에 사실적인 착시 현상을 일으킨다.

5) 교수는 복도에 있는 문을 왜 언급하는가?
    A) 학생의 아이디어를 교정하기 위해
    B) Trompe-l'oeil 기법의 예시를 제공하기 위해.
    C) 건물 보수 목록을 작성하기 위해
    D) 그곳에 벽화 그리기를 추천하기 위해.

ANSWERS AND SCRIPT

6) 대화를 마칠 때, 교수는 어떤 제안을 하는가?

A) 학생들은 보수 공사를 무시하고 벽에다가 그들의 프로젝트를 계속해야 한다.
B) 학생들은 그들의 벽화를 나무판에 그려야 한다.
C) 학생들은 그들의 프로젝트를 하기 위해 방학 후까지 기다려야 한다.
D) 학생들은 Trompe-l'oeil 아트를 연습해야 한다.

Part 1 – lecture (professor – WOMAN)

ANSWERS – 7(B) 8(A) 9(B) 10(B) 11(A,C) 12(C)

Alright everyone, let's get started. Last time we were discussing about mass extinction. As you recall, we talked about different scientific theories concerning large populations of living organisms suddenly disappearing at certain times in history. Today we are going to continue our lecture on mass extinction by looking at a specific case that occurred on the continent of Australia, roughly around 50,000 years ago. Scientists estimate that nearly 85% of the organisms inhabiting this continent perished. However, scientists are not sure what exactly caused such a mass extinction.

One ecological theory revolves around an accelerated climate change. As you are aware, this type of environmental change is suspected of starting the disappearance of many other creatures throughout the Earth's timeline, including the dinosaurs. It is without a doubt that plants and animals are susceptible to dramatic changes in temperature, however this could not have been the cause related to our particular disappearance. Geological facts have shown that there has been no glacial movement anywhere on Australia at around 50,000 BC. So, it is safe to rule out that climate change caused the mass extinction.

Another hypothesis is that mass extinction occurred due to excessive hunting. The mastodons are a great example. These elephant like creatures were so powerful, it was almost impossible for primitive humans to successfully hunt them down. As time passed, our ancestors developed tools and weaponry that would have allowed successful hunting. Unfortunately, primitive Australians did not master such tool making skills until thousands of years later.

So where does this leave us? If all the aforementioned hypothesis are disproven, then what could have caused the mass extinction in Australia? Well… a third hypothesis has been proposed: rampant fires. Primitive Australians had discovered fire and could have started wildfires at will. Also, there is the possibility that nature could have started the fires spontaneously. Under the right conditions, a lightening striking a vegetated area during a dry season could start a fire.

자 여러분, 시작해 봅시다. 지난 번에 우리는 대량 멸종에 대해 토론하고 있었습니다. 여러분이 기억하듯이, 우리는 역사상 어떤 시기에 갑자기 사라져 버린 많은 생물체들에 관한 다양한 과학적 이론들에 대해 이야기 했습니다. 오늘 우리는 대략 5만년 전에 오스트레일리아 대륙에서 일어난 특정 사건을 살펴봄으로써 대량 멸종에 대한 강의를 계속할 것입니다. 과학자들은 이 대륙에 서식하는 유기체의 거의 85%가 멸종했다고 추정합니다. 하지만, 과학자들은 정확히 무엇이 그러한 대량 멸종의 원인이 되었는지 확신하지 못합니다.

한 생태 이론은 가속화된 기후 변화를 중심으로 전개됩니다. 여러분도 알다시피, 이런 종류의 환경 변화는 지구의 연대기에 걸쳐 공룡을 포함하여 많은 다른 생물체들을 멸종 시켰다는 의심을 받고 있습니다. 동식물이 급격한 온도 변화에 민감하다는 것은 의심의 여지가 없지만, 이것이 특정한 멸종과 관련된 원인이 될 수는 없었습니다. 지질학적 사실들은 기원전 5만년 경에 오스트레일리아 어디에서도 빙하의 움직임이 없었다는 것을 보여주었습니다. 그러므로, 기후 변화가 대량 멸종의 원인이라는 것을 배제해도 될 겁니다.

또 다른 가설은 과도한 사냥으로 인해 대량 멸종이 발생했다는 것입니다. 마스토돈은 좋은 예입니다. 이 코끼리 같은 생물체들은 매우 강력해서 원시인들이 성공적으로 그들을 사냥하는 것은 거의 불가능했습니다. 시간이 흐르면서, 우리의 조상들은 사냥을 성공적으로 할 수 있는 도구와 무기를 개발했습니다. 불행하게도, 원시 오스트레일리아인들은 수 천 년이 지나도록 그러한 도구 제작 기술을 익히지 못했습니다.

그러면 우리는 어떤 결론에 다다를 수 있을까요? 만약 앞서 언급한 모든 가설들이 반증되었다면, 무엇이 오스트레일리아에서 발생한 대량 멸종의 원인이 될까요? 음… 걷잡을 수 없는 화재가 세 번째 가설로 제안되었습니다. 원시 오스트레일리아인들은 불을 발견했고 마음대로 산불을 일으킬 수도 있었습니다. 또한 자연에서 스스로 불이 발생했을 가능성도 있습니다. 적절한 조건 하에서, 건기 동안에는 번개가 초목 지역을 강타하여 불을 일으킬 수 있습니다.

Who or what caused the fire will never be known. But research shows that this hypothesis is the likely answer for Australia's mass extinction. The most convincing evidence comes from scientific observations of dry regions where vegetation is scarce. For example, scientists have dug deep into dried up lakebeds to investigate ancient fossil remains and sediments. By observing the different geological layers, scientists noticed not only that vegetation flourished at one time, but there were traces of charred decompositions that date back to the same period as the mass extinction. This confirms that an enormous fire had destroyed the area. Another interesting find is what scientists learned from fossilized egg shells. After analyzing the genetic makeup of these prehistoric shells, scientists were able to determine the ancient bird's diet, and conclude what species of plants existed at the time. They specifically compared the egg shells of two bird species: the emu and the genyorm. The emu egg shell showed greater diversity in vegetation in their diet before the mass extinction. After the event, the emu seemed to consume fibrous desert shrubbery, which the modern emu still eats. In contrast, the genyorm egg shells showed that this bird had a limited diet that restricted them to eat only certain types of plants. Therefore, when the fires started and burned their primary food source, the genyorm could not adapt and ultimately became extinct. These evidence show why the Emu survived to this day by adjusting their diet when their environment changed.

누가, 혹은 무엇이 화재를 일으켰는지는 결코 알려지지 않을 것입니다. 그러나 연구는 이 가설이 오스트레일리아의 대량 멸종에 대해 가능한 정답이라는 것을 보여줍니다. 가장 설득력 있는 증거는 초목이 부족한 건조 지역에 대한 과학적인 관찰에서 나옵니다. 예를 들어, 과학자들은 고대 화석 잔해와 퇴적물을 조사하기 위해 말라버린 호반들을 깊이 파냅니다. 서로 다른 지질 층을 관찰함으로써, 과학자들은 초목이 한때 무성했을 뿐만 아니라, 대량 멸종과 같은 시기에 발생한 검게 그을린 부패의 흔적이 있다는 것을 알아챘습니다. 이것은 거대한 화재가 그 지역을 파괴했다는 것을 확인시켜 줍니다. 또 다른 흥미로운 발견은 과학자들이 화석화된 알 껍질을 통해 알아낸 점입니다. 이 선사시대 조개껍데기의 유전자 구성을 분석한 후, 과학자들은 고대 새의 식단을 확인할 수 있었고, 그 당시 어떤 종의 식물이 존재했는지를 결론지을 수 있었습니다. 그들은 특히 두 종의 새, 에뮤와 게니오르니스의 알 껍질을 비교했습니다. 에뮤 알 껍질은 대량 멸종이 일어나기 전, 그들의 초목 식단이 훨씬 다양함을 보였습니다. 그 일이 벌어진 후, 에뮤는 오늘날의 에뮤가 먹는 섬유질이 풍부한 사막 관목림을 섭취하는 것처럼 보였습니다. 이와 대조적으로, 이 게니오르니스의 알 껍질은 이 새가 특정한 종류의 식물만을 먹도록 하는 제한적인 식단을 가지고 있다는 것을 보여주었습니다. 그러므로, 불이 나서 그들의 주요 식량원을 태웠을 때, 게니오르니스는 적응할 수 없었고 결국 멸종되었습니다. 이러한 증거들은 에뮤가 환경이 변했을 때 그들의 식단을 조절함으로써 오늘날까지 살아남을 수 있었던 이유를 보여줍니다.

7) 강의의 핵심은 무엇인가?

   A) 두 종류의 새 비교
   B) 오스트레일리아 대량 멸종을 야기한 원인
   C) 암석 및 호반의 과학적 분석 방법
   D) 대량 멸종에 대한 다양한 과학적 가설

8) 강의 내용을 다시 한 번 들어보라. 그리고 질문에 답하라.
   교수는 왜 이런 말을 하는가?

   A) 다른 가설을 소개하기 위해
   B) 학생들이 주의 깊게 듣고 있는지 확인하기 위해
   C) 과학자들이 어떻게 대량 멸종이 일어났는지 전혀 모른다는 것을 보여 주기 위해
   D) 학생이 앞의 예시들을 이해했는지 확인하기 위해

9) 교수는 오스트레일리아 원시인들이 어떤 지식을 가지고 있었다고 말하는가?

   A) 대형 포유류 사냥 방법
   B) 불을 피우는 방법
   C) 도구 및 무기 제조 방법
   D) 알들을 수집하는 방법

10) 교수에 따르면, 무엇이 자연적으로 불을 일으킬 수 있었는가?

   A) 급격한 온도 변화
   B) 낙뢰
   C) 호수의 고갈
   D) 제한적인 식생

**11) 과학자들은 5만 년 전에 어떤 종류의 식물이 존재했는지 어떻게 아는가?
2개의 답을 선택하라.**

A) 새알 껍질을 분석함으로써
B) 물 시료를 채취함으로써
C) 호반 밑 토양에서 발견된 잔해로부터
D) 원시 무기와 도구로부터.

12) 에뮤에 대한 교수의 의견은?

A) 그는 에뮤가 따뜻한 기후를 견딜 수 있었다고 믿는다.
B) 그는 에뮤가 날 수 있기 때문에 불길을 피했다고 생각한다.
C) 그는 에뮤의 적응하는 능력이 생존을 가능하게 했다고 믿는다.
D) 그는 에뮤와 다른 새들 사이에 어떠한 차이점도 없다고 본다.

Page.79~87

Part 2 – Conversation

ANSWERS – 1(C) 2(B) 3(C) 4(D) 5(B,D)

A – Hello! What can I help you with today? S – Hi! I'm here to ask some questions regarding the transfer of my credits from the classes I took while I was at Hartford University last year. I think there has been a mistake because most of the class credits have not been transferred to my current transcript. A – Alright, let's see what the problem is. Can I have your name please? S – My name is David Woode. Last name is spelled W-O-O-D-E. I think the mistake was made because I was studying mechanics when I first entered this school, but I recently switched my major to electrical engineering. But, I don't see what the problem is. Most of the classes I took are related to electrical engineering. Some of the classes even meet the major's graduation requirements. A – I agree, so I don't think that's the problem here. Ok, here is your file. Can you give me the name of the college you attended last year again? S – It was Hartford University. A – Alright. I see that two of the classes you took there has been transferred. One course is in applied propulsion systems and the other class is mechanical fabrications. S – Yes that's correct. But I don't get it! I have a year's worth of credits that should have been transferred! Why didn't the school accept the other credits!? A – OK, Ok calm down. I understand your frustration, but there is no need for that. Did you turn in a formal transfer credit request form to the administration? S – Actually no… I didn't even know there was a transfer credit form to turn in. A – Well, all transfer students are recommended to fill out the form when entering our school. Since the registrar staff are not academic experts, we cannot be expected to comprehend every class that comes to us, especially the ones that are not associated with our school. So, it's the student's responsibility to make sure the transfer credit request forms are turned in.	A - 안녕하세요! 무엇을 도와드릴까요? S - 안녕하세요! 작년에 하트포드 대학에 다닐 때 들었던 수업에서 학점을 옮긴 것에 대해 몇 가지 질문을 하려고 왔습니다. 대부분의 학점이 제 현재 성적표에 옮겨지지 않은 실수가 있었던 것 같습니다. A - 네. 어떤 문제가 있는지 알아보겠습니다. 성함이 어떻게 되시죠? S - 제 이름은 David Woode입니다. 성의 철자는 W-O-O-D-E입니다. 제가 처음 이 학교에 입학했을 때 기계 공학을 공부하다가 최근에 전공을 전기 공학과로 바꾸면서 실수가 있었던 것 같아요. 하지만 뭐가 문제인지 모르겠어요. 제가 들은 대부분의 수업은 전기 공학에 관련된 것이에요. 일부 수업은 심지어 이 전공의 졸업 요건까지 충족시키고 있거든요. A - 알겠습니다. 저는 우리 대학 측에서 발생한 문제가 아니라고 생각해요. 좋아요, 여기 학생의 파일이 있어요. 작년에 다녔던 대학의 이름을 다시 말씀해 주시겠어요? S - 하트포드 대학교였습니다. A - 알겠습니다. 거기서 수강하신 강의 중 두 과목이 옮겨졌군요. 한 과목은 응용 추진 시스템이고, 다른 과목은 기계 제작이네요. S - 예, 맞습니다. 하지만 이해가 안 돼요! 저는 옮겨졌어야 할 1년치 학점을 가지고 있어요! 왜 이 학교는 다른 학점들을 받아들이지 않았을까요!? A - 네, 진정하세요. 학생의 불만은 이해하지만 그렇게까지 하실 필요는 없어요. 공식적인 학점 인정 신청서 양식을 교학처에 제출했나요? S - 아니요… 제출해야 할 학점 인정 서식이 있는지도 몰랐습니다. A - 음, 모든 편입생들은 입학할 때 이 양식을 작성하도록 요청됩니다. 교학처 직원들은 학문적인 전문가가 아니기 때문에, 저희에게 오는 모든 수업, 특히 우리 학교와 관련이 없는 수업들을 이해할 것이라고 기대해서는 안 됩니다. 그러므로, 학점 인정 요청서를 제출하는 것은 학생의 책임입니다.

S – Ok, I understand. But why did only two of my classes get transferred, and not the others?
A – The likely scenario is that the two class names match closely with the classes we offer at our university. This is the usual case because the administration has an easier time connecting them.
S – OK. I better start filling out the form then. Where do I start?
A – First, visit the Dean of the Engineering College. Also visit the head professor of the department you are majoring in. You need to get their signatures. **I'm sure you're familiar with where the offices are, right?**
S – Yes I do.
A – Good. They will most likely ask for your course credentials, so take all of your academic documents with you. Be prepared to show your Hartford University transcripts and copies of the syllabus for the classes you took.
S – I will, thank you. Anything else?
A – I think that's it. After you are finished, bring the form back to us. Oh, wait a minute. We did overlook a requirement you still need.
S – And what's that?
A – You haven't satisfied your physical education requirement yet. In order to graduate, all students must take P.E. class.
S – You mean sports? Is that necessary?
A – Yes it is. It's the school's mission to offer a holistic education and have well-rounded students with knowledge across diverse subjects. You can take an easy badminton class or even a semester of tap dance. In fact, a lot of students enjoy this compulsory class because it gives them a relaxing break from their major studies.

S - 네, 알겠습니다. 그런데 다른 과목들은 안 됐는데, 왜 두 과목의 학점은 인정되었을까요?
A - 아마도 그 두 과목명이 우리 대학에서 제공하는 과목명과 일치하는 것 같습니다. 일반적으로 그 과목들은 교학처에서 매칭하기 더 쉽기 때문이에요.
S - 네. 그럼 양식을 작성하는 게 좋겠어요. 무엇부터 시작할까요?
A - 먼저 공대 학장실을 방문하세요. 또한 학생이 전공하고 있는 과의 수석 교수실에도 방문하세요. 학생은 그 분들의 서명을 받아야 합니다. 사무실이 어디 있는지 잘 알고 계실 거예요, 그렇죠?
S - 네, 그렇습니다.
A - 좋습니다. 강의 자격 증명을 요구할 가능성이 높으므로 모든 학업 관련 서류들을 지참하세요. 학생이 수강한 강의에 대한 하트포드 대학의 성적표와 강의계획서 사본을 보여줄 준비를 하세요.
S - 감사합니다. 또 다른 건 없나요?
A - 그러면 될 겁니다. 다 끝내고 나면, 양식을 저희에게 가져오세요. 아, 잠깐만요. 학생에게 필요한 요건을 간과했네요.
S - 그게 뭐죠?
A - 아직 체육 관련 요구 사항을 충족하지 못했습니다. 졸업을 하기 위해서는 모든 학생들이 체육 수업을 들어야 합니다.
S - 스포츠요? 그게 필요해요?
A - 네, 그렇습니다. 종합적인 교육을 제공하고 다양한 과목에 걸쳐 지식을 갖춘 학생들을 양성하는 것이 우리 학교의 임무입니다. 학생은 쉬운 배드민턴 수업을 들을 수도 있고 한 학기 동안 탭댄스를 출 수도 있어요. 사실, 전공 수업으로부터 휴식을 주기 때문에 많은 학생들이 필수 수업을 즐깁니다.

1) 학생은 왜 사무실을 방문했는가?

   A) 졸업 요건에 대한 질문을 하기 위해
   B) 체육 수업에 등록하기 위해
   C) 학점 인정에 대해 문의하기 위해
   D) 학장과의 만남을 위해

2) 그 학생은 무엇을 전공합니까?

   A) 기계 공학
   B) 전기 공학
   C) 체육
   D) 철학

3) 교학처장이 그 학생이 왜 다른 수업에 학점 인정이 안 되는지 설명하기 위해 제시한 이유는 무엇인가?

   A) 컴퓨터 시스템에 보관하는 것을 잊어버렸다.
   B) 대학이 그의 수업을 거부하였다.
   C) 해당 직원이 수업 변경에 대한 충분한 지식을 가지고 있지 않다.
   D) 학생이 과정 요건을 충족하지 못했다.

4) 여자가 이것을 물었을 때 무엇을 알아내려고 하는가?

   A) 사무실의 위치
   B) 학생이 이미 사무실을 방문했는지의 여부.
   C) 현재 위치에서 사무실까지의 거리
   D) 그녀가 사무실의 위치를 알려줄 필요가 있는지에 대한 여부

5) 교학처장은 학생에게 무엇을 하라고 권하는가? 정답을 2개 고르세요.

   A) 조기 등록을 신청하라.
   B) 학점 인정 서식을 작성하라.
   C) 학점 인정 미승인을 반박할 항의서를 제출하라.
   D) 그의 이전 성적표와 강의 계획표를 준비하라.

Part 2 – Lecture

ANSWERS – 6(C) 7(B) 8(A) 9(B,C) 10(D) 11(B)

So far, we have been talking about different types of marketing techniques regarding the sale of products and services. Today, we are going to focus our class on the topic of public relations. From a marketing perspective, the goal of a successful public relations department is to keep the company's positive image consistent. This is different from the profit aim we discussed earlier. The focus here is more on resources, human resources to be exact. The general public should always have a good impression of the company. Without a doubt, you can all understand why this is important to a business's survival. There are two categories of human resources. The first, which provides the most benefit, is employees. Employees are an important asset because they can spread news to maintain the company's image. However, they can also become a liability if they pass on the wrong message. For example, let's say an employee is misinformed about the business they work for. They will pass on this harmful knowledge to five of their friends, or worse, to five family members. Each of the family members will then inform five of their friends of the bad information. As you can see, this causes a ripple effect and shows the results of a mal-informed employee. The second category of human resource is the company's audience. This refers to the general public who happen to be the business's customers. Let me give you a personal example from when I worked at a different school a few years back. The school administration decided to start on a huge construction project on campus. Before construction, the public relations department did a fantastic job notifying the students, parents, and staff members about the new construction project. However, the department completely overlooked the rest of the audience. No information was given to the school's neighbors and its surrounding community that there would be a great amount of demolishing and constructing. Does that seem strange to anyone?

지금까지 우리는 제품과 서비스의 판매에 관한 다양한 마케팅 기술에 대해 이야기 해왔습니다. 오늘, 우리는 우리 수업을 홍보하는 것에 관한 주제에 집중하려고 합니다. 마케팅의 관점에서, 성공적인 홍보 부서의 목표는 회사의 긍정적인 이미지를 일관되게 유지하는 것입니다. 이는 앞서 논의한 수익 목표와는 다릅니다. 여기에서 초점은 자원, 정확히 말하면 인적 자원에 더 맞춰져 있습니다. 일반 대중은 항상 그 회사에 대해 좋은 인상을 가져야만 합니다.
의심할 여지 없이, 여러분은 이것이 왜 기업의 생존에 중요한지 이해할 수 있습니다.
인적 자원에는 두 가지 범주가 있습니다. 첫째로, 가장 큰 이점을 안겨 주는 것은 직원들입니다. 직원들은 회사의 이미지를 유지시키는 소식들을 퍼뜨릴 수 있기 때문에 중요한 자산입니다. 하지만, 그들이 잘못된 메시지를 전달한다면, 그들은 또한 골칫거리가 될 것입니다. 예를 들어, 직원이 자신이 맡고 있는 사업에 대해 잘못 알고 있다고 가정해 봅시다. 그들은 이 해가 되는 지식을 친구 다섯 명, 더 안 좋게는 다섯 가정에게 전할 것입니다. 그리고 나서 각 가족 구성원들은 각각 다섯 명의 친구들에게 나쁜 정보를 알려줄 것입니다. 보시다시피, 이는 파급 효과를 일으키고, 잘못된 정보를 가진 직원의 결말을 보여줍니다.
인적 자원의 두 번째 범주는 그 회사의 고객들입니다. 이것은 우연히 그 사업의 고객이 된 일반적인 대중을 가리킵니다. 제가 몇 년 전에 다른 학교에서 근무했던 때의 개인적인 예를 하나 들어보겠습니다. 학교 교학처는 캠퍼스에서 대규모 건설 프로젝트를 시작하기로 결정했습니다. 공사 전에, 홍보 부서에서는 새로운 건설 프로젝트를 학생들과 학부모, 직원들에게 잘 알렸습니다. 하지만, 그 부서는 다른 청중들을 완전히 간과해 버렸습니다. 학교의 이웃들과 주변 지역 사회에 엄청난 양의 파괴와 건설이 있을 것에 대한 어떠한 정보도 주어지지 않았습니다. 이게 이상해 보이나요?

When the trucks and construction equipment started to move in, the neighborhood residents became enraged by the noise disturbances and the traffic it caused. The community members soon filed a complaint to local authorities and voted for an immediate halt in the building campaign. This situation made an excellent example for the business management class I was teaching that year. Some of my students even chose to write their thesis about the school's public relation's mistake. Nevertheless, this entire predicament could have been avoided if the school had notified the community members about the construction project. Then, the community members could have prepared for the troubles the construction would cause ahead of time. They could have also learned that the new buildings would provide a renovated performing arts theater and a gigantic fitness center that would be open to the public.

So, as you can see, it is important to always remember these two human resources at all times. It is also imperative that companies routinely reflect on their public relations plans. All companies should reflect on their previous engagements and consider what they did well and what they could improve on. It is also important to rethink and update a company's audience since they change constantly with time. This includes age, location, trends, and any other factors. Then, the company can create a new marketing plan to make sure that their positive image is maintained.

트럭과 건설 장비가 투입되기 시작했을 때, 인근 주민들은 소음과 그로 인한 교통 체증에 격분했습니다. 지역 주민들은 곧 지역 당국에 항의했고 건설 활동의 즉각적인 중단을 투표에 부쳤습니다. 이 상황은 내가 그 해에 가르치던 경영학 수업에서 훌륭한 본보기가 되었습니다. 제 학생들 중 일부는 심지어 학교의 홍보 실수에 대한 논문을 쓰기로 결정하기도 했습니다. 그렇긴 하지만, 학교가 만약 그 건설 프로젝트에 대해 지역 주민들에게 통지했다면 이 모든 곤경은 피할 수 있었을지도 모릅니다. 그러면, 그 지역 주민들은 그 공사가 일으킬 문제에 미리 대비할 수 있었을 것입니다. 그들은 또한 이 새로운 건물들이 대중들에게 개방될 개조된 공연 예술 극장과 거대한 휘트니스 센터로 제공될 것이라는 것을 알 수 있었을 것입니다.

보시다시피, 항상 이 두 가지 인적 자원을 기억하는 것이 중요합니다. 기업들이 정례적으로 홍보 계획에 대한 반성을 하는 것도 필수적입니다. 모든 회사는 이전의 업무를 반성하고 그들이 무엇을 잘했고 무엇을 개선할 수 있는지 고려해야 합니다. 시간과 함께 지속적으로 변하는 회사의 고객들을 재고하고 업데이트하는 것도 중요합니다. 여기에는 연령, 위치, 트렌드 및 기타 모든 요인이 포함됩니다. 그러면, 회사는 자신들의 긍정적인 이미지가 확실히 유지되도록 하기 위한 새로운 마케팅 계획을 세울 수 있습니다.

6) 강의의 핵심은 무엇인가?

   A) 기업이 긍정적인 이미지를 유지할 수 있는 방법
   B) 기업이 건축 프로젝트에 착수하기 전에 취해야 할 조치
   C) 인적 자원이 기업에 얼마나 중요한지
   D) 제품 및 서비스를 위한 시장 전략

7) 교수에 따르면, 기업은 어떻게 긍정적인 이미지를 유지하는가?

   A) 이익에 집중함으로써
   B) 자원에 주의를 기울임으로써
   C) 성공적인 홍보 담당자를 고용함으로써
   D) 효과적인 광고 캠페인을 시작함으로써

8) 교수는 왜 이런 말을 하는가?

   A) 학교의 실수가 비논리적이며 피할 수도 있었다는 점을 강조하기 위해
   B) 학교 건축 프로젝트의 목적을 의심하기 위해
   C) 학생들이 홍보에 대해 얼마나 중대하게 생각해야 하는지를 지적하기 위해
   D) 다음 예로 넘어가기 위해

9) 학교는 어떤 시설을 새로 짓고 있다고 하는가?

   A) 지역센터
   B) 헬스장
   C) 극장
   D) 강의실

10) 학교 이웃에 대해 유추할 수 있는 것은?

A) 그들은 이전에 학교 때문에 방해를 받았었다.
B) 학교 관련 정기적인 공동체 모임을 희망하고 있다.
C) 그들은 지방 당국이 아무 소용이 없을 것이라고 생각했다.
D) 그들은 건축 프로젝트가 그들에게 가져다 줄 이익에 대해 알지 못했다.

11) 학교 건설 프로젝트에 대한 교수의 의견은 무엇인가?

A) 그는 소음이 그녀의 강의를 방해해서 짜증이 났다.
B) 그는 홍보에 대해 가르칠 수 있는 좋은 기회라고 생각했다.
C) 그는 그것을 더 잘 홍보할 수 있었을 것이라고 믿는다.
D) 그는 학교가 새로운 시설을 짓고 있다는 사실을 알고 충격을 받았다.

ANSWERS AND SCRIPT

Part 2 – Lecture

ANSWERS – 12(B) 13(B) 14(A) 15(A,B) 16(C) 17(YES: Oxygen for astronauts, Hydrogen to fuel rockets/NO: an energy source for electricity, irrigation for moon colony crops)

P - So far in class, we have been discussing about various celestial objects by looking at asteroids, comets, and nebulas. Today, we will begin our discussion on the planets of our solar system. Let's first turn our attention to something close to our home planet – the Moon. When humans first landed on the moon, it forever changed our history. These days, astronomers are fascinated with the Moon's South Pole Aitken Basin, also known as SPA Basin. When we look at the topography of the Moon's surface, the SPA Basin lies in the darker area, which points out that the basin is extremely deep. The SPA Basin's size is roughly 2500 kilometers in diameter and 13 kilometers deep. This makes it one of the largest impact craters discovered in our galaxy. It is the deepest and probably the oldest crater on the Moon. In 1994, a surprising discovery was made during the Clemente Mission, where astronomers found frozen ice in the Basin. But, let's come back to this later.

P - In the SPA Basin, there are tiny craters inside, which concludes to its old age. This is because the craters had to be made before a projectile collided with the Moon and made the SPA Basin. To find out the Basin's true origin, scientists have created virtual simulations to try to find the answers. Some argue that the impact was so enormous that it actually dug deep into the Moon's mantle. Others argue that the Basin was formed by a low-velocity object due to the presence of crustal materials found beneath the Basin's floor. This shows that whatever smashed into the Moon did not come close to the core as astronomers once thought. In the end, we cannot come up with a complete hypothesis without going back to the Moon for additional dust samples. You have a question Jennifer?

S – If NASA has such sophisticated photographic equipment, why do astronauts have to go back to the Moon? Can't we gather the information from the pictures?

P - 지금까지, 우리는 소행성, 혜성, 성운을 관찰하면서 다양한 천체들에 대해 논의해 왔습니다. 오늘, 우리는 태양계의 행성에 대해 토론을 시작할 겁니다. 먼저 우리의 고향 행성에 가까운 것부터 눈을 돌려봅시다. 달입니다. 인간이 달에 처음 착륙했을 때, 그것은 우리의 역사를 영원히 바꾸어 놓았습니다. 요즘 천문학자들은 SPA 분지로도 알려진 달의 남극 에이트켄 분지에 매료되었습니다. 달 표면의 지형을 볼 때, SPA 분지는 어두운 구역에 있고 이것은 분지가 매우 깊다는 것을 보여줍니다.

SPA 분지의 크기는 지름이 약 2500km이고 깊이가 13km입니다. 이것은 우리 은하에서 발견된 가장 큰 충돌 분화구 중 하나입니다. 그것은 달에서 가장 깊고 아마도 가장 오래된 분화구일 것입니다. 1994년, 천문학자들이 분지에서 얼음을 발견한 클레멘테 임무가 진행되는 중에 놀라운 발견이 이루어졌습니다. 하지만, 이것에 대해서는 나중에 다시 이야기합시다.

P - SPA 분지에는 이것이 오래되었음을 보여주는 작은 분화구들이 내부에 있습니다. 왜냐하면 이 분화구들은 발사체가 달과 충돌하여 SPA 분지를 만들어 내기 전에 형성되어야 했기 때문입니다. 이 분지의 진짜 기원을 알아내기 위해, 과학자들은 해답을 찾기 위한 가상 시뮬레이션을 만들었습니다. 어떤 사람들은 그 충격이 너무 커서 실제로 달의 맨틀 깊숙이 파고들었다고 주장합니다. 다른 사람들은 분지의 바닥 아래에서 발견된 지각 물질의 존재 때문에 분지가 속도가 낮은 물체에 의해 형성되었다고 주장합니다. 이것은 달에 충돌한 것이 무엇이었든지 간에 천문학자들이 한 때 생각했던 것처럼 중심부에 근접하지 않았음을 보여 줍니다. 결국, 우리는 추가적인 먼지 샘플을 얻기 위해 달로 돌아가지 않고는 완전한 가설을 세울 수 없습니다. 제니퍼씨 질문 있습니까?

S - NASA가 그렇게 정교한 사진 장비를 가지고 있다면, 왜 우주 비행사들이 다시 달에 가야 하나요? 사진들에서 정보를 수집할 수는 없나요?

P – Well, photos do not always provide accurate information. Another mission to the moon would be more beneficial, especially since the astronauts can gather geological samples. This would be the most accurate method for confirming the origins of the SPA Basin. It would also help obtain more information about the water situated in the Moon's poles. If another lunar mission were to be sent, it would greatly benefit mankind with its endless scientific knowledge.
S – You mentioned frozen ice on the moon. Does that mean there is the possibility of life on the moon?
P – <u>**Hahaha, wouldn't that be something?** Maybe the Moon is not just a floating piece of rock, empty of alien life. Nonetheless, this is a completely different topic.</u> The topic I'm trying to focus on is the practicality of the Moon's water and how valuable it could be for future space explorations. After all, the possible uses of water found on the moon is limitless. For instance, astronauts can drink water purified from the lunar ice. Also, hydrogen can be extracted from the water molecule and turned into fuel for rockets or other space vehicles. The leftover oxygen from the water molecule can be changed into breathable air. Just by carrying out the aforementioned procedures, the Moon can be converted into a launching station for deeper voyages into space.
S – But professor, such endeavors seem extremely expensive. Wouldn't the costs be coming out of the taxpayer's pockets? Wouldn't that money be better spent on solving global problems such as hunger or poverty?
P – You're absolutely right. The lunar mission would cost additional resources as well as government funding. A space station like this is actually still decades away from becoming a reality. However, nations coming together to send another man to the moon will help mankind step closer to space adventures. I mean, I personally would pay a fortune just to get my hands on a sample of moon dust.

P – 사진이 항상 정확한 정보를 제공하는 것은 아닙니다. 달에 가는 또 다른 임무는 특히 우주비행사들이 지질학적 샘플을 수집할 수 있기 때문에 더 이로울 것입니다. 이 방법은 SPA 분지의 기원을 확인하는 가장 정확한 방법입니다. 그것은 또한 달의 극지방에 있는 물에 대해 더 많은 정보를 얻는 데 도움이 될 것입니다. 만약 또 다른 달 탐사선이 보내진다면, 그것은 끝없는 과학 지식으로 인류에게 큰 도움을 줄 것입니다.
S – 교수님은 달에 있는 얼음을 언급하셨죠. 그것은 달에 생명체가 존재할 가능성이 있다는 것을 의미하나요?
P – 하하하, 뭔가 있지 않을까요? 어쩌면 달은 외계 생명체가 없는 단순하게 떠다니는 바위 조각이 아닐지도 모릅니다. 그럼에도 불구하고, 이것은 완전히 다른 주제입니다. 제가 초점을 맞추고자 하는 주제는 달에 있는 물의 실용성과 그것이 미래의 우주 탐사에 얼마나 가치가 있을지에 관한 것입니다. 결국, 달에서 발견되는 물의 사용 가능성은 무한합니다. 예를 들어, 우주 비행사들은 달의 얼음에서 정제된 물을 마실 수 있습니다. 또한, 수소는 물 분자에서 추출되어 로켓이나 다른 우주선의 연료로 바뀔 수 있습니다. 물 분자에서 남은 산소는 숨쉴 수 있는 공기로 바뀔 수 있습니다. 앞서 언급한 절차를 수행하는 것만으로도, 달은 우주로 떠나는 더 깊은 항해를 위한 발사장으로 바뀔 수 있습니다.
S – 하지만 교수님, 이런 노력은 비용이 많이 드는 것 같습니다. 비용은 납세자의 주머니에서 나오는 것 아닌가요? 그 돈이 기아나 빈곤과 같은 세계적 문제를 해결하는 데 쓰이는 게 더 낫지 않을까요?
P – 학생의 말이 전적으로 옳아요. 달 탐사에는 정부 자금뿐만 아니라 추가 자원이 들 것입니다. 이와 같은 우주 정거장이 실제로 현실화되기까지는 아직 수십 년이 남았습니다. 하지만, 다른 사람을 달에 보내기 위해 함께 협력하는 국가들은 인류가 우주 모험에 더 가까이 다가가는 것을 도울 것입니다. 제 말은, 저는 달 먼지 샘플을 손에 넣기 위해 개인적으로 많은 돈을 지불할 것입니다.

ANSWERS AND SCRIPT

12) 이 강의의 핵심은 무엇인가?

A) 달에 있는 물의 사용 가능성
B) SPA분지와 달로 돌아가는 것
C) SPA분지의 기원
D) 클레멘테 임무에 의한 발견

13) 교수는 왜 SPA 분지에서 발견된 작은 분화구를 언급하는가?

A) 그것의 크기를 강조하기 위해
B) 그것의 연대의 증거를 보여주기 위해
C) 달의 얼음물의 위치를 보여주기 위해
D) 그것이 어떻게 형성되었는지 말하기 위해

14) 강의의 일부를 다시 들으시오. 그리고 질문에 답하시오.
   교수는 왜 이런 말을 하는가?

A) 그는 학생의 관심에 동의한다.
B) 그는 그 학생의 질문이 유머러스하다고 생각한다.
C) 그는 학생들이 이 주제에 관심을 갖기를 바란다.
D) 그는 학생의 질문에 허를 찔렸다.

15) 교수는 왜 또 다른 달 탐사 임무를 지지하는가?
   정답을 2개 고르시오.

A) 달 먼지 샘플을 회수하기 위해
B) 달에서 발견된 물에 대해 더 자세히 알아보기 위해
C) 우주를 더 깊이 탐험하기 위해
D) 더 많은 사진을 찍기 위해

16) 교수는 달 먼지에 대해 무엇을 시사하는가?

    A) 달을 연구할 수 있는 유일한 실용적인 방법이다.
    B) 첫 번째 달 탐사 임무의 이유였다.
    C) 좀처럼 손에 얻기 힘들다.
    D) 연중 특정 시기에만 이용할 수 있다.

17) 강의에 따르면, 교수는 달의 물과 과학자들을 위한 물의 활용 가능성에 대해 이야기한다. 각 구절에서 알맞은 칸에 체크하라.

달에 있는 물의 사용 가능성	Yes	No
우주 비행사를 위한 산소		
전기 에너지원		
달의 군집 작물을 위한 관개		
로켓 연료로 쓰일 수소		

Actual Test 02

Page.95~100

Part 1 – Conversation

ANSWERS – 1(B) 2(D) 3(B,C) 4(C) 5(B)

P – Good morning Ashley. Thanks for stopping by. So did you reconsider about joining my translation project? We could really use an extra hand in translating the articles.
S – Well professor, I don't think I'll have the extra time to participate. My part time job at the library circulation desk takes up a lot of my time these days. Does your project require full time obligation?
P – Well to be honest, I do have a lot of articles that need to be translated. The goal is to retrieve as much information as possible and analyze all the findings. Luckily, the state has offered me a government grant to compensate students who can help me with the translation task.
S – Well, I did do a lot of translation in the past and I must say, it was a good experience. However, it was tedious and took up a lot of my time. Another problem I have is I've got a full schedule this term, with six classes and all….
P – I agree that translating is quite a monotonous task and labor intensive. However, I'm pretty sure the content of the article will be quite intellectually stimulating than other translations you did in the past. I mentioned the articles are interviews with farm families across the Midwest right? For me, it's been a very fulfilling task so far. The families were especially eager to take part and it shows in their responses.
S – It does sound fascinating. Plus, I'm sure it will help bolster my resume when I start applying for research assistant positions next semester.

P - 좋은 아침입니다 Ashley. 들러 주어 고마워요. 그래서 학생은 제 번역 프로젝트에 참여하는 것에 대해 재고해 봤나요? 우리는 그 기사들을 번역하는 데 정말 일손이 더 필요해요.
S - 글쎄요, 교수님, 저는 참여할 시간이 없을 것 같아요. 요즘 도서관 대출 데스크에서 아르바이트를 하는데 시간이 많이 걸리거든요. 교수님 프로젝트에는 전일제 의무가 있나요?
P - 솔직히 말하면, 번역해야 할 기사가 많이 있어요. 목표는 가능한 한 많은 정보를 검색하고 모든 결과를 분석하는 것입니다. 운 좋게도, 주 정부는 번역 작업을 도와줄 수 있는 학생들에게 보상할 수 있도록 정부 보조금을 내게 제안했어요.
S - 음, 저는 과거에 많은 번역을 했었고, 그것은 좋은 경험이었습니다. 하지만, 그것은 지루했고 많은 시간이 걸렸습니다. 또 다른 문제는 이번 학기에 일정이 꽉 차서 여섯 과목의 수업과 모든….
P - 번역 일이 상당히 단조롭고 많은 노동이 든다는 것에 동의합니다. 하지만, 저는 그 기사의 내용이 학생이 과거에 번역했던 것보다 지적으로 상당히 자극적일 것이라고 확신해요. 제가 그 기사들이 중서부 전역의 농장 가족들과 한 인터뷰라고 언급했었죠? 제게는, 지금까지 이 일이 매우 성취감을 주는 일이었습니다. 그 가족들은 특히 열성적으로 참여했고 그것은 그들의 응답에서 드러나요.
S - 정말 매력적으로 들리네요. 게다가, 다음 학기에 연구 보조직에 지원하게 되면 제 이력서를 보강하는 데 도움이 될 거라고 확신해요.

P – Indeed. And concerning pay, my funding is more than enough. I will be able to offer a competitive wage compared to what you're making at the library job. Did I mention that you'll be able to translate the articles anytime you want? So you will have more flexibility and work around your class schedule.
S – That would be great. So how long do you think this project will last? I mean, when do you need the translations to be finished?
P – I am actually flexible in this regard. <u>Of course, I would like them sooner than later, but at the same time, I don't want you to work so hard or risk losing your library job. Also, remember that you're not the only student participating. Hopefully, that will lessen the burden.</u>
S – You make a persuasive point professor. It's a very tempting offer, but I'm still not sure. I'd feel horrible if I did a terrible job.
P – Ok, how about this. Let's set the bar low and aim for you to finish one article every other week. Then, we can adjust the number of articles if you think you can do more work. How's that?
S – I'm still nervous even with that level of commitment. If it's ok with you, can I try doing one article first and see how that works out?
P – I guess that would be ok. Still, I will need your final say by next week. Once you confirm your participation, I can loan you the equipment you need for translating. It's very easy to operate. Just set up the machines and the keyboard…
S – Pardon me professor, but I don't think that should be a problem. I did translating in the past, remember?
P – Oh that's right! Good to know. Alright then, I look forward to your response next week!

P - 그렇고 말고요. 그리고 급여에 관해서라면, 제 자금은 충분하고도 남습니다. 학생이 도서관 일을 통해 버는 것보다 경쟁력 있는 임금을 제공할 수 있을 겁니다. 학생이 원하는 시간에 언제든지 그 기사들을 번역할 수 있을 거라고 말했나요? 학생은 더 많은 융통성을 갖게 될 것이고 수업 일정을 피해 일할 수 있을 거예요.
S - 정말 멋지네요. 이 프로젝트가 얼마나 오래 지속될 거라고 생각하세요? 제 말은, 번역을 언제까지 끝내야 하나요?
P - 이 점에 있어서 저는 사실 융통성이 있습니다. 물론, 저는 그것이 더 빨리 되기를 원하지만, 동시에 저는 학생이 너무 힘들게 일하거나 도서관 일자리를 잃는 위험을 감수하는 것을 원하지 않아요. 또한, 학생만이 참여자인 건 아니라는 것을 기억하세요. 바라건대, 그것이 짐을 덜 수 있으면 좋겠네요.
S - 교수님 설득력 있는 요점이네요. 매우 솔깃한 제안이지만, 전 여전히 확신할 수가 없어요. 제가 일을 엉망으로 한다면 끔찍한 기분이 들 거예요.
P - 그럼 이건 어때요? 목표를 낮춰서 격주로 기사 하나를 끝내도록 합시다. 그 다음에, 학생이 더 많은 일을 할 수 있겠다는 생각이 들면 기사 수를 조정할 수 있어요. 어떻습니까?
S - 그 만큼의 배려에도 불구하고 저는 여전히 불안합니다. 괜찮으시다면, 제가 먼저 기사 하나를 시도해보고 어떻게 되는지 볼 수 있을까요?
P - 괜찮을 것 같아요. 그래도 다음 주까지는 최종 결정이 나야 합니다. 일단 학생이 참가한다는 것이 확정되면, 저는 학생에게 번역에 필요한 장비를 빌려줄 수 있어요. 그것은 조작하기 매우 쉽습니다. 기계와 키보드를 설치하기만 하면 됩니다.
S - 교수님, 죄송하지만, 저는 그것이 문제가 될 것이라고는 생각하지 않습니다. 제가 과거에 번역을 했었던 것, 기억하시나요?
P - 아 맞아요! 알려줘서 고마워요. 좋아요, 그럼 다음주에 답장 기다리겠습니다!

ANSWERS AND SCRIPT

1) 교수는 왜 그 학생을 보자고 했는가?

   A) 그녀의 프로젝트 진행 상태를 확인하기 위해
   B) 그녀가 그의 연구 프로젝트를 도와줄 수 있는지 알아보기 위해.
   C) 그녀의 미래 취업 전망에 대한 조언을 해주기 위해.
   D) 그녀가 기사를 번역했던 이전 작업에 대해 논의하기 위해

2) 교수가 번역 작업에 자금을 대는 방법은 무엇인가?

   A) 그는 개인적인 자금을 보탰다.
   B) 학부에서 자금을 지원했다.
   C) 학교가 보조금을 주었다.
   D) 정부가 지원했다.

3) 교수가 학생을 설득하기 위해 언급하는 이점은 무엇인가? 정답을 2개 고르시오.

   A) 그 일은 그녀가 다음 학기에 연구직을 얻는 데 도움을 줄 것이다.
   B) 그녀는 자신의 작업 일정을 짤 수 있다.
   C) 그 일은 그녀의 다른 아르바이트보다 보수가 더 좋다.
   D) 그 프로젝트는 그녀에게 번역 경험을 줄 것이다.

4) 대화의 일부를 들어라. 그리고 질문에 답하시오.
   교수가 이 말을 할 때 무엇을 시사하는가?

   A) 그는 자신이 학생에게 부담을 주었다고 생각한다.
   B) 학생은 시간을 더 벌기 위해 다른 일을 그만두어야 한다.
   C) 다른 학생들의 도움이 작업량을 줄일 것이다.
   D) 학생은 그 프로젝트의 중요성을 과소평가해서는 안 된다.

5) 학생이 교수를 위해서 번역하기로 동의한 글의 개수는 몇 개인가?

   A) 없다.
   B) 오직 1개
   C) 1주에 1개
   D) 2주에 1개

Part 1 – Lecture

ANSWERS – 6(A) 7(A,B) 8(C) 9(D) 10(C) 11(Leopard – A,D)(Eagle – B)(Snake – C)

P – Alright, let's get started. Today we will be looking at a method of communication animals use to relay information. This method is called "alarm calling". Animals will use this calling to alert others that a predator is nearby. The most famous example of an animal that uses alarm calling is the Diana monkey, which has different alarm calls for different predators. The Diana monkey lives in a habitat where predators can attack from all sides. Snakes and leopards can attack the monkeys from the ground, and eagles can swoop down from the air to hunt them. Each predator elicits a distinct alarm call from the monkeys, which are high frequency sounds. The monkeys actually make these high pitched sounds because the predators have a harder time suspecting them. For example, the alarm call for a leopard is brief and tonal, as the monkey produces the sound while inhaling and exhaling. The alarm call for an eagle is a grunt that is low pitched. A snake's alarm calls are chutters that are high pitched.

As you can see, the alarm calls for each predator is unique because each alarm produces a different reaction from the Diana monkeys. For instance, if neighboring Diana monkeys receive a leopard alarm call, they would run up a tree to avoid getting caught by the leopard from the ground. The monkeys would also sit on the branches farthest from the tree trunk since leopards can climb trees, but the weight of the predator will not be supported by the smaller branches. On the other hand, when Diana monkeys hear the alarming call for an eagle, the monkeys will immediately look up towards the sky and then find the nearest bush to hide under and avoid an aerial attack from the hunter.

Finally, when a Diana monkey hears the alarm call for a snake, the monkey will stand on both hind legs and look around the ground.

P – 이제 시작해 보겠습니다. 오늘 우리는 동물들이 정보를 전달하기 위해 사용하는 의사소통 방법을 살펴볼 것입니다. 이 방법을 "경보 호출"이라고 합니다. 동물들은 다른 동물들에게 포식자가 근처에 있다는 것을 알리기 위해 이 호출을 사용할 것입니다. 경보 호출을 사용하는 동물의 가장 유명한 예는 다이애나 원숭이로, 다른 종류의 포식자들에 대해 다른 경보 호출을 가지고 있습니다. 다이애나 원숭이는 사방에서 포식자들이 공격할 수 있는 서식지에서 살고 있습니다. 뱀과 표범은 땅에서 원숭이를 공격할 수 있고, 독수리는 그들을 사냥하기 위해 공중에서 급강하할 수 있습니다. 각각의 포식자는 원숭이들로부터 뚜렷하게 구분되는 고주파 소리인 경보 호출을 이끌어냅니다. 원숭이들은 실제로 높은 음을 내는데, 포식자들이 그 소리를 감지하는 것이 더 어렵기 때문입니다. 예를 들어, 원숭이가 숨을 들이쉬고 내쉬면서 소리를 내기 때문에 표범에 대한 경보는 간결하고 음조가 있습니다. 독수리 경보 호출은 낮은 음의 끙끙대는 소리입니다. 뱀의 경보 호출은 높은 음의 절단음입니다.

보시다시피, 각 포식자에게 보내는 경보 호출은 독특합니다. 그 이유는 각각의 경보가 다이애나 원숭이들로 하여금 다른 반응을 만들어 내기 때문입니다. 예를 들어, 이웃 다이애나 원숭이가 표범 경보 호출을 들으면, 그들은 땅에서 표범에게 잡히는 것을 피하기 위해 나무 위로 뛰어 올라갈 것입니다. 표범 또한 나무에 오를 수 있기 때문에 원숭이들은 나무 줄기에서 가장 멀리 떨어진 가지에 앉아있지만, 더 작은 나무 가지는 포식자의 무게를 지탱하지 못할 것입니다. 반면에, 다이애나 원숭이가 독수리의 경보 호출을 들으면, 원숭이들은 즉시 하늘을 올려다보고 나서 사냥꾼의 공중 공격을 피하기 위해 가장 가까이 있는 덤불을 찾을 것입니다.

마지막으로, 다이애나 원숭이가 뱀의 경보 호출을 듣게 되면, 원숭이는 양 뒷다리로 서서 땅을 살펴 볼 것입니다

It's actually very interesting that the Diana monkey can understand these different types of communications. Besides their communication skills, Diana monkeys are a valuable asset in understanding animal behavior because their behavior is also similar to that of certain social behavior found in humans. There has been an ongoing debate between scientists concerning the Diana monkey's alarm calls. The controversy is whether or not the alarm calls are a selfless act or a selfish act. In other words, when a Diana monkey cries an alarm for others to hear, it is at risk of exposing its location to the predator, thus the selfless act. Scientists have called this sort of behavior as altruistic behavior. However, others have pointed out that the Diana monkeys will only make the alarm calls if they find out that their immediate family member is in danger. For example, young monkeys will make the alarm call for their mother, but not for a monkey that is not related to them. This shows that alarm calls are basically an instinctual response to make sure that the family gene pool is carried on.	사실 다이애나 원숭이가 이런 다른 종류의 의사소통을 이해할 수 있다는 것은 매우 흥미로운 일입니다. 그들의 의사소통 기술 외에도, 다이애나 원숭이는 동물의 행동을 이해하는 데 있어 귀중한 자산입니다. 왜냐하면 그들의 행동은 또한 인간에게서 발견되는 특정한 사회적 행동과 비슷하기 때문입니다. 다이애나 원숭이의 경보 호출에 관한 과학자들 사이의 논쟁은 계속되고 있습니다. 논쟁 사항은 경보 알림이 이타적인 행동인지 아니면 이기적인 행동인지 여부입니다. 즉, 다이애나 원숭이가 다른 동물들이 들을 수 있도록 경보음을 울리면, 그것은 포식자에게 자신의 위치를 노출시킬 위험이 있고, 따라서 이타적인 행동이 됩니다. 과학자들은 이런 종류의 행동을 이타적인 행동이라고 불렀습니다. 하지만, 다른 사람들은 다이애나 원숭이가 그들의 직계 가족이 위험에 처해 있어야만 경보 호출을 울릴 것이라고 지적했습니다. 예를 들어, 어린 원숭이들은 그들의 어미를 위해 경보 호출을 울리지만, 그들과 관련이 없는 원숭이는 울리지 않습니다. 이것은 경보 호출이 기본적으로 가족 유전자 풀을 보존 하기 위한 본능적인 반응이라는 것을 나타냅니다.

6) 교수는 왜 다이애나 원숭이의 서식지를 언급하는가?

A) 경보 호출이 다양한 이유를 설명하기 위해
B) 포식자의 서식지와 비교하기 위해
C) 지리적 이점을 지적하기 위해
D) 왜 이타적 행동이 필요한지 설명하기 위해

7) 교수에 따르면, 다이애나 원숭이가 경보 호출에 어떤 반응을 보이는가?

A) 두 다리로 서서 아래를 내려다본다.
B) 덤불 속에 몸을 숨긴다.
C) 또 다른 다이애나 원숭이를 붙잡고 있는다.
D) 가장 가까운 강으로 뛰어든다.

8) 교수는 왜 이타적 행동을 언급하는가?

A) 새로 발견된 다이애나 원숭이의 행동을 묘사하기 위해
B) 그 행동의 장점을 보여주기 위해
C) 경보 호출에 관한 두 가지 다른 관점을 비교하기 위해
D) 다이애나 원숭이의 인생관을 지적하기 위해

9) 어린 다이애나 원숭이에 대해 유추할 수 있는 것은?

A) 그들은 기꺼이 희생하는 원숭이가 될 것이다.
B) 어떤 경보 호출을 내야 하는지 혼동하는 경우가 많다.
C) 경보 호출을 개발하는 데 시간이 더 오래 걸린다.
D) 그들은 어머니와 강한 애착 관계를 맺고 있다.

10) 다이애나 원숭이에 대한 교수의 의견은?

A) 그는 그들의 의사소통 방식을 의심한다.
B) 그는 그들의 지능 수준을 조롱한다.
C) 그는 그들이 공부할 가치가 있다고 생각한다.
D) 그는 그들이 가장 진화한 유인원이라고 믿는다.

11) 강의에서 교수는 다이애나 원숭이의 몇 가지 다른 경보 호출을 설명한다. 포식자와 관련된 경보를 표시하라.

각 구문에 대해 올바른 상자를 클릭합니다.

	표범	독수리	뱀
A) 음조 경보			
B) 낮고 끙끙댐			
C) 고음의 절단음			
D) 짧은 경보			

Page.101~109

Part 2– Conversation

ANSWERS – 1(C) 2(B) 3(B,D) 4(A) 5(A)

A – Hello! How can I help you today?
S – Hello, I was wondering if it was possible to move into the dormitory. Who should I speak to concerning this matter?
A – I can assist you with that, although, I'm afraid this late into the semester, it will be difficult to move in. Is there a particular reason you want to move to the dormitory?
S – Well, currently, I'm living in a studio apartment across the university because I thought it would be wonderful to have my own personal space. But now I realized that living on campus would actually be better since I would have more chance to meet new people and become friends with them since I'm not from around these parts.
A – Ah ha, I see. Well let's see if there are any empty rooms you can move in to…. You're in luck! A student will be moving out next week, so it looks like you will be able to move in. Unfortunately, the elevators will be reserved for the weekend, so you'll have to move in during the weekday. Will that be a problem?
S – Oh no. Is there any way to move in during the weekend? My class schedule is pretty hectic so it will be almost impossible for me to move during the weekdays.
A – I'm afraid so. Do you have a lot of belongings to move?
S – Not really. I have my clothes and some small personal items. However, I have a lot of books. Oh, and a desk which is probably heavy. Does the school provide any moving services to help students move?
A – Unfortunately no. It's the student's responsibility to find one. However, if you have trouble finding a moving company, I can always help you out.
S – Thank you so much. I'm still clueless on where everything is.

A - 안녕하세요! 무엇을 도와드릴까요?
S - 안녕하세요, 기숙사로 이사할 수 있는지 궁금해요. 이 문제에 관해서 누구한테 말하면 될까요?
A - 제가 도와드릴 수는 있지만, 학기 후반에는 이사하기가 어려울 것 같습니다. 기숙사로 이사하고 싶은 특별한 이유가 있나요?
S - 음, 현재, 저는 대학 건너편에 있는 원룸에 살고 있습니다. 왜냐하면 저는 제 개인적인 공간을 갖는 것이 좋을 거라고 생각했기 때문이에요. 하지만 이제 저는 캠퍼스에서 사는 것이 더 낫다는 것을 깨달았어요. 왜냐하면 저는 이 지역 출신이 아니어서 캠퍼스에 사는 것이 새로운 사람들을 만나고 그들과 친구가 될 수 있는 더 많은 기회를 가질 수 있어서 이것이 더 나을 거라고 생각했어요.
A - 아하, 그렇군요. 그럼 학생이 이사할 수 있는 빈 방이 있는지 한번 봅시다. 운이 좋으시군요! 다음 주에 학생 한 명이 이사할 예정이니, 학생이 이사 갈 수 있을 것 같군요. 안타깝게도 엘리베이터는 주말 동안 예약되어 있어서 주중에 입주하셔야 합니다. 괜찮으시겠어요?
S - 오 이런… 주말에 이사 할 수 있는 방법이 있나요? 수업 스케줄이 너무 바빠서 주중에는 이사하기가 거의 불가능할 것 같아요.
A - 힘들 것 같아요. 이삿짐이 많이 있나요?
S - 그렇지 않아요. 저는 제 옷과 작은 개인 용품들을 가지고 있어요. 하지만, 저는 많은 책을 가지고 있습니다. 아, 그리고 책상은 아마 무거울 거예요. 학교에서는 학생들의 이사를 돕기 위해 이삿짐 서비스를 제공하고 있나요?
A - 안타깝게도 아니에요. 그것을 찾는 것은 학생의 책임입니다. 하지만, 만약 학생이 이사하는 회사를 찾는 것이 어렵다면, 저는 언제든지 학생을 도울 수 있어요.
S - 대단히 감사합니다. 저는 아직도 어떻게 해야할 지 모르겠어요.

Answers and Script 48

A – Well then, I'll start looking right away. The room you'll be moving to is a descent size. Everything you mentioned should be able to fit in nicely.
S – That's good to hear. **I was curious, can I decorate the room to my personal taste?**
A – What kind of decoration were you thinking?
S – Nothing's set yet. I was just wondering if there were any rules before I decorated.
A – Well, the school does not permit room decorations, such as wall papers, but you can hang up pictures if you want to. Just make sure to mount them firmly so that the pictures don't fall off. The school's policy is that students are welcome to decorate their rooms, as long as they can return the room to its original status when they check out of the dormitory. Also, be careful not to damage the built-in furniture, or else you will have to pay a fine. Do you have any other questions?
S – No, that's about it.
A – Ok then, why don't we get started on the paperwork and help you move to the dormitory.

A - 그럼, 지금 바로 알아보겠습니다. 학생이 이사 갈 방은 적당한 크기입니다. 학생이 말한 모든 것이 잘 들어맞을 수 있을 거에요.
S - 듣던 중 반가운 소리네요. 궁금한 점이 있는데, 제 취향에 맞게 방을 꾸며도 될까요?
A - 어떤 장식을 생각하고 있나요?
S - 아직 아무 것도 정하진 않았어요. 단지 장식하기 전에 어떤 규칙이 있는지 궁금해서요.
A - 음, 학교에서는 벽지와 같은 실내 장식을 허용하지 않지만, 원한다면 그림을 걸어둘 수도 있습니다. 그림이 떨어지지 않도록 단단히 고정하세요. 기숙사에서 퇴실할 때 방을 원래 상태로 되돌릴 수 있는 정도만큼만 학생들이 방을 장식하는 것을 허락한다는 것이 학교의 방침입니다. 또한, 설치된 가구가 손상되지 않도록 주의하세요. 그렇지 않으면 벌금을 내야 할 수도 있어요. 다른 질문 없으세요?
S - 없어요, 그게 다에요.
A - 그럼 서류 작업을 시작하고 기숙사 이사를 도와드리는 건 어떨까요?

1) 주로 무엇에 관한 대화인가?

   A) 실내 장식 방법에 대한 안내
   B) 룸메이트 구하기
   C) 학교 기숙사에서 방 구하기
   D) 이삿짐 업체에 예약하기

2) 왜 현재의 생활 방식에서 벗어나고 싶은가?

   A) 그는 집세를 내는데 어려움을 겪고 있다.
   B) 그는 친구를 사귀고 싶어한다.
   C) 그는 원룸의 엄격한 규칙에 반대한다.
   D) 그의 계약 기간이 만료되었다.

3) 대화 내용에 따르면 기숙사 이용에 관한 대학의 방침은 무엇인가?
   정답 2개를 클릭하십시오.

   A) 주중에만 기숙사에 이사하는 것이 허용된다.
   B) 학생이 방을 비울 때는 방을 원상태로 돌려놔야 한다.
   C) 이사는 이삿짐 업체만 해야 한다.
   D) 설치된 가구가 파손되었을 경우 학생들은 학교에 배상해야 한다.

4) 대화의 부분을 듣고 질문에 답하시오.
   학생이 이렇게 말했을 때, 그것은 무엇을 의미하는가?

   A) 학생은 어떤 특정한 계획이 있지 않다.
   B) 학생은 그 벽이 충분히 단단하지 않을까 봐 걱정하고 있다.
   C) 학생은 완전히 벽을 덮을 계획이다.
   D) 학생은 언제 이사할지 결정하지 않았다.

5) 대화에 의하면, 학생은 다음에 무엇을 할 것인가?

   A) 그는 기숙사로 이사하기 위한 서류를 작성할 것이다.
   B) 그는 기숙사의 대기자 명단에 이름을 올릴 것이다.
   C) 그는 장식품을 사기 위해 쇼핑하러 갈 것이다.
   D) 그는 이사 업체와 약속을 할 것이다.

Answers and Script

ANSWERS AND SCRIPT

Part 2– Lecture

ANSWERS – 6(D) 7(A) 8(B) 9(C) 10(B) 11(A)

Welcome back to class everyone! I hope you all had a wonderful weekend. Let's start right away because we have a lot of materials to cover. We will be continuing our lesson on the sculptures of the ancient world. Today, we will focus our attentions on the sculptures and statues that the ancient Romans made. Now, for someone who is not artsy, these works will look no different from one another. Some might say they are identical to the classical statues we have covered from ancient Greece. Well actually, there's a very good reason for this. As some of you are aware, the ancient Romans imitated the styles of the ancient Greeks. The Greeks came up with many sculpting techniques that showed people in their natural forms. Some of these techniques showed realistic proportions and others made the statues look as if they were moving. Of course, the Romans copied these techniques into their own sculptures.

However, we should not rule out that the Romans failed to contribute their own inventions. In spite of the influence the ancient Greeks had on Roman sculpture, the two styles had stark differences. A reason for this is because of their subject matter. Greek sculptures focused primarily on mythological subjects, and their artwork was created mainly for aesthetic reasons. On the other hand, Roman sculptures portrayed subjects that were actual individuals and were made for political or social reasons. For example, Julius Caesar commissioned many sculptures of himself to show off his reputation. Actually, many of the Roman politicians did the same at the time.

Now because the Roman sculptures portrayed actual people, they struggled with limitations than their counterparts.

If a Roman artist attempted to idealize his subject, the image might become so twisted that the public would not be able to recognize the subject in the sculpture, which would then serve no purpose for its creation.

여러분, 다시 수업에 온 것을 환영합니다! 여러분 모두 즐거운 주말을 보내셨기를 바랍니다. 우리가 다뤄야 할 자료가 많으니 바로 시작합시다. 우리는 고대의 조각에 대한 수업을 계속할 것입니다. 오늘, 우리는 고대 로마인들이 만든 조각품과 조각상에 관심을 집중시킬 겁니다. 자, 예술적 소양이 부족한 사람들에게는, 이 작품들이 서로 다르지 않게 보일 것입니다. 어떤 사람들은 그것들이 우리가 고대 그리스에서 다뤘던 고전적인 조각상들과 동일하다고 말할지도 모릅니다. 사실, 여기에는 아주 그럴싸한 이유가 있습니다. 여러분 중 몇몇이 알고 있듯이, 고대 로마인들은 고대 그리스인들의 스타일을 모방했습니다. 그리스인들은 사람을 자연스러운 형태로 보여주는 많은 조각 기법을 고안해 냈습니다. 이 기술들 중 일부는 현실적 비율을 보여주었고 다른 것들은 동상이 마치 움직이는 것처럼 보이게 했습니다. 물론, 로마인들은 이 기술들을 그들 자신의 조각품들에 적용했습니다.

하지만, 우리는 로마인들이 그들 자신의 발명에 이바지한 점이 있다는 것을 배제해서는 안됩니다. 고대 그리스인들이 로마 조각에 끼친 영향에도 불구하고, 두 스타일은 뚜렷한 차이를 보였습니다. 그 이유는 그들의 주제 때문입니다. 그리스 조각들은 주로 신화적인 주제에 초점을 맞췄고, 예술작품은 주로 미적인 이유로 만들어졌습니다. 반면에, 로마 조각상들은 실제 개개인과 정치적, 사회적 이유로 만들어진 주제를 묘사했습니다. 예를 들어, 줄리어스 시저는 자신의 명성을 과시하기 위해 많은 조각품들을 의뢰했습니다. 사실, 많은 로마 정치인들이 그 당시에 동일하게 했습니다.

로마 조각상들이 실제 사람들을 묘사했기 때문에, 그것들은 그리스 조각상보다 이상화의 한계에 직면해야 했습니다. 만약 로마 예술가가 그의 주제를 이상화하려고 시도한다면, 이미지가 너무 뒤틀려서 대중들이 해당 조각품에서 그 주제를 인식하지 못할 것이고, 그것은 그 작품을 만든 목적을 알려주지 못할 것입니다.

Therefore, Roman sculptures became more realistic. The sculptures showed the subjects as they were in real life. For instance, many of Caesar's sculptures show that he was balding. Cicero's sculptures do not show him as a handsome man, contrary to written records. Of course, the sculptors did perform minor plastic surgery, but they tended to show the subjects as they were.

On the contrary, Greek sculptures revolved around mythological figures and was meant to express beauty in its artwork. Thus, it came to no surprise that Greek sculptures idealized its images. For example, if a sculptor was carving a statue of a goddess, he had the complete freedom to sculpt her in any way he wished. Furthermore, the Greeks showed off the human body as ideal, in other words, the bodies appeared the way a human body should look, often exaggerating from reality. Because Greek sculptors emphasized ideal beauty so much, they tended to gloss over many of the non-idealistic features found in the Roman sculptures.

Although sculptures from these two time frames are different, mainly in the area of exaggeration and realism, they have come to be appreciated by many art critics after their time. Modern sculptors have even mixed the technique of these two eras to show new creations. For example, a recent sculpture made by an amateur shows the mythological Zeus on top of a mountain, holding a bolt of lightning, while his stomach bulges out with wrinkles covering his entire body. This is a great example of modern art that has incorporated the styles of the past.

따라서, 로마의 조각들은 더욱 사실적인 형태가 되었습니다. 그 조각품들은 대상들을 실제 삶 그대로 보여주었습니다. 예를 들어, 시저의 많은 조각품들은 그가 대머리였음을 보여줍니다. 키케로의 조각상들은 쓰여진 기록과는 달리 그를 잘생긴 사람으로 보여주지 않습니다. 물론, 조각가들은 작은 성형 수술을 하기는 했지만, 그들은 대상의 있는 그대로의 모습을 보여주는 경향이 있었습니다.

반대로, 그리스 조각들은 신화적인 인물들을 중심으로 다뤄졌고, 예술 작품의 아름다움을 표현하기 위한 것이었습니다. 따라서, 그리스 조각들이 이미지를 이상화했다는 것은 놀랄 일이 아닙니다. 예를 들어, 조각가가 여신상을 조각하고 있다면, 그는 자신이 원하는 어떤 방법으로든 그녀를 조각할 수 있는 완전한 자유를 가졌습니다. 게다가, 그리스인들은 인간의 몸을 이상적이라 여기고 과시했는데, 다시 말해, 신체를 종종 현실보다 과장하여 보았습니다. 그리스 조각가들은 이상적인 아름다움을 너무 강조했기 때문에, 로마 조각상들에서 발견되는 많은 사실적인 특징들을 얼버무리는 경향이 있었습니다.

비록 이 두 시대의 프레임 속 조각품들은 주로 과장과 사실주의 분야에서 서로 다르지만, 그 시대 이후 많은 미술 비평가들에게 감명을 주었습니다. 현대 조각가들은 새로운 창작물을 보여주기 위해 이 두 시대의 기술을 혼합하기도 했습니다. 예를 들어, 아마추어들에 의해 만들어진 최근의 조각은 온몸이 주름으로 덮여 배가 불룩 튀어나온 채 번개를 들고 산꼭대기에 서 있는 신화적인 제우스를 보여줍니다. 이것은 과거의 스타일들을 접목시킨 현대 미술의 좋은 예입니다.

6) 강의의 핵심은 무엇인가?

    A) 로마 조각상에 숨어있는 이유
    B) 그리스 및 로마 조각의 주요 예
    C) 그리스인들이 로마 조각에 어떤 영향을 끼쳤는가
    D) 그리스와 로마 조각상의 차이점

7) 교수는 강의를 어떻게 구성하는가?

    A) 조각의 주제와 묘사 방법을 비교함으로써
    B) 먼저 그리스인의 조각 기법을 논의한 후 로마인의 조각 기법을 논의함으로써
    C) 로마 조각의 유래를 언급하고 그 예를 언급함으로써
    D) 그리스 신화를 살펴보고, 조각에서 어떻게 묘사되었는지 살펴봄으로써

8) 로마 조각상은 어떤 용도로 사용되었는가?

    A) 로마 신화의 이야기를 다시 들려주는 것
    B) 로마의 각 개인을 찬양하는 것
    C) 인체의 이상적인 아름다움을 표현하는 것
    D) 건물 내부를 장식하는 것

9) 왜 많은 로마 조각품들이 덜 매혹적인 특성을 가지고 있는가?

    A) 예술가들은 그리스의 영향을 따르지 않겠다는 입장을 고수하고 있었다.
    B) 예술가들은 이상을 보여주기 위해 과장된 표현을 사용했다.
    C) 대상에 대한 사실적 이미지 제시했다.
    D) 아마추어 조각가들이 그것을 만들었다.

10) 강의 일부를 다시 들으시오. 그리고 질문에 답하시오.
   교수가 이 말을 할 때 무엇을 시사하는가?

   A) 로마의 조각가들은 종종 실수를 했기 때문에, 그들은 돌아가서 그것들을 고쳐야 했다.
   B) 로마의 조각가들은 그들의 대상의 이미지를 향상시키기 위해 약간의 노력을 기울였다.
   C) 로마의 조각가들은 그들의 조각품이 묘사된 방식에 만족하지 않았다.
   D) 로마의 조각가들은 그들의 조각품의 대상을 신중하게 선택한다.

11) 현대 제우스 조각의 어떤 부분이 대상과 일치하지 않았는가?

   A) 배와 주름들
   B) 번개
   C) 산꼭대기에 위치함
   D) 아마추어에 의해 조각됨

ANSWERS AND SCRIPT

Part 2– Lecture

ANSWERS – 12(A,C) 13(B) 14(A,B,E) 15(A) 16(B) 17(C)

If you have ever taken an architecture class, then you know the importance of a keystone. A keystone is a rock that is positioned at the top of an arch to make sure the structure stays fixed. Without it, the entire arch and the structure itself would topple. Like architecture, a keystone species in biology play an important role in the ecosystems. Keystone species can be plants or animals. Of course, every organism in an ecosystem rely on each other in some way. However, the keystone species play an important role by creating or maintaining the biodiversity of the ecosystem. Please note that the keystone species does not necessarily dominate in numbers. And just as a structure would fall down without the keystone in place, the keystone species will bring down the ecological community if misplaced.

So what are these keystone species and how do they work in their natural habitats. Well, there are several categories of keystone species that we will now discuss. First, the top predators. The top predators eat the smaller animals lower than them in the food chain. By doing this, they permit other species to survive. A good example of this keystone species is the Alaskan Wolf in North America. These gentle yet ferocious predators hunt all sorts of animals in the woods, including other predators. If they didn't hunt the other predators, the small and cuddly wood inhabitants of the forest, like rabbits and squirrels, would cease to exist in the area. So without the Alaskan wolf, other small predators will take over and the biodiversity of North America would decrease.

만약 여러분이 건축 수업을 들어봤다면, 키스톤의 중요성을 알고 있을 것입니다. 키스톤은 아치 꼭대기에 위치하여 구조가 고정되어 있는지 확인하기 위한 바위입니다. 그것이 없다면, 전체 아치와 구조물은 스스로 붕괴될 것입니다. 건축처럼, 생물학의 핵심 종들은 생태계에서 중요한 역할을 합니다. 핵심 종은 식물이나 동물이 될 수 있습니다. 물론, 생태계의 모든 생물들은 어떤 식으로든 서로에게 의존합니다. 하지만, 그 핵심 종들은 생태계의 생물 다양성을 만들거나 유지시킴으로써 중요한 역할을 합니다. 핵심 종이 반드시 수적으로 우세하지는 않다는 것을 알아두세요. 그리고 키스톤이 제자리에 있지 않은 구조물이 무너지듯이, 만약 핵심 종이 제자리에 있지 않다면, 생태계는 붕괴될 것입니다.

그럼 이 핵심 종들은 무엇일까요? 그리고 어떻게 자연 서식지에서 작동할까요? 자, 몇 가지 종류의 핵심 종에 대해 논의해 보겠습니다. 첫째, 최상위 포식자들입니다. 최상위 포식자들은 먹이 사슬에서 자기들보다 더 작은 동물들을 잡아먹습니다. 이렇게 함으로써, 그들은 다른 종들이 생존하도록 합니다. 이 핵심 종의 좋은 예는 북아메리카에 있는 알래스카 늑대입니다. 이 온화하지만 사나운 포식자는 숲에서 다른 포식자들을 포함하여 모든 종류의 동물들을 사냥합니다. 만약 그들이 다른 포식자들을 사냥하지 않는다면, 토끼나 다람쥐와 같은 숲 속의 작고 사랑스러운 나무 서식 동물들은 그 지역에 더 이상 존재하지 못할 것입니다. 그래서 알래스카 늑대가 없다면, 다른 작은 포식자들이 그 자리를 차지할 것이고, 북아메리카의 생물 다양성은 줄어들 것입니다.

The next keystone species we will discuss are the mutualists. As the name implies, it carries a mutually beneficial relationship with many other species. Many of the fruit trees found in the rainforest are keystone mutualists because the trees not only provide shelter to other animals like monkeys and birds, but they also provide them with food. In return, the animals help disperse the seeds by eating the fruit and their feces containing the seed being dropped onto the ground.

Finally, there are some keystone species that are called the ecosystem engineers since they change their physical environment. The elephants in the African savannahs are a great example. Elephants will knock down trees to look for fruit, which indirectly controls the tree population. If the elephants refrain from knocking down trees, the grass in the savannahs would not flourish and the plains would turn into woodlands. Without grass to feed on, grazing animals like the antelopes and zebras would cease to exist.

As a supporter of environmental preservation, it is imperative we identify the keystone species in every ecosystem. Conservationists must understand which species to target to save and promote biodiversity. Sadly, time is running out in many of the habitats. I mean, doesn't it make sense to protect only one species rather than protect the variety of life forms to sustain a whole ecosystem?

Having said that, let's look at some of the keystone species we have identified in North America. The Great Northwest is home to many animals, but some of these creatures are dying out from over predation. The Florida swamplands are home to many birds that migrate seasonally, but time has shown that some of these birds stopped coming. Let's see which keystones species are affected here.

다음으로 논의할 핵심 종은 공생 생물들입니다. 이름에서 알 수 있듯이, 그것은 다른 많은 종들과 상호 이익이 되는 관계를 가지고 있습니다. 열대 우림에서 발견되는 많은 과일 나무들은 핵심 공생 생물들입니다. 그 나무들은 원숭이나 새와 같은 다른 동물들에게 은신처를 제공할 뿐만 아니라 먹이도 제공하기 때문입니다. 그에 대한 보답으로, 동물들은 땅에 떨어진 씨 가진 과일과 배설물을 먹음으로써 씨앗을 퍼트리는 것을 도와줍니다.

마지막으로, 자신들의 물리적 환경을 바꾼다는 이유로 생태계 기술자라고 불리는 몇몇 핵심 종들이 있습니다. 아프리카 사바나에 사는 코끼리들이 좋은 예입니다. 코끼리들은 과일을 찾기 위해 나무를 쓰러뜨리고, 이것은 간접적으로 나무 개체 수를 조절합니다. 코끼리가 나무를 쓰러뜨리지 않으면, 사바나의 초원은 번성하지 못하고 평야는 삼림 지대로 변하게 될 것입니다. 먹을 풀이 없다면, 영양소와 얼룩말과 같은 방목 동물들은 더 이상 존재할 수 없을 것입니다.

환경 보존의 지지자라면, 모든 생태계의 핵심 종들을 파악하는 것이 필수적입니다. 환경 보호론자들은 생물 다양성을 살리고 촉진하기 위해 어떤 종을 목표로 삼아야 하는지 이해해야 합니다. 슬프게도, 많은 서식지들에서는 시간이 촉박합니다. 결국, 생태계 전체를 유지하기 위해 다양한 생명체를 보호하기 보다는 딱 한 종만을 보호하는 것이 타당하지 않을까요?

방금 배운 내용을 가지고, 우리가 북아메리카에서 확인한 핵심 종들을 살펴봅시다. 그레이트 노스웨스트에는 많은 동물들이 서식하고 있지만, 이 생물들 중 일부는 지나친 포식 때문에 죽어가고 있습니다. 플로리다의 늪지대는 계절적으로 이주하는 많은 새들의 서식지이지만, 시간이 지나면서 이 새들 중 일부는 더 이상 오지 않는 것으로 나타났습니다. 여기에 어떤 핵심 종들이 영향을 받는지 살펴봅시다.

ANSWERS AND SCRIPT

12) 강의의 주된 아이디어는 무엇인가? 정답 2개를 선택하시오.

A) 핵심 종의 생태학적 중요성
B) 핵심 종에 의한 해악과 이익
C) 핵심 종의 다양한 분류
D) 멸종 위기 핵심 종을 살리는 방법

13) 왜 교수는 건축에 사용된 키스톤에 대해 언급하는가?

A) 서로 다른 두 분야 간의 연결을 강조하기 위해
B) 그것의 역할과 생태계에서의 유사성을 보여주기 위해
C) 생물학을 다른 관점에서 이해하기 위해
D) 다른 과목을 공부해야 하는 중요성을 보여주기 위해

14) 교수에 따르면, 다음 중 핵심 종에 대한 설명으로 옳은 것은? 3개의 답을 선택하시오.

A) 이들의 부재는 생태계의 붕괴로 이어질 수 있다.
B) 특정 생물들이 밀려나는 것을 방지할 수 있다.
C) 개체 수가 너무 적어서 다른 종에 미치는 영향은 미미하다.
D) 육식 동물이 대부분이고 식물은 거의 없다.
E) 물리적 환경을 재구성하거나 유지할 수 있다.

15) 아프리카 사바나 지역에서 코끼리의 먹이 습성이 중요한 이유는?

A) 다양한 방목 동물을 먹이는 풀을 관리한다.
B) 작은 포유동물을 보호하는 나무의 개체 수 확대에 도움이 된다.
C) 나무의 씨앗을 분산시키고 식물의 다양성을 증진시킨다.
D) 지배적인 포식자의 수를 감소시킨다.

16) 핵심 종에 집중해 환경을 살린다는 교수의 의견은 무엇인가?

    A) 전반적 영향력은 아직 미심쩍다.
    B) 매우 중요하며 긴급하다.
    C) 시간이 너무 길어서 효과가 없다.
    D) 다른 멸종 위기종 보호의 필요성을 무시한다.

17) 교수는 다음에 무엇을 할 것인가?

    A) 수업을 마침
    B) 수업 숙제를 배정함
    C) 핵심 종에 대해 계속 이야기함
    D) 자연 보호론자로서 일한 자신의 경험에 대해 이야기함

Actual Test 03

Page.117~122

Part 1 – Conversation

ANSWERS – 1(B) 2(C) 3(D) 4(A) 5(B)

S – Hello, Professor. Do you have a minute to spare? P – Hey Sarah, what can I do for you? S – Well, I heard that next semester you are teaching a course on economics in Third World countries. P – Yes I am. I'm actually looking forward to teaching it. People are aware of the economic influence that powerful countries hold against the world, like the United States and China. But few realize the importance that Third World countries have and how they can tip the scales. Are you perhaps interested in joining the class? S – As a matter of fact, I am. But the problem is my schedule for next semester is already full. I'm taking the maximum number of classes allowed. And I have to take all those classes in order to graduate. But at the same time, I have keen interest in economics…. So I was wondering if I could audit your class without doing the assignments. P – **Well, if it was up to me, I would definitely let you sit in and listen to the class. But there is one problem. The economics department only allows students to audit classes that are not completely filled. But I suppose the department can make an exception for you, since you have an outstanding reputation in the department.** S – That would be great! I have always enjoyed taking your classes, but this time it will be for free! P – Just a second… I think you might have jumped to conclusions. The class will not be free. There will be a standard fee for registering, even for an audited course. Of course, it will be cheaper than a formal course.	S – 안녕하세요, 교수님. 혹시 잠시 시간이 되시나요? P – 새라, 무엇을 도와줄까요? S – 음, 다음 학기에 제3세계 국가의 경제학 강의를 하신다고 들었어요. P – 네, 맞아요. 저는 정말 그것을 가르치기를 기대하고 있어요. 사람들은 미국과 중국처럼 강대국이 세계에 미치는 경제적 영향에 대해 알고 있죠. 그러나 제3세계 국가들이 갖는 중요성과 그들이 어떻게 상황을 바꿀 수 있는지 깨닫는 사람은 거의 없어요. 혹시 그 수업에 관심이 있나요? S – 사실 그렇습니다. 하지만 문제가 되는 게, 다음 학기 스케줄이 이미 꽉 찼어요. 저는 허용되는 최대치의 수업을 수강하고 있습니다. 졸업을 하기 위해서는 이 모든 수업을 들어야 해요. 하지만 동시에 경제에도 관심이 많습니다. 그래서 과제를 하지 않고 교수님 수업을 청강할 수 있을까 해서요. P – 글쎄요, 그 결정이 저에게 달렸다면, 저는 분명 학생이 앉아서 수업을 듣도록 할 거예요. 그러나 한가지 문제가 있어요. 경제학부는 수강생이 완전히 채워지지 않은 수업만 청강할 수 있도록 허용하고 있어요. 하지만 경제학부에서 학생의 평판이 좋으니까 예외로 해줄 수 있을 것 같아요. S – 정말 좋은데요! 저는 항상 교수님의 수업을 듣는 것을 즐겼지만, 이번에는 공짜가 되겠네요! P – 잠깐만요… 저는 학생이 성급하게 결론을 내린 거라 생각해요. 이 수업은 무료가 아니에요. 청강일지라도 등록 시에 기본 요금은 부과될 거예요. 물론 정식 코스보다는 훨씬 저렴할 것이지만요.

S – Are you serious? I have to pay for the course, even when I'm not getting any credits? P – Well, it's only fair. Students who audit the classes still receive information from the professor. During discussion time, their questions can also be answered. They shouldn't be given a freebee because they're not getting any credits. Wouldn't you agree? S – I guess you're right. I'm just a bit surprised. I don't see the point of paying for a course if you're not going to get a grade. P – I understand. Money is hard to come by these days, but it looks like you really want to take the class. Since I don't teach it every semester, it is a rare opportunity. Why don't you sign up first, and if you're still not happy you have to pay for the class, you can drop out. I believe you will get a full refund if you drop out before the second week of the semester is done. S – You're right. I'm sure what I pay will be incomparable to the information I learn in class. I guess I'll sign up for the class and see how it turns out. Thank you professor. P – Anytime. And come by later with the class registration form so I can post a comment to have you take the class.	S – 정말요? 학점을 이수하는 게 아닌데도 수업료를 내야 한다고요? P – 음, 그게 공평해요. 그 수업을 청강하는 학생들도 교수로부터 정보를 얻어요. 토론 시간 동안, 그들의 질문에 대답할 수도 있어요. 그들이 학점을 따지 않는다고 해서 공짜가 될 수는 없어요. 동의하지 않나요? S – 교수님 말이 맞는 것 같아요. 조금 놀랐을 뿐이에요. 학점을 따지 못해도 수업에 대한 비용을 지불해야 한다는 점을 알지 못했어요. P – 이해합니다. 요즘 경제가 많이 어렵지만, 학생은 정말 그 수업을 듣고 싶어하는 것 같군요. 제가 매 학기마다 가르치지는 않으니, 정말 드문 기회이긴 해요. 먼저 등록을 하고, 여전히 수업료를 내야 하는 것이 마음에 들지 않으면, 청강을 취소해도 됩니다. 학기 둘째 주 전에 그만두면 전액 환불 받을 수 있을 거예요. S – 교수님 말씀이 맞아요. 지불하는 돈이 수업 시간에 배우는 정보와는 비교가 안 될 거라고 확신해요. 수업에 등록해서 결과가 어떤지 봐야겠어요. 교수님 감사합니다. P – 언제라도 좋습니다. 그리고 나중에 수업 등록 양식을 가지고 오시면 강의를 들을 수 있도록 추천서를 써줄 수 있어요.

ANSWERS AND SCRIPT

1) 학생은 왜 교수를 보러 가는가?

   A) 다음 학기에 그의 수업에 수강 등록이 되었다는 것을 말하기 위해
   B) 학점을 따지 않고 다음 학기에 수업을 듣는 것에 대해 이야기하기 위해서
   C) 언제 경제학 수업을 할 것인지 문의하기 위해
   D) 다음 학기에 어떤 수업을 들을 것인지 조언을 구하기 위해

2) 왜 학생은 정식 수강 대신 청강을 원하는가?

   A) 그 비용을 지불할 돈이 없다.
   B) 수업에서 낙제할까 봐 걱정한다.
   C) 이미 최대 개수의 수업을 등록했다.
   D) 자신의 연구 논문을 위한 정보가 필요하다.

3) 청강 수업에 수업료를 지불하는 것에 대한 교수의 의견은 무엇인가?

   A) 경제적인 어려움을 겪는 학생들에게 불공평하다고 생각한다.
   B) 학생들에게 요금을 부과한 대학 측에 화가 나 있다.
   C) 정책에 명시되어 있기 때문에 받아들여야 한다고 생각한다.
   D) 교수들이 하는 역할이기 때문에 필요하다고 생각한다.

4) 교수는 무엇을 시사하고 있는가?

   A) 수업은 이미 꽉 찼다.
   B) 그 학생은 경제학을 지긋지긋해한다.
   C) 교수는 그 학생이 청강할 수 있을지 의심스럽다.
   D) 교수는 학생을 돌보지 않는 것 같다.

5) 학생은 무엇을 할 것인가?

   A) 학점이 필요할 때 수업을 들음
   B) 청강생으로 등록함
   C) 청강에 대한 비용 지불에 대해 학교 관리자와 상의함
   D) 다음 학기에 대해서 교수와 계속 이야기함

Part 1 – Lecture

ANSWERS – 6(C) 7(D) 8(C) 9(D) 10(A) 11(B)

P – Now that everyone has taken their seat, let's get started. Today, we will begin our discussion on desalination, which is the process of removing salt from ocean water and marsh water. I noticed a lot of you guys taking some great notes in the previous classes. Can someone tell me what desalination is?

S1 – I remember that dumping the previously removed salt caused some environmental issues. It upset the balance between salt and water, so it killed off a lot of plants and the fish that eat them.

S2 – There's an easy solution to that. Just find another place to dump the salt.

P – I guess that could work. However, I believe that the bigger problem is humanity is left with only a finite amount of fresh water that is made naturally. Desalination is a solution to this problem. It will provide all the drinking water we need, especially in this unstable weather and environmental condition we live today.

Now let's get into the specific details of desalination. Most of the desalination processes we use incorporate a phenomenon found in nature: evaporation. We all know that the sun produces heat in nature and it will cause liquid water to change into water vapor at certain temperatures. When salt water is evaporated, only water turns to vapor, and salt is left behind. When the evaporated water cools, it will condense and turn back to liquid water. But this time, it will be salt-free.

Our planet performs this naturally on a daily basis in a process called the rain cycle. Desalination factories use the same principles. The factory will boil water until the water evaporates and leaves behind the salt. Then it will cool the evaporated water to make fresh liquid water. Although there are many other methods for desalination, this is the most widely used method. However, what do you think might be some of the problems with this method of desalination?

S1 – It requires a lot of energy to heat the water and cool it.

P - 이제 모두가 자리에 앉았네요. 시작하겠습니다. 오늘, 우리는 해수 및 습지 물에서 염분을 제거하는 과정인 담수화 과정에 대해 논의를 시작할 겁니다. 저는 많은 분들이 이전 수업에서 멋지게 필기 하는 것을 보았습니다. 담수화가 무엇인지 누가 말해줄 수 있을까요?

S1 - 저는 앞서 제거된 소금을 버리는 것이 여러 환경 문제를 일으켰던 것으로 기억합니다. 그것은 소금과 물 사이의 균형을 깨뜨렸고, 그래서 많은 식물과 그것을 먹고 사는 물고기들을 죽게 했습니다.

S2 - 쉬운 해결책이 있습니다. 소금을 버릴 다른 장소를 찾는 것입니다.

P - 가능할 것 같습니다. 하지만, 저는 더 큰 문제는 인류가 자연적으로 만들어지는 한정된 양의 담수만 가지고 남겨진 것이라 생각해요. 담수화는 이 문제의 해결책입니다. 그것은 특히 오늘날 우리가 살고 있는 불안정한 날씨와 환경 조건에서 우리가 필요로 하는 모든 식수를 제공할 겁니다.

이제 담수화의 세부 사항에 대해 알아 봅시다. 우리가 사용하는 대부분의 담수화 과정에는 자연에서 발견되는 현상인 증발이 포함되어 있습니다. 우리 모두는 태양이 자연에서 열을 발생시키고 그 열이 특정한 온도에서 액체 상태의 물을 수증기로 변하게 할 것이라는 걸 알고 있습니다. 소금물이 증발할 때, 물만 수증기로 변하고, 소금은 남습니다. 증발된 물이 식으면, 그것은 응축되어 다시 액체인 물로 변할 겁니다. 하지만 이 때는, 소금기가 없을 거예요.

우리 행성은 비의 순환이라고 불리는 과정에서 이것을 매일매일 자연적으로 행합니다. 담수화 공장도 같은 원리를 사용합니다. 공장은 물이 증발해서 소금이 남겨질 때까지 물을 끓일 겁니다. 그리고 나서 증발된 물을 식혀서 신선한 물을 만들어 냅니다. 담수화에는 많은 다른 방법들이 있지만, 이것이 가장 널리 사용되는 방법입니다. 하지만, 여러분은 이 담수화 방법에 어떤 문제가 있다고 생각하나요?

S1 - 물을 가열하고 냉각하려면 많은 에너지가 필요합니다.

P – Excellent. Millions of gallons of saltwater are boiled and cooled all day, which do require tremendous amounts of energy. This is the reason why a lot of the desalination factories are built next to power plants to supply them with energy. However, technicians have come up with some methods to reduce the energy needed. It focuses on two principles.

The first is recycling heat. Heat-exchange technology is used in desalination factories that integrates the evaporation and condensation processes. At the desalination factory, there are several evaporation chambers. In the first chamber, an energy source, such as electricity or fossil fuel, is used to boil the salt water. The steam that is produced will have to be cooled so that it can turn into fresh water. Of course a cooling system can be used, but that would cost additional energy. So instead, factories will direct the steam using a series of pipes, and they spray cold water on the pipes. Then heat from the steam will be transferred to the salt water. Using this method, it's like killing two birds with one stone. Not only does it save energy by using steam to heat the saltwater, but it also cools the steam so that it can condense into fresh water. Of course, some heat will be lost in each chamber, so those that come later in the series will be cooler and the temperature will be lower than the water's boiling point. So what would be the solution to boil the saltwater in each chamber, without having to heat up every single chamber?

The second principle takes effect here: factories using low pressure evaporation chambers. Can someone tell me why this is so creative?

S1 – Oh, it's because water at lower pressure will evaporate at a lower temperature.

P – You are correct. So by transporting the salt water to lower pressurized chambers, less energy will be used to boil the water since the evaporation temperature will be lower. Actually, if the pressure difference from one chamber to the next is big enough, the water will immediately evaporate. This is called flash evaporation and the collection of chambers with low pressure are called flash generators. By using flash generators and heat-exchange technology, a desalination factory can just use a single central heat source. So that explains why this method is so popular and using this method produces more than half of the desalinized water the world uses.

P - 훌륭합니다. 수백만 갤런의 소금물이 하루 종일 끓고 식혀지는데, 이것은 엄청난 양의 에너지를 필요로 합니다. 많은 담수화 공장들이 에너지를 공급하기 위해 발전소 옆에 지어지는 이유입니다. 하지만 기술자들은 필요한 에너지를 줄이기 위한 몇 가지 방법을 생각해 냈어요. 그것은 두 가지 원리에 초점을 맞춥니다.

첫 번째는 열을 재활용하는 겁니다. 열 교환 기술은 증발과 응축 과정을 통합시키는 담수화 공장에서 사용됩니다. 담수화 공장에는 몇 개의 증발 챔버들이 있어요. 첫 번째 챔버에서, 전기나 화석 연료와 같은 에너지원은 소금물을 끓이는 데 사용됩니다. 생산되는 증기는 담수로 변할 수 있도록 냉각 되어야 합니다. 물론 냉각 시스템을 사용할 수 있지만, 그것은 추가적인 에너지를 필요로 하죠. 그래서 대신, 공장들은 일련의 파이프를 사용하여 증기를 유도하고, 파이프에 차가운 물을 뿌립니다. 그러면 증기의 열은 소금물로 옮겨질 겁니다. 이 방법을 사용하면 일석이조입니다. 증기를 이용해 소금물을 가열함으로써 에너지를 절약할 뿐만 아니라 증기를 냉각시켜 담수로 응축시킬 수 있습니다.

물론, 각 챔버에서 열의 일부가 손실될 것이고, 따라서 뒤따라 오는 열은 더 차갑고 온도가 물의 끓는점보다 낮을 겁니다. 그러면 소금물을 각 챔버에서 데우지 않고도, 끓일 수 있는 해결책은 무엇일까요?

두 번째 원리가 여기에서 적용됩니다. 저압 증발 챔버를 사용하는 공장입니다. 이것이 왜 그렇게 창의적인지 누가 말해줄 수 있나요?

S1 - 더 낮은 압력에서는 물이 더 낮은 온도에서 증발하기 때문입니다.

P - 정답입니다. 소금물을 더 압력이 낮은 챔버로 운반함으로써, 증발 온도가 더 낮아지기 때문에 물을 끓이는 데 더 적은 에너지가 사용될 겁니다. 사실, 만약 한 챔버와 다른 챔버 사이의 압력 차이가 충분히 크면, 물은 즉시 증발합니다. 이를 플래시 증발(순간 증발)이라고 하며, 압력이 낮은 챔버를 모은 것을 플래시 발생기라고 합니다. 플래시 발전기와 열 교환 기술을 사용하여 담수화 공장은 단일 중앙 열원을 사용할 수 있습니다. 이것이 이 방법이 왜 그렇게 인기가 있는지 말해주며 이 방법을 사용하면 전 세계가 사용하는 담수화 물의 절반 이상이 생산됩니다.

6) 강의의 핵심은 무엇인가?

　　A) 담수화에서 저압의 적용
　　B) 열 교환 기술의 활용
　　C) 에너지 절약을 돕는 담수화 기법
　　D) 담수화 효과가 환경에 미치는 영향

7) 담수화와 관련한 교수의 의견은?

　　A) 그녀는 그것이 그렇게 믿을 수 있는 것이 아니라고 생각한다.
　　B) 그녀는 그것이 자연에 긍정적인 영향을 미칠 지에 대해 주저한다.
　　C) 그녀는 그것이 더 효율적일 수 있다고 믿는다.
　　D) 그녀는 그것이 지금 그 어느 때보다 더 필요하다고 느낀다.

8) 교수는 담수화 과정을 어떻게 소개하는가?

　　A) 기존 담수화 공정과 비교함
　　B) 그것이 가장 많이 사용되는 나라들을 명명함으로써
　　C) 그것이 기초로 하는 자연 발생에 대한 언급을 함으로써
　　D) 전통적인 담수화 방법의 결함을 지적함으로써.

9) 담수화에서 플래시 발전기는 왜 실용적인가?

　　A) 증기를 담수로 빠르게 냉각시킨다.
　　B) 바닷물에서 더 많은 소금을 제거한다.
　　C) 바닷물을 빨리 끓도록 예열한다.
　　D) 물의 끓는 점을 낮춘다.

ANSWERS AND SCRIPT

10) 교수는 열 교환 기술과 플래시 발전기에 대해 뭐라고 하는가?

A) 함께 사용되는 경우가 많다.
B) 더 완벽해져야 한다.
C) 기존 방식보다 더 많은 에너지를 필요로 한다.
D) 환경 문제를 야기한다.

**11) 강의 일부를 다시 들어보시오. 그리고 질문에 답하시오.
교수가 이 말을 할 때 무엇을 시사하는가?**

A) 열 교환은 환경에 큰 도움이 된다.
B) 열 교환은 하나 이상의 문제에 대한 해결책을 제공한다.
C) 열 교환은 다른 방법에 비해 2배 빠른 속도로 작동한다.
D) 열 교환은 두 개의 에너지원에 의존한다.

Page.123~131

Part 2 – Conversation

ANSWERS – 1(C) 2(D) 3(B) 4(A,B) 5(included – C,D)(not included – A,B)

S – Good morning professor. Sorry to drop by at such a short notice, but could I ask for some advice on a movie I'm making on global warming? P – Of course! You know I love to help students, even on short notice. Let me finishing typing this document first. S – Oh, if you're busy at the moment, I can always come back when you're free. P – No no, I just finished. All I have to do is save it. Done. Now, what do you need advice on? S – I just needed some help on the movie I'm making. It's about the effects that global warming has on migrating birds. P – Oh yes, I remember! You told me you'd be working on that a while back. How is that going? S – I'm actually having a tough time. I've been working on what to film and how to present it, but I still can't seem to organize everything together. P – It's understandable. Filming a movie is a detailed process, even for professional filmmakers. S – I don't even know where to begin… Filming an interview even seems complicated. I mean coming up with thought-provoking questions that the interviewee will answer with insight is easy. But I'm not sure how I will capture their responses from different angles. When you shoot interviews, do you record the interview multiple times, or do you have multiple cameras recording from different angles in one interview? P – Well it depends on the interview. There is no real answer. Depending on the location of the interview and the set, you might have to film the same thing several times. For instance, if you're conducting the interview in a small room where multiple cameras cannot be placed, you'll have to record the interview several times. Also, you have to consider the sound quality if you decide to interview the person outdoors, since natural environment can influence how the sound comes out in one shot.	S – 안녕하세요 교수님. 이렇게 잠깐 들려서 죄송하지만, 제가 만들고 있는 지구 온난화에 관한 영화에 대해 조언을 구할 수 있을까요? P – 물론이죠! 알다시피 저는 학생들을 잠깐이라도 돕는 것을 좋아해요. 그 전에 이 문서 타이핑을 마저 끝내겠습니다. S – 아, 지금 바쁘시면 언제든지 시간 되실 때 방문할 수 있어요. P – 아니요, 방금 끝냈어요. 저장만 하면 돼요. 다 됐어요. 자, 무슨 조언이 필요하세요? S – 지금 만들고 있는 영화에 도움이 좀 필요했어요. 지구 온난화가 철새들에게 미치는 영향에 관한 것입니다. P – 네, 기억나요! 얼마 전에 그 작업을 할 거라고 하셨잖아요. 어떻게 진행되고 있나요? S – 사실 저는 좀 힘들어요. 무엇을 촬영하고 어떻게 발표해야 할 지 고민했는데, 아직도 모든 것을 다 정리 할 수 없는 것 같아요. P – 이해할 수 있습니다. 영화 촬영은 전문적인 영화 제작자들에게도 섬세한 과정이거든요. S – 어디서부터 시작해야 할지… 심지어 인터뷰 녹화는 복잡해 보여요. 통찰력을 지닌 면접 대상자의 생각을 이끌어 내는 질문들을 생각해내는 것은 어렵지 않다고 생각합니다. 하지만 저는 다른 각도에서 어떻게 그들의 반응을 포착해야 할지 잘 모르겠어요. 인터뷰 장면을 찍을 때, 인터뷰를 여러 번 녹화하나요, 아니면 한 번의 인터뷰를 여러 각도에서 카메라 녹화를 하나요? P – 인터뷰에 따라 다릅니다. 정답은 없어요. 인터뷰 장소와 촬영 장소에 따라 같은 내용을 여러 번 촬영해야 할 수도 있습니다. 예를 들어, 여러 대의 카메라를 설치할 수 없는 작은 방에서 인터뷰를 진행하는 경우, 여러 번 인터뷰를 촬영해야 합니다. 또한, 만약 야외에서 그 사람을 인터뷰하기로 결정한다면, 학생은 음질을 고려해야 합니다. 왜냐하면 자연 환경은 그 소리가 장면에 나오는데 영향을 줄 수 있기 때문입니다.

S – Wow, these are some great points professor. So how about placing the interviews in between the films. Maybe I should split the interview into different parts and insert each section in the appropriate part of the film. Or would it better to leave the interview as it is so that viewers can better understand the overall opinion of the interviewee? P – Again, that depends on the situation. But in my opinion, since your movie is on birds and how global warming affects them, I would cut the interview into smaller sections and attach it to the parts relevant to the topic you are covering. Your movie is an informative media that attempts to explain a particular phenomenon. On the other hand, if you were making a movie focusing on the opinions of the general public and how they feel about the negative effects of global warming while enjoying the benefits it has to offer, then your interview should be left as is. S – I see. Your analogies helped me so much professor. I think I know which direction I want my movie to go. Before coming here, I felt unsure of even pursuing a career in film making… P – There will be times when we doubt our abilities, but don't let it get to you! Come by the office again if you have any other questions. S – Thank you so much professor.	S - 와, 그 점들은 정말 중요한 것 같아요. 그러니 영화들 사이에 인터뷰 내용을 넣는 것은 어떨까요. 인터뷰를 다른 부분으로 나누고 각 섹션을 영화의 적절한 부분에 삽입해야 할 것 같습니다. 아니면 시청자들이 인터뷰 대상자의 전반적인 의견을 더 잘 이해할 수 있도록 인터뷰를 있는 그대로 두는 것이 더 나을까요? P - 다시 한 번 말하지만, 상황에 따라 달라요. 하지만 제 생각에는, 학생의 영화가 새에 관한 것이고 지구 온난화가 새들에게 어떤 영향을 미치는지에 대한 것이기 때문에, 저라면 인터뷰를 더 작은 부분으로 나누고 학생이 다루고 있는 주제와 관련된 부분에 첨부할 겁니다. 학생의 영화는 특정한 현상을 설명하려고 하는 정보 제공의 수단입니다. 반면, 학생이 일반 대중의 의견과 지구 온난화가 주는 혜택을 누리는 가운데 느끼는 지구 온난화의 부정적인 영향에 대해 초점을 맞춘 영화를 만들고 있다면, 인터뷰는 그대로 남겨두어야 합니다. S - 그렇군요. 교수님의 비유는 많은 도움을 주었어요. 제 영화가 어떤 방향으로 흘러가길 원하는지 알게 된 것 같아요. 여기 오기 전까지, 저는 영화 제작의 길을 갈 확신이 없었습니다. P - 우리의 능력을 의심하는 때가 간혹 있지만, 걱정하지 마세요! 다른 질문이 있으면 연구실에 다시 오세요. S - 교수님 감사합니다.

1) 대화의 주제는?

   A) 지구 온난화 관련 영화 촬영 승인 받기
   B) 지구 온난화의 부정적 영향에 대해 사람들에게 알리는 방법
   C) 가장 좋은 방법은 새들이 지구 온난화에 어떻게 영향을 받는지에 대한 영화를 만드는 것이다.
   D) 정보 영화에서 사람들을 인터뷰하는 가장 좋은 방법

2) 영화 제작에 대한 교수의 의견은?

   A) 세심하게 계획한다면 어렵지 않다.
   B) 영화 전공자만 감독할 수 있다.
   C) 모든 것이 정리될 때까지 촬영에 착수하지 않아야 한다.
   D) 어렵고 힘든 작업이다.

3) 그 학생의 영화에 대해 유추할 수 있는 것은?

   A) 그는 여전히 그 주제에 대해 더 많은 정보를 찾아야 한다.
   B) 그는 이미 좋은 질문을 생각해 놓았다.
   C) 그는 인터뷰 대상자를 구하는 데 어려움을 겪고 있다.
   D) 그는 지구 온난화에 대한 찬반론을 포함 시킬 계획이다.

4) 같은 인터뷰를 여러 번 찍을지 말지를 결정할 때 고려해야 할 사항은 무엇인가? 정답 2개를 선택하시오.

   A) 인터뷰 세트의 크기.
   B) 음질
   C) 인터뷰가 나뉘게 되는 경우.
   D) 인터

ANSWERS AND SCRIPT

5) 대화에서는 교수와 학생이 학생의 영화의 다른 면을 이야기한다. 다음 사항을 언급했는지의 여부를 표시하라.

각 구에 대해 올바른 상자를 선택하시오.

	포함 됨	포함되지 않음
A) 장비 준비 방법		
B) 관련 자원을 찾는 장소		
C) 인터뷰를 효과적으로 삽입할 수 있는 위치		
D) 여러 대의 카메라를 사용하는 경우		

Part 2 – Lecture

ANSWERS – 6(B) 7(D) 8(B) 9(B) 10(C) 11(Homogeneous A,D)(Heterogeneous B,C,E)

Chemistry is the study of the substances that make up everything in the universe and how they interact with one another. Scientists refer to these substances as matter, which is described as anything with mass and volume. Today, we will be focusing on different ways that matter can mix or blend with one another. First of all, a mixture is made up of two or more different kinds of matter that are mechanically combined, but not chemically. In other words, the matter is physically mixed together, but they are not chemically bonded at an atomic or molecular level. There are two different types of mixtures: homogenous and heterogeneous. Within each of these two types, mixtures are further categorized by the number of phases they have. Remember that there are four different phases matter can exist in: liquid, solid, gas, or plasma. Homogeneous mixtures are only made up of one phase. Heterogeneous mixtures can contain more than one phase.

Ok, moving on. Homogeneous mixtures appear uniform in their composition. Let me give you an example. Water that is mixed with salt is a homogeneous solution since the concentration of salt is the same within the solution. If you were to pour out half of the water, there would be the same amount of salt in each half of the water. Furthermore, a salt water solution only has one phase, which is liquid.

On the other hand, sandy water is a heterogeneous mixture because its components can be identified by simple observation. When some of the sand in the water settle, it will not dissolve completely Also, sandy water has two phases: the sand being a solid phase and the water as a liquid phase.

What is interesting is that sand is a heterogeneous mixture. Sand is made up of tiny grains of rocks and minerals. Some sand may contain seashells or the remains of other marine lifeforms.

화학은 우주의 모든 것을 구성하는 물질과 그것들이 서로 어떻게 상호 작용하는지 연구하는 학문입니다. 과학자들은 이 근본 물질(substance)들을 물질(matter)이라고 부르는데, 이것은 질량과 부피가 있는 것으로 묘사됩니다. 오늘, 우리는 물질이 서로 섞이거나 혼합될 수 있는 다른 방법에 초점을 맞출 것입니다.

우선, 혼합물은 기계적으로 결합되지만 화학적으로 결합되지는 않는 두 가지 이상의 다른 물질로 이루어져 있습니다. 다른 말로 하자면, 물질은 물리적으로 섞이지만, 원자나 분자 수준에서 화학적으로 결합되어 있지는 않습니다. 혼합물은 균일, 불균일의 두 가지 다른 유형이 있습니다. 이 각각의 두 가지 유형에서 혼합물은 단계에 따라 추가로 분류됩니다. 물질은 액체, 고체, 기체 또는 플라즈마의 네 가지 상태로 존재할 수 있다는 것을 기억하세요. 균일 혼합물은 한가지 상태로만 이뤄집니다. 불균일 혼합물은 둘 이상의 상태를 포함할 수 있습니다.

자, 다음 단계로 넘어갑시다. 균일 혼합물은 구성이 균일하게 나타납니다. 예를 하나 들어 보죠. 소금과 혼합된 물은 용액 내 염분 농도가 동일하기 때문에 균일 용액입니다. 만약 여러분이 물의 절반을 쏟아낸다면, 물의 절반에는 같은 양의 소금이 있을 것입니다. 게다가, 소금물 용액은 액체인 단 하나의 상태만 가지고 있습니다.

반면에 모래를 섞은 물은 단순한 관찰로도 성분을 식별할 수 있기 때문에 불균일 혼합물입니다. 물에 있는 모래 중 일부가 가라앉으면, 그것은 완전히 녹지 않을 것입니다. 또한, 그 물은 두 개의 상태가 있습니다: 모래는 고체 상태이고 물은 액체 상태입니다. 흥미로운 것은 모래가 불균일 혼합물이라는 것입니다. 모래는 돌과 미네랄의 작은 알갱이로 이루어져 있습니다. 어떤 모래는 조개껍질이나 다른 해양 생물의 잔해를 포함할 수 있습니다.

In our natural environment, some substances can alternate from being a homogeneous mixture to a heterogeneous mixture. Air is an example. In its purest, breathable form, air is in its homogeneous gas phase. However, when air is combined with smog or smoke, it will contain solid materials that are unevenly distributed. This will make the air heterogeneous. This reminds me of another characteristic of heterogeneous mixtures: their constituents can be filtered out. This filtration is impossible with homogeneous mixtures. Many factories these days have installed a filtration system on their chimneys because the factory had let out too much smoke which was harming the environment. The filtration system collects most of the solid harmful materials, and only lets out the semi-pure air into the environment.

Finally, when we consider the characteristics of mixtures, it is also important to consider their variable properties. One variable property is how the quantity of each part within a mixture determines its character. A great example is tea. Tea is a homogeneous mixture. When we leave the tea bag in the water longer, the tea become darker and more flavorful. This is due to the plant leaves in the tea bag homogeneously dissolving into the water with the passing time. Another example is the density of smoke. As smoke is heterogeneous, the smoke's density is dependent upon the amount of airborne liquid and the solid particles it is composed of. Also, we mustn't forget the influence temperature has on the melting and freezing points. Going back to the example of salt water, this type of water requires lower temperatures to freeze than regular water. This is because the salt content lowers the freezing point, with more salt decreasing the temperature even more. This is actually why ocean water requires such extreme cold climates for it to freeze than a freshwater lake.

Understanding the properties of different kinds of mixtures actually help us a lot in our everyday lives. We know sugar melts faster at higher temperatures and is distributed more evenly in coffee, so we have learned to add sugar cubes only in hot coffee. We have also learned in winter, ice forms slower when salt is added to the water, so cities have covered the streets with pinches of salt to prevent icy roads from forming.

우리의 자연 환경에서, 일부 물질은 균일 혼합물에서 불균일 혼합물로 대체될 수 있습니다. 공기가 그 예입니다. 가장 순수하고, 숨쉴 수 있는 형태에서, 공기는 균일한 기체 상태에 있습니다. 그러나, 공기가 스모그나 연기와 결합될 때, 그것은 고르게 분포되지 않은 고체 물질을 포함하게 될 것입니다. 이것은 공기를 불균일하게 만들 것입니다. 이러한 점은 불균일 혼합물은 그 성분들을 걸러낼 수 있다는 또 다른 특징을 상기시킵니다. 균일 혼합물에서는 이 필터링이 불가능합니다. 요즘 많은 공장들은 굴뚝에 여과 장치를 설치했습니다. 왜냐하면 공장들은 환경을 해치는 연기를 너무 많이 배출했기 때문입니다. 여과 시스템은 대부분의 고체 유해 물질을 포집하며 일부 청정한 공기만 자연으로 배출합니다.

마지막으로, 혼합물의 특성을 고려할 때, 변수 특성을 고려하는 것도 중요합니다. 한 가지 변수 특성은 혼합물 내 각 부분의 양이 해당 특성을 결정하는 방법입니다. 좋은 예는 차입니다. 차는 균일한 혼합물입니다. 찻주머니를 물 속에 더 오래 두면, 차는 더 진해지고 더 풍미가 더해집니다. 이것은 찻주머니의 식물 잎이 시간이 지남에 따라 물 속에 균일하게 용해되기 때문입니다. 또 다른 예는 연기의 밀도입니다. 연기가 불균일하기 때문에, 연기의 밀도는 공기 중의 액체와 연기로 구성된 고체 입자의 양에 따라 달라집니다. 또한, 우리는 어는점과 끓는점 온도에 미치는 영향을 잊어서는 안 됩니다. 소금물의 예로 돌아가서, 이런 종류의 물은 보통 물보다 더 낮은 온도를 필요로 합니다. 이것은 소금 함량이 온도를 더 낮추면서 어는점을 낮추기 때문입니다. 실제로 이것이 바닷물이 얼기 위해서는 민물 호수보다 더 추운 기후가 필요한 이유입니다.

다른 종류의 혼합물의 특성을 이해하는 것은 사실 우리의 일상 생활에 많은 도움을 줍니다. 우리는 설탕이 더 높은 온도에서 더 빨리 녹고 커피에 더 고르게 분포된다는 것을 알고 있습니다. 그래서 우리는 뜨거운 커피에서만 각설탕을 넣습니다. 우리는 또한 겨울에 소금을 물에 넣으면 얼음이 더 느리게 형성된다는 것을 알게 되었습니다. 그래서 도시들은 빙판길이 형성되는 것을 막기 위해 소금 덩어리로 거리를 덮었습니다.

6) 강의의 핵심은 무엇인가?

A) 다양한 종류의 물질의 가변적 특성
B) 두 가지 유형의 혼합물의 특성.
C) 특정 종류의 혼합물의 장점
D) 현대 화학에 관한 연구

7) 강의에 따르면 다음 중 균일 혼합물에 대한 설명으로 옳은 것은?

A) 두 가지 이상의 상태로 구성될 수 있다.
B) 여과 장치는 그 안에 있는 물질을 분리시킬 수 있다.
C) 대부분 액체 용액이다.
D) 구성 물질을 고르게 펴 바른다.

8) 다음 중 공기에 대한 설명으로 옳은 것은?

A) 항상 균일하다.
B) 불균일하게 될 수 있다.
C) 스모그 발생 시 균일하다.
D) 순수한 공기는 불균일하다.

9) 교수는 왜 차를 언급하는가?

A) 불균일 혼합물의 예를 제공한다.
B) 구성 변화가 혼합물에 어떤 영향을 미칠 수 있는지 보여 준다.
C) 불균일 물질이 어떻게 균일하게 변하는지 설명한다.
D) 균일 혼합물은 여과할 수 없음을 지적한다.

10) 교수는 강의를 어떻게 조직하였는가?

A) 역사적 발견에 대해 연대순으로 논의한다.
B) 자연적, 인공적 조합의 목록을 작성한다.
C) 정의를 제공하고 그 성질을 설명한다.
D) 상태 수에 따라 순위를 매긴다.

ANSWERS AND SCRIPT

11) 강의에서 교수는 다양한 종류의 혼합물에 대해 이야기한다.
각 구에 대해 올바른 상자를 선택하시오.

	균일 혼합물	불균일 혼합물
A) 소금물		
B) 모래물(모래섞인물)		
C) 모래		
D) 차		
E) 연기		

Part 2 - Lecture

ANSWERS – 12(C) 13(A,B) 14(C) 15(C) 16(A) 17(B)

P – In our last class, we discussed how the immune system works. Let's move on to our next topic. But before we begin, it's important that we go over some fundamental parts of our brains. If you recall, our brain contains over one trillion cells called neurons. Fun fact, that's more than the stars in our own Milky Way galaxy, and that's a lot! We also went over their important role in processing and delivering information to the rest of our body. Would anyone like to volunteer and answer how they do this?
S – If I remember correctly, neurons form a network that send signals to different internal organs in order for them to work properly. So these neurons control the conscious activities we perform, like the muscular movements in running or swimming. They also take over the involuntary actions in the body like breathing and digesting.
P – Well done. This systematic process is called neurotransmission. Let me describe it in more detail. First, a neuron cell receives a nerve impulse, which is an electrical current that moves from one neuron cell to the next. Every neuron is specialized to carry out these signals to the next cell. Neurons do this using structures called synapses. Synapses connect the neurons so the signals are passed along. When the electrical nerve impulse finally arrives at its target neuron, chemical signals called neurotransmitters are released, which can cause different biological effects. It may cause our arm to move away from the fire or signal the stomach to release more stomach acid to digest the food faster. Thus, the communication network is completed.

P - 지난 수업에서, 우리는 면역 체계가 어떻게 작동하는지에 대해 토론했습니다. 다음 주제로 넘어가도록 하겠습니다. 시작하기 전에, 뇌의 몇 가지 핵심적인 부분들을 살펴보는 것이 중요합니다. 기억하실지 모르겠지만, 우리의 뇌는 뉴런이라고 불리는 1조개 이상의 세포를 가지고 있습니다. 재미있는 사실은, 그것이 우리 은하계에 있는 별들 이상으로 아주 많다는 것입니다! 우리는 또한 정보를 처리하고 그 정보를 우리 몸의 나머지 부분으로 전달하는데 있어서 뉴런의 중요한 역할을 검토했습니다. 그것들이 어떻게 이런 일을 하는지 누가 자원해서 대답해 줄 사람 있나요?
S - 제 기억이 정확하다면, 뉴런은 그들이 적절하게 작동하기 위해 서로 다른 내부 기관으로 신호를 보내는 네트워크를 형성합니다. 그래서 이 뉴런들은 우리가 행하는 의식적인 활동들을 통제합니다. 달리기나 수영을 할 때 근육의 움직임처럼 말이죠. 그들은 또한 호흡과 소화 같은 무의식적인 신체 활동에 관여합니다.
P - 잘했습니다. 이 체계적인 과정을 신경 전달이라고 부릅니다. 좀 더 자세히 설명하겠습니다. 우선, 뉴런 세포는 신경 자극을 받는데, 이것은 하나의 뉴런 세포에서 다음 뉴런 세포로 이동하는 전류입니다. 모든 뉴런은 이 신호를 다음 세포로 전달하도록 특화되어 있습니다. 뉴런은 시냅스라고 불리는 구조를 사용하여 이것을 합니다. 시냅스는 뉴런을 연결하여 신호가 전달되도록 합니다. 전기 신경 자극이 마침내 목표한 뉴런에 도착했을 때, 신경 전달 물질이라고 불리는 화학적 신호가 방출되는데, 이것은 다른 생물학적 영향을 일으킬 수 있습니다. 그것은 우리의 팔이 불에서 멀어지게 하거나 위가 음식을 더 빨리 소화시키기 위해 더 많은 위산을 방출하도록 신호를 보낼 수 있습니다. 그렇게 해서 의사소통 네트워크가 완료되는 것입니다.

Aside from neurons, there is another cell that is critical in neurotransmission. They are called glia. In Greek, it means glue, and appropriately so. When it was first discovered, scientists thought that the sole purpose of glia was to act as connective tissue in the brain, gluing all the neurons in place. One thing to note is that the number of neurons and glial cells in our brain are equal. But, their frequency ratio differs, which is dependent on their location in the brain. For instance, there are three times the amount of glial cells in the cerebral cortex of the brain than neurons, while there are four time the amount of neurons in the cerebellum than the number of glial cells. The numbers here are not important, just remember that their frequency ratios differ.

Research has shown that glial cells are far more important than once thought. They serve a higher purpose than simply acting as glue in the brain. We now understand that glial cells perform several critical roles. First, they resupply the neurons with oxygen and necessary nutrients. Second, they act as insulators for each neuron. Third, they keep the brain healthy by removing harmful pathogens and throwing out dead neurons. The most recent research has shown that glial cells sometimes participate in neurotransmission, and like neuron cells, they will release neurotransmitters when having received an electrical signal. Now that's something!

These discoveries have forever changed neuroscience! Previously, neuroscientists focused only on the neuron cells, however, their gaze has shifted towards glial cells. Another interesting find was that glial cells possess the ability to reproduce through cell division, something neurons are incapable of. Although there are some exceptions to this characteristic, it is generally observed to be true. You have your hand up? Do you have a question?
S – Excuse me professor. Are you saying that there are potential discoveries to be made in the field of neuroscience? That neuroscientists don't know everything about the human brain yet?
P – That's exactly what I'm saying. When you guys graduate, modern research will have heightened our knowledge about the brain, especially of glial cells. There simply seems to be no end! I have no doubt in my mind that there is more to learn about these special cells and its role in our brain.
Now open your textbooks to page 422. Let's look at some pictures of glial cells in action.

뉴런 외에도 신경전달에 또 다른 중요한 세포가 있습니다. 그것들은 글리아라고 불립니다. 그리스어로, 접착제라는 의미로서 너무 적절합니다. 그것이 처음 발견되었을 때, 과학자들은 글리아의 유일한 목적이 뇌에서 결합 조직 역할을 하여 모든 뉴런을 제자리에 붙어있게 하는 것이라고 생각했습니다. 한 가지 주목할 것은 우리 뇌의 뉴런의 숫자와 글리아의 숫자가 같다는 것입니다. 하지만, 그들의 진동수 비율은 다른데, 이는 뇌의 위치에 따라 다릅니다. 예를 들어, 뇌 대뇌 피질에서는 뉴런보다 글리아 세포가 3배 많은 반면, 소뇌에서는 글리아 세포보다 뉴런의 수가 4배 더 많습니다. 여기서 중요한 것은 숫자가 아니라 진동수 비율의 차이라는 것을 기억하십시오.

연구는 한 때 생각했던 것보다 글리아 세포가 훨씬 더 중요하다는 것을 보여줍니다. 그것들은 단순히 뇌의 접착제 역할보다 더 중요한 목적을 제공합니다. 우리는 이제 글리아 세포가 몇 가지 중요한 역할을 수행한다는 것을 이해했습니다. 첫째, 그들은 뉴런에 산소와 필요한 영양분을 재공급합니다. 둘째로, 그들은 각 뉴런의 절연체 역할을 합니다. 셋째, 그들은 해로운 병원균을 제거하고 죽은 뉴런을 제거함으로써 뇌를 건강하게 유지합니다. 가장 최근의 연구는 글리아 세포가 뉴런 세포처럼 때때로 신경 전달에 참여한다는 것을 보여 주었고, 그들은 전기 신호를 받았을 때 신경 전달 물질을 방출할 것입니다. 굉장하죠!

이러한 발견들은 신경 과학을 영원히 바꾸어 놓았습니다! 이전에는 신경 과학자들이 뉴런 세포에만 초점을 맞췄지만, 그들의 시선은 글리아 세포 쪽으로 옮겨갔습니다. 또 다른 흥미로운 발견은 글리아 세포가 뉴런은 할 수 없는 어떤 세포 분열을 통해 번식할 수 있는 능력을 가지고 있다는 것입니다. 이 특징에는 몇 가지 예외가 있지만, 일반적으로 사실로 여겨집니다. 손 든 사람? 질문 있으세요?
S – 실례합니다만 교수님. 교수님께서는 신경 과학 분야에서 잠재적 발견이 있을 거라고 말씀하시는 건가요? 신경 과학자들이 아직 인간의 뇌에 대해 모든 것을 알지 못한다는 건가요?
P – 바로 그 말입니다. 여러분이 졸업할 때 즈음엔, 현대의 연구는 뇌에 대한 우리의 지식을 고양시켜줄 것입니다. 특히 글리아 세포에 대한 지식 말입니다. 끝이 없는 것 같아요! 저는 이 특별한 세포와 그것이 우리 뇌에서 어떤 역할을 하는지에 대해 더 많은 것을 배울 수 있다는 것을 확신합니다.
이제 교과서 422페이지를 펴세요. 활동 중인 글리아 세포의 사진을 살펴봅시다.

12) 강의의 핵심은 무엇인가?

    A) 신경 전달의 작동 방식
    B) 글리아 세포 연구의 역사
    C) 글리아 세포와 뇌에서 수행하는 다양한 역할
    D) 글리아 세포 및 뉴런의 비교 및 대조

13) 다음 중 뉴런에 대한 설명으로 옳은 것은? 정답을 2개 고르시오.

    A) 우리의 의식적이고 무의식적인 움직임을 통제한다.
    B) 전기 신호를 서로 전달한다.
    C) 뇌의 결합 조직에서 활동한다.
    D) 이를 시냅스라고 한다.

14) 신경 과학자들이 갖고 있던 글리아 세포의 초기 이해에 대해 교수는 무엇을 암시하는가?

    A) 그들은 글리아 세포가 뇌의 특정 부분에만 영향을 준다고 생각했다.
    B) 그들은 글리아 세포가 신경 전달 물질을 포함하고 있다는 잘못된 믿음을 가졌다.
    C) 그들은 글리아 세포의 역할이 미미한 것으로 생각했다.
    D) 장비를 제대로 갖추지 못했음에도 글리아 세포를 발견하는 어려움을 극복했다.

15) 글리아 세포와 뉴런의 차이점은 무엇인가?

    A) 글리아 세포가 뉴런보다 더 많다.
    B) 신경 전달 물질은 뉴런만이 만들 수 있다.
    C) 글리아 세포는 재생산 할 수 있다.
    D) 뉴런이 글리아 세포를 함께 붙인다.

16) 교수는 어떻게 글리아 세포의 기능에 대한 강의를 조직했는가?

    A) 연대기 순으로 된 발견들
    B) 단순한 것에서 복잡한 것으로
    C) 그것들이 뇌에서 일어나는 순서
    D) 생물학적 중요도에 따라.

ANSWERS AND SCRIPT

17) 교수는 글리아 세포 연구에 대해 어떻게 생각하는가?

A) 뉴런 연구보다 덜 중요하다고 생각한다.
B) 뇌 연구의 중심이 될 것이라고 확신한다.
C) 더 중요한 발견이 이루어질 것인지를 궁금해 한다.
D) 과학자들이 너무 많은 실수를 해서 불안해 한다.

Actual Test 04

Page.139~144

Part 1 – Conversation

ANSWERS – 1(D) 2(C) 3(C) 4(A) 5(A)

S – Excuse me, is this the housing office?
E – Yes it is. What can I help you with?
S – My name is Jonathan Smith and I live over at Raven Hall on the second floor. Well… I'm not so comfortable talking to you about this, but it's come to a point where I can't take it any longer. It's about my RA. Someone needs to check up on him.
E – Uh oh, sounds pretty serious. So what seems to be the problem?
S – Well, it's not just one thing that occurred, it's actually a lot of smaller things that built up over the semester. Ok so first, someone on my floor played their stereo really loud, day and night. As you know, the walls in our dormitory are pretty thin, so we could hear everything. I went over and asked the student to turn it down, but he wouldn't listen. **So I asked the RA to talk to the student. He went over and talked to him, but the student continued to play the music loud. I asked my RA about what happened, and he said that I should just relax and not let the music bother me! It was as if I was in the wrong here!**
E – **And there were other events, I presume?**
S – **Well, yes! Students are always running down the halls, throwing frees bees in the hallways, holding loud parties, and being loud all the time. These things happen all day long.** I used to file my complaint to the RA, but he never did anything. Later, I found out that he was actually quite close with the rowdy students, and even participated creating the ruckus.

S - 실례합니다만, 여기가 기숙사 사무실인가요?
E - 네, 그렇습니다. 무엇을 도와 드릴까요?
S - 제 이름은 조나단 스미스이고 2층 레이븐 홀에 살고 있습니다. 음… 이 문제에 대해 당신과 이야기하는 것이 그렇게 편하지는 않지만, 더 이상 참을 수 없는 지경에 이르렀어요. 관리인에 관한 거예요. 누군가가 그를 점검할 필요가 있어요.
E - 어, 꽤 심각한 것 같네요. 그래서 무엇이 문제인가요?
S - 음, 한 가지 일이 일어난 게 아니라, 한 학기 동안 실제로 작은 일들이 아주 많이 일어났습니다. 먼저, 우리 층에 있는 누군가가 밤낮으로 스테레오 소리를 크게 냈습니다. 당신도 알다시피, 우리 기숙사 벽이 꽤 얇아서, 우리는 모든 것을 들을 수 있었어요. 내가 가서 그 학생에게 소리를 꺼 달라고 했지만, 그는 듣지 않았어요. 그래서 저는 관리인에게 그 학생에게 말해달라고 요청했습니다. 그가 가서 학생에게 말을 걸었지만, 그 학생은 계속해서 음악을 크게 틀었어요. 나는 무슨 일이 일어났는지 관리인에게 물었고, 그는 그냥 내가 긴장을 풀고 음악에 신경 쓰지 말라고 말했어요! 마치 제가 잘못한 사람인 것 말이죠!
E - 그리고, 다른 일들도 있었나요?
S - 네! 학생들은 항상 복도에서 달리고, 복도에서 원반을 던지고, 큰 파티를 열고, 항상 시끄럽게 합니다. 이런 일들은 하루 종일 일어나요. 나는 불만 사항을 관리인에게 제출하곤 했지만, 그는 아무것도 하지 않았어요. 나중에, 저는 그가 실제로 소란을 피우는 학생들과 꽤 친하다는 것과, 심지어 소란을 피우는 데 참여하기도 했다는 걸 알게 됐어요.

ANSWERS AND SCRIPT

E – I guess he thought that he could get away with anything with his friends once he became an RA. Or maybe the other students are taking advantage of him.
S – I don't care. But this is giving me too much stress. It's unbelievable I'm actually paying money to live in this sort of environment.
E – I'll tell you what. I'm going to formally file this complaint and see if other students are having similar problems on that floor. If so, then the RA is in violation against school regulations and the school will have to remove him from his position. We have to investigate the matter though, and we might ask you to speak to us again.
S – That's fine. However, I have something that is bothering me. I don't want to be the one that is over-dramatic, but let's say the RA does get in trouble. I'm afraid his friends will harass me in the dorms. I wouldn't want that.
E – Of course not. If anything like that happens, you should immediately report it to campus security. And if the RA gets out of control, report that to the campus security as well. They have higher authority than the RAs. Now, if you don't feel comfortable in your current dorm room, I can have you switch to another floor or room. We have a lot of empty rooms, so after you fill out the paperwork, you can move to your new room right away.
S – Oh yea? I think I will do that.
E – Also, keep in mind that the school might punish some of the other trouble makers too by having them move out. Depending upon our investigation, you might end up staying in your current room.
S – Thanks, but hopefully I'm the one that moves out.
E – Alright then, let's get the paperwork started.

E - 제 생각엔 그가 일단 관리인이 되면 친구들과 그 어떤 벌도 받지 않을 거라 생각했던 것 같아요. 아니면 다른 학생들이 그를 이용하고 있는 걸지도 몰라요.
S - 전 관심 없어요. 하지만 이건 제게 너무 많은 스트레스를 주고 있어요. 이런 환경에서 살기 위해서 실제로 돈을 지불한다는 것은 믿을 수 없는 일이에요.
E - 제가 말씀 드리겠습니다. 정식으로 이 불만사항을 접수해서 다른 학생들도 그 층에서 비슷한 문제를 겪고 있는지 알아보겠습니다. 만약 그렇다면, 그 관리인은 학교 규정을 위반하는 것이고, 학교는 그를 직위에서 제외시켜야 할 거예요. 하지만 우리는 그 문제를 조사해야 합니다. 그리고 우리는 학생에게 다시 우리에게 이야기하도록 요청할 수도 있습니다.
S - 괜찮습니다. 하지만, 신경 쓰이는 게 있어요. 전 지나치게 극단적인 사람이 되고 싶지는 않지만, 관리인이 곤경에 처한다고 합시다. 그의 친구들이 기숙사에서 나를 괴롭힐까 봐 걱정돼요. 전 그걸 원하지 않아요.
E - 물론 아닙니다. 그런 일이 생기면 즉시 캠퍼스 경비실에 신고해야 합니다. 그리고 만약 관리인이 통제 불능이 된다면, 캠퍼스 경비실에도 보고하세요. 그들은 그 관리인보다 더 높은 권한을 가지고 있습니다. 현재 기숙사에서 불편하시면 다른 층이나 방으로 바꿔 드릴 수 있습니다. 빈 방이 많아서 서류 작성 후 바로 새 방으로 옮길 수 있습니다.
S - 아, 그래요? 전 그렇게 하고 싶어요.
E - 또한, 학교에서는 다른 문제 학생들을 강제 퇴거시킴으로써 그들을 처벌할 수도 있다는 것을 명심하세요. 조사 결과에 따라서는 당신이 현재 방에 머무르게 될 수도 있습니다.
S - 고맙지만, 이사를 갔으면 좋겠어요.
E - 좋아요, 그럼 서류 작업을 시작합시다.

1) 학생은 왜 기숙사 사무실에 갔는가?

    A) 새 기숙사 방으로 바꾸는 요청을 하기 위해
    B) 기숙사 사무실의 조사에 응하기 위해
    C) 기숙사 메이트 몇 명을 퇴거시키도록 요구하기 위해
    D) 기숙사 생활에 대한 불만을 제기하기 위해

2) 관리인이 기숙사 내 나쁜 행실을 허용하는 이유는?

    A) 그는 그것을 막을 권한이 없다.
    B) 그는 그것이 아무에게도 폐가 되지 않는다고 믿는다.
    C) 그는 나쁜 행실을 일으키는 사람들과 친구다.
    D) 그는 문제 학생들을 두려워한다.

3) 직원은 이 상황을 어떻게 대처할 계획인가?

    A) 즉시 관리인을 해고한다.
    B) 기숙사 규정을 검토한다.
    C) 문제에 대한 조사를 약속한다.
    D) 학생의 기숙사비 일부를 환불해 준다.

4) 그 학생은 다음에 무엇을 할 것인가?

    A) 방을 바꿀 서류를 작성한다.
    B) 기숙사의 질서를 잡도록 관리인에게 이야기한다.
    C) 캠퍼스 경비실에 관리인의 행동에 대해 알린다.
    D) 관리인이 조사 받기를 기다린다.

5) 대화의 일부를 들으시오. 그 후 질문에 답하시오.
   직원이 이 말을 할 때 이것은 무엇을 의미하는가?

    A) 그녀는 다른 유사한 사례가 있었다고 의심한다.
    B) 그녀는 한 가지 잘못된 행동에 만족하지 않는다.
    C) 그녀는 학생이 상황을 자세히 설명하기를 원한다.
    D) 그녀는 그 학생이 그 상황을 견뎌야 했던 것에 대해 유감스러워한다.

Answers and Script

ANSWERS AND SCRIPT

Part 1 – Lecture

ANSWERS – 6(B) 7(B) 8(A) 9(C) 10(C) 11(C)

P - I know that many of you want to become business owners. The fact that you're majoring in business administration proves it. Well, you have to understand how difficult it is to start a new business. Did you know that more than half of the new businesses that open fail in the first year? And almost all of them disappear after five years? So what can you do as a business owner to make sure that your establishment survives? The solution is clear: if you are able to distinguish your merchandise from the other products that are sold in the market, you will gain an upper hand. One way you can do this is by differentiation. What that means is making your company unique compared to the rest of the companies out there. In other words, make your company stand out.
The best way to differentiate is through pricing. I'm sure you have heard of premium pricing. Customers are willing to pay extra money for something they see as better than other comparable products. The interesting thing about premium pricing is that it all depends on customer perception. For instance, a company is in the paper business. They can say that their paper is of higher quality than others so they can charge a higher price. The company's paper may or may not be better than the competition. However, the premium price is enough to persuade customers that the paper is better. So if the product is unique or if the customer thinks it is, you can differentiate your product and have the advantage. At the same time, however, you can differentiate and have a competitive advantage by offering lower prices. This method is called a financial incentive. For instance, another company is making laptops. Since there are dozens of laptops in the market, they are all around the same price. But what if the company uses cheaper parts and sell the laptop at a lower cost? Since the company is using cheaper parts to make the product, the company is able to sell at a lower price. So the lower prices of the laptops will differentiate them from the competition, and the company will be able to attract more customers.
Can anyone else think of another way businesses can differentiate?

P - 전 여러분 중 많은 이가 사업주가 되고 싶어 한다는 것을 알고 있습니다. 학생이 경영학을 전공하고 있다는 사실이 그것을 증명하죠. 글쎄요, 학생은 새로운 사업을 시작하는 것이 얼마나 어려운 일인지 이해해야 합니다. 새로 문을 연 사업의 절반 이상이 첫 해에 망한다는 사실을 알고 있었나요? 그리고 거의 대부분이 5년 후에 사라진다는 건요? 그러면 사업주로서 당신의 사업체가 살아남을 수 있도록 하기 위해 무엇을 할 수 있을까요? 해결 방법은 명확합니다. 시장에서 판매되는 다른 제품과 당신의 제품을 구별할 수 있다면 우위를 점할 수 있습니다. 이것을 가능하게 하는 한 가지 방법은 차별화입니다. 즉, 다른 기업들과 비교해 볼 때 당신의 회사를 특별하게 만드는 것입니다. 다시 말해, 여러분의 회사를 돋보이게 하세요.
차별화하는 가장 좋은 방법은 가격 책정입니다. 프리미엄 요금에 대해 들어보셨을 겁니다. 고객들은 다른 비교 가능한 제품들보다 더 나아 보이는 것에 기꺼이 추가 비용을 지불합니다. 프리미엄 가격의 흥미로운 점은 모든 것이 고객의 인식에 달려 있다는 것입니다. 예를 들어, 한 제지업 회사가 있습니다. 그들은 자신의 종이가 다른 종이에 비해 품질이 뛰어나서 더 높은 가격을 청구할 수 있다고 말할 수 있습니다. 회사의 종이가 경쟁사보다 나을 수도 있고 그렇지 않을 수도 있습니다. 하지만, 프리미엄 가격은 종이가 더 낫다고 소비자들을 설득하기에 충분합니다. 따라서 제품이 특별하거나 고객이 그렇다고 생각하는 경우 제품을 차별화하고 이득을 취할 수 있습니다. 그러나 이와 동시에 가격 인하를 통해 차별화를 꾀하고 경쟁 우위를 확보할 수 있습니다. 이 방법을 재정적 장려책이라고 합니다. 예를 들어, 다른 회사는 노트북을 만듭니다. 수십 대의 노트북이 시장에 나와 있기 때문에, 그것들은 모두 같은 가격입니다. 하지만 만약 그 회사가 더 싼 부품을 사용하고 노트북을 더 싼 가격에 팔면 어떻게 될까요? 그 회사는 제품을 만들기 위해 더 싼 부품을 사용하기 때문에, 더 낮은 가격에 팔 수 있습니다. 따라서 노트북 가격이 낮아지면 경쟁 제품과 차별화되며, 더 많은 고객을 유치할 수 있을 것입니다.
기업이 차별화할 수 있는 또 다른 방법을 생각해 낼 수 있는 사람이 있을까요?

S – How about offering special deals or promotions?

P – That's a great idea! Special deals and promotions are a great way to differentiate businesses. Do you remember seeing product commercials with life time warranties? This is a great example of how to set your business apart from others and bring in customers. **For instance, a consumer needs to buy a dish washer. He will go to Store A and find some good dish washers at affordable prices. But when he looks across the street, he will see in bright letters "life time warranty on all dish washers" in Store B's sign. Do you think he will buy the product from Store A? No way. He will immediately head over to Store B because he will feel secure knowing that there is a life time warranty on the dishwasher if anything wrong were to happen to it.** This shows that you can differentiate and bring in customers by giving special deals and promotions that the competition cannot.

Everything we mentioned so far are great strategies to make your business stand out. However, it's important to maintain the strategies. Using the laptop's example, what do you think would happen if I changed the pricing? I could get greedy and decide to increase the prices on the laptops so that it becomes similar to the competition's prices. What would happen then?

S – I think that would upset your customers. They would start buying the laptops from someone else who offered lower prices or unique laptops.

P – Absolutely. Therefore, it's imperative that you stick with whatever policy that differentiated you from the others. If you stop doing this, your business will no longer stand out and your business is likely to end up failing within the next few years.

S - 특가 상품 또는 프로모션을 제공하는 것은 어떻습니까?

P - 좋은 생각이에요! 특가 상품과 프로모션은 사업을 차별화할 수 있는 좋은 방법입니다. 당신은 평생 보증이 되는 상품 광고를 본 것을 기억하나요? 이것은 당신의 사업을 다른 기업과 차별화하고 고객을 유치하는 방법의 좋은 예입니다. 예를 들어, 소비자는 식기세척기를 사야 합니다. 그는 A 상점에 가서 적당한 가격의 좋은 식기세척기를 찾습니다. 하지만 그가 길 건너편을 바라보니, 상점 B의 간판에서 "모든 식기 세척기에 대한 평생 보증"이라는 빛나는 글자를 보게 됩니다. 당신은 그가 A가게에서 그 제품을 살 것이라고 생각합니까? 말도 안되죠. 만약 잘못된 일이 생기면 식기 세척기에 평생 보증이 있다는 것을 알고 안심할 수 있기 때문에 그는 즉시 가게 B로 향할 것입니다. 이는 경쟁업체가 할 수 없는 특가 상품과 프로모션을 제공함으로써 차별화하고, 고객을 끌어들일 수 있음을 보여줍니다.

지금까지 언급한 모든 내용은 당신의 사업을 돋보이게 하기 위한 훌륭한 전략입니다. 하지만, 전략을 유지하는 것이 중요합니다. 노트북의 예를 들어, 내가 만약 가격을 변경하면 어떻게 될 것 같습니까? 내가 욕심을 부려서 노트북 가격을 인상해 경쟁사의 가격과 비슷해지도록 할 수도 있어요. 그러면 어떻게 될까요?

S - 제 생각에 그것은 당신의 고객들을 화나게 할 것입니다. 그들은 더 낮은 가격이나 독특한 노트북을 제공하는 다른 사람에게서 노트북을 사기 시작할 것입니다.

P - 물론이죠. 그러므로, 여러분은 다른 사람들과 차별화 시키는 어떠한 정책이든 계속 지키는 것이 필수적입니다. 이것을 중단하면 사업이 더 이상 눈에 띄지 않고 향후 몇 년 이내에 사업이 중단될 가능성이 높습니다.

6) 강의의 핵심은 무엇인가?

A) 신규 사업자가 저지르는 실수
B) 새로운 사업을 차별화하는 방법
C) 다양한 유형의 신규 사업 전략
D) 잠재 고객에게 광고하는 방법

7) 강의 내용에 따르면, 재정적 장려책은 어떤 역할을 하는가?

A) 고가의 상품을 구매하도록 소비자를 설득한다.
B) 경쟁사보다 낮은 가격으로 소비자를 유혹한다.
C) 경쟁사가 제공하지 않는 서비스를 제공한다.
D) 소비자에 대한 경쟁력을 유지한다.

8) 토론의 일부를 다시 한 번 들어보시오. 그 후 질문에 답하시오.
교수가 이 말을 할 때 무엇을 시사하는가?

A) 특가 상품 및 프로모션의 효과를 말하기 위해
B) 제품 비용과 품질을 차별화하기 위해
C) 다른 상점에서 쇼핑해야 하는 이유를 제시하기 위해
D) 소비자의 관점에서 문제를 언급하기 위해

9) 강의에 따르면, 사업 전략에서 중요한 부분은 무엇인가?

A) 경쟁 업체와 경쟁할 수 있는 가격 제시
B) 수익이 날 때까지 고유성 유지
C) 사업이 돋보이는 경우 정책 유지
D) 그 사업체에서 쇼핑하는 고객에게 안정성 제공

10) 교수는 소비자에 대해 무엇을 시사하는가?

A) 특별한 상품보다는 특가 상품 및 판촉 행사를 선호한다.
B) 가격 변동에 관계 없이 회사에 대한 충성도를 유지한다.
C) 품질에 따라 구매하지 않는다.
D) 새 가게보다 오래 가는 가게에서 쇼핑할 가능성이 높다.

11) 강의는 어떻게 구성되는가?

A) 사업의 유형을 분류함
B) 이론을 기술하고 그 이론의 결점을 언급함
C) 용어의 정의를 예시와 함께 제공함
D) 전략들을 비교하고 대조함

ANSWERS AND SCRIPT

Page.145~153

Part 2 – Conversation

ANSWERS – 1(C) 2(B) 3(B) 4(D) 5(C)

P – Hello Michelle, how can I help you today? S – Hello professor. I came over to talk to you about next week's play. I think it's wonderful how you managed to persuade the theater department to hold a play of Corneille's Cinna. It's also great that the campus theater is allowing students to watch plays for free this month. P – I think you and I can both agree that studying historical playwrights through textbooks is not as entertaining as watching their works performed on the stage. Having a discussion on tragedy is completely different from watching it in the audience and feeling all sorts of emotions. S – I completely agree and I was looking forward to watching it, but I'm sort of worried about attending. The thing is, I don't know how to speak French. I did take a class in high school, but I don't remember too much. You mentioned that attending the play is mandatory, but since I won't be able to understand what they're saying, do you think you can make an exception? P – I'm sorry but I don't think I can do that. I did make it clear in class that I can't make any exceptions. Also, you will be tested on the play on our first exam. Were you not in class when I made the announcement? S – No, I had to pick up my sister at the train station and it overlapped with your class time. I'm sorry. P – Well, another student did raise the same concerns you have about attending the play. The thing is, you don't have to worry about understanding the language during the play. What we actually plan to do is go over the entire play before attending the actual performance. So when you go to the play, you will already know everything about the characters and the storyline. You shouldn't have too much trouble following the performance. Also, there will be supertitles during the play.	P - 안녕하세요, Michelle, 무엇을 도와드릴까요? S - 안녕하세요 교수님. 다음 주 연극에 대해 얘기하러 왔어요. 교수님이 극장 부서가 Corneille's Cinna 연극을 열도록 설득하신 것이 정말 멋지다고 생각해요. 또한 이번 달에 캠퍼스 극장이 학생들에게 연극을 무료로 관람할 수 있게 한 것도 멋진 일이에요. P - 저와 학생 둘 다 교과서를 통해 역사극 작가들을 공부하는 것보다 무대 위에서 공연되는 그들의 작품을 보는 것이 더 재미있다는 것에 동의할 수 있다고 생각해요. 비극에 대해 토론하는 건 청중 속에서 그것을 보고 모든 종류의 감정을 느끼는 것과는 완전히 달라요. S - 전적으로 동의하고 관람하는 걸 기대했지만, 참석하는 것이 좀 걱정됩니다. 중요한 점은, 저는 프랑스어를 할 줄 모릅니다. 고등학교 때 수업을 들었는데, 기억이 잘 안 나요. 연극 관람은 의무라고 말씀하셨는데, 전 그 사람들 말을 알아듣지 못할 것 같은데, 예외로 해 주실 수 있나요? P - 죄송하지만 그렇게 할 수 없을 것 같습니다. 전 수업 시간에 어떤 예외도 없다는 것을 분명히 했습니다. 또한, 학생은 우리의 첫 시험에서 연극에 대한 테스트를 받을 겁니다. 제가 공지 했을 때 수업에 없었나요? S - 없었어요, 여동생을 기차역에서 태워야 했는데, 교수님의 수업 시간과 겹쳤어요. 죄송해요. P - 글쎄요, 또 다른 학생이 연극에 참석하는 것에 대해 학생과 같은 우려를 제기했습니다. 중요한 점은, 학생은 연극에서 언어를 이해하는 것에 대해 걱정할 필요가 없다는 겁니다. 우리가 실제로 계획하고 있는 것은 실제 공연에 참석하기 전에 전체 연극을 살펴보는 것입니다. 그래서 학생이 극장에 갈 때, 이미 등장인물들과 줄거리에 대한 모든 것을 알고 있을 겁니다. 학생은 공연을 따라가기가 크게 어렵지 않을 거예요. 또한, 연극 중에 수퍼 타이틀이 있을 겁니다.

S – The what?
P – Supertitles. They're like subtitles. Even through the actors will speak in French, their dialogue will be projected on a screen in English.
S – Oh! I just finished watching a Chinese movie in my film club. Although the entire movie was spoken in Chinese, there were English subtitles, so I was able to understand what was going on. Actually it was really surprising how easy it was to read the subtitles while watching the film.
P – You see? It won't be so bad.
S – Ok, that's good to hear. I would hate to miss the material since it will appear on the test. By the way, when are we having the test?
P – On the syllabus I handed out the first day of class, there is a calendar showing everything that's going on this semester.
S – **Oh… I'm afraid I lost my syllabus. I recently moved to a new apartment and I had some school papers lying around on the table. They must have gotten lost while I was moving.**
P – **I happen to have an extra copy here. Here you go. Make sure to hang on to this one. Regarding the test, it will be two weeks from today.** You should go over everything we've discussed in class, the reading assignments, and the play we will be watching.
S – Ok. What aspects of the play will be on the questions?
P – Make sure you understand the basic outline and characteristics of classic French tragedies. I might include a few phrases from the play and ask you who said them and what the real motive behind the words are.
S – Alright. Thank you so much for your help professor. I'll see you in class next week!

S - 뭐라고요?
P - 수퍼 타이틀. 자막 같은 거예요. 배우들이 프랑스어로 말할지라도, 그들의 대화는 영어로 스크린에 투영될 거예요.
S - 아! 전 방금 영화 동아리에서 중국 영화를 다 봤어요. 비록 영화 전체에서 중국어로 말했지만, 영어 자막이 있어서 무슨 일이 일어나고 있는지 이해할 수 있었어요. 사실 영화를 보면서 자막을 읽는 것이 얼마나 쉬운지 정말 놀라웠어요.
P - 그렇죠? 그렇게 나쁘지는 않을 거예요.
S - 네, 듣던 중 반가운 소리네요. 그 자료가 시험에 나올 거기 때문에 전 놓치고 싶지 않아요. 그런데 저희 시험은 언제 치나요?
P - 제가 수업 첫날 나눠준 강의 계획표에는 이번 학기에 진행되는 모든 것을 보여주는 달력이 있습니다.
S - 아… 강의 계획표를 잃어버렸어요. 제가 최근에 새 아파트로 이사했는데 탁자 위에 몇 개의 학교 신문이 놓여 있었어요. 제가 이사하는 동안 잃어버린 게 분명해요.
P - 마침 여기 한 부 더 있어요. 여기 있습니다. 이걸 꼭 잘 보관하세요. 시험은 오늘부터 2주 후가 될 거예요. 학생은 우리가 수업에서 논의한 모든 것, 읽기 과제, 그리고 우리가 보게 될 연극을 살펴 봐야 해요.
S - 네. 문제에서 연극의 어떤 면을 다루나요?
P - 프랑스 고전 비극의 기본 개요와 특징을 확실히 이해하십시오. 저는 연극의 몇 구절을 포함시켜 누가 그런 말을 했는지, 그 말의 진짜 동기는 무엇인지 물어볼 수도 있어요.
S - 알겠습니다. 교수님 도와 주셔서 정말 감사합니다. 다음 주 수업에서 뵙겠습니다!

ANSWERS AND SCRIPT

1) 학생은 왜 교수에게 갔는가?

   A) 그녀가 왜 마지막 강의에 참석하지 못했는지 변명하기 위해
   B) 같은 반 친구를 위한 여분의 티켓을 요청하기 위해
   C) 연극 관람에 불참할 수 있는 허가를 받기 위해
   D) 연극에 대한 더 많은 정보를 요청하기 위해.

2) 대화 내용에 따르면, 여자는 무엇에 대해 걱정하는가?

   A) 예술 극장까지 차를 타고 가는 것
   B) 외국 영화를 이해하는 것
   C) 연극 티켓을 구입하는 것
   D) 수퍼 타이틀을 읽을 수 있는 것

3) 이번 시험에 대해 무엇을 추론할 수 있는가?

   A) 시험은 불어로 치른다.
   B) 시험 일자는 강의 계획서에 기재되어 있다.
   C) 테스트는 연극이 끝나고 2주 후에 실시된다.
   D) 문제는 중국 영화에 관한 것이 될 것이다.

4) 대화 내용을 다시 한 번 들어보시오. 그 후 질문에 답하시오.
   교수는 왜 이런 말을 하는가?

   A) 다른 강의 계획표를 찾을 때 학생에게 기다리라고 하기 위해
   B) 강의 계획서에 있는 중요한 날짜를 학생에게 알리기 위해
   C) 학생이 마지막 복사본을 가지고 있다는 것을 말하기 위해
   D) 학생이 강의 계획표를 다시 잃어버리지 않도록 하기 위해

5) 교수는 학생들에게 시험에서 무엇을 물어볼 것인가?

   A) 비극적인 연극의 역사를 설명한다.
   B) 연극의 대사 부분을 번역한다.
   C) 연극에서 누가 그 대사를 말했는지 알아낸다.
   D) 공연의 세트와 구조를 기술한다.

Part 2 - Lecture

ANSWERS – 6(B) 7(D) 8(D) 9(C) 10(A) 11(catastrophism – B,C / uniformitarianism – A,D)

P – So far in class, we have been discussing about Earth's physical features and the various processes that are continuously taking place on our planet. All of this would be categorized as physical geology. Let's turn our attention to something called historical geology. Historical geology is the application of physical geology to understand the history of our planet. Something that has been debated for a long time is the history and evolution of our geosphere. Throughout most of human history, scholars believed that our planet was only several thousand years old. Does anyone know why they would think like this?
S – Probably because the length of time humans can live makes it difficult for us to comprehend much longer periods of time.
P – Exactly! Class, what your classmate just described is called human bias in scale. Let me explain.
The average lifespan of a modern person is less than a hundred years. In ancient times however, humans lived even shorter than that. This is actually very important since it changes our perspective on everything surrounding us. In other words, human life span restricts us to a timescale of several thousand years. A timescale of millions and billions of years is beyond our understanding. It's like imagining a fourth dimension. It's impossible for us to imagine such a dimension exists because everything we do takes place in three dimension. Yes, you have a question?
S – But didn't scientists observe formations in rocks and sediments that appeared to be much older than thousands of years?

P - 지금까지 우리는 지구의 물리적 특징과 지구에서 지속적으로 일어나고 있는 다양한 과정에 대해 논의해 왔습니다. 이 모든 것은 자연 지질학으로 분류될 것입니다. 우리의 관심을 역사 지질학이라고 불리는 것으로 돌려 봅시다. 역사 지질학은 우리 행성의 역사를 이해하기 위해 자연 지질학을 적용하는 것입니다. 오랫동안 논쟁이 되어 온 것은 지구권의 역사와 진화입니다. 대부분의 인류 역사 내내, 학자들은 우리 행성이 불과 몇 천 년 밖에 되지 않았다고 믿었습니다. 그들이 왜 이런 생각을 했는지 아는 사람 있나요?
S - 아마도 인간이 살 수 있는 시간의 길이가 우리가 훨씬 더 긴 시간을 이해하는 것을 어렵게 하기 때문일 것입니다.
P - 바로 그겁니다! 여러분의 친구가 방금 말한 것을 규모에 대한 인간의 편견이라고 합니다. 제가 설명해 드릴게요. 현대인의 평균 수명은 100년 미만입니다. 그러나 고대에는 인간이 그보다 더 짧게 살았습니다. 이것은 우리를 둘러싼 모든 것에 대한 우리의 관점을 바꾸기 때문에 사실 매우 중요합니다. 다시 말해서, 인간의 수명은 우리를 수 천 년의 시간적 범위로 제한합니다. 수 백 만, 수 십 억 년의 기간은 우리가 이해할 수 없는 것입니다. 이것은 마치 4차원을 상상하는 것과 같습니다. 우리가 하는 모든 일이 3차원으로 이루어지기 때문에 그런 차원이 존재한다고 우리가 상상하는 것은 불가능합니다. 네, 질문 있으세요?
S - 하지만 과학자들은 수 천 년보다 훨씬 오래된 것으로 보이는 바위와 퇴적물들의 형태를 관찰하지 않았나요?

P – Yes they did. And that brings me to my second point. Long ago, people always assumed that earth was only several thousand years old and always had the same appearance. But, they started to discover new findings that questioned their beliefs. For instance, Greek philosophers unearthed fossils of marine animals in rock formations. Interestingly, these rocks were nowhere near water. So a conclusion was reached that at some point, a great flood covered the entire land. This was the start of a theory called catastrophism. They theory developed over time and basically said that geological structures on our plant were created by catastrophic events like floods, earthquakes, and volcanoes. This actually fit well with the idea that to their understanding, earth was only several thousand years old, so it remained popular for a long time. However, another theory surfaced that challenged it. Anyone know what I'm referring to?

S – I think it was called uniformitarianism.

P – Correct. The renowned geologist James Hutton proposed the idea. Uniformitarianism theory states that the geologic features on Earth were created by continuous geologic processes, instead of a catastrophic event, that lasted for billions of years and still continues to this day. This theory directly contradicted with the theory of catastrophism. Hutton stated that the history of Earth could only be understood by looking at what is happening on Earth now. He stated that the geological processes that happen on Earth are uniform, and these processes have not changed throughout earth's history.

S – **But professor, didn't catastrophic events happen on earth? Let's look at the facts. Volcanoes erupt every year and earthquakes topple landscapes all the time. These events continuously change the earth's surface.**

P – Of course, you are correct again. And your comment leads us to the modern view of historical geology. It is undeniable that catastrophic events did occur in Earth's geological history. Volcanic eruptions, earthquakes, and even meteor impacts have occurred for billions of years, and still occur today. These events do change the structure of the planet. So the catastrophism theory actually resurfaced and the name has been changed to neo-catastrophism. Geologists have agreed that both neo-catastrophism and uniformitarianism play important roles in the structuring of our planet.

P – 네, 그렇습니다. 그리고 그것이 제 두 번째 요점을 말해줍니다. 오래 전에, 사람들은 항상 지구가 몇 천 년 밖에 되지 않았고 항상 같은 모습을 하고 있다고 생각했습니다. 하지만, 그들은 그들의 믿음에 의문을 제기하는 새로운 발견을 찾아내기 시작했습니다. 예를 들어, 그리스 철학자들은 바위 모양으로 된 해양 동물의 화석을 발굴했습니다. 흥미롭게도, 이 바위들은 물 근처 어디에도 없었습니다. 그래서 어느 순간 큰 홍수가 온 땅을 덮었다는 결론에 도달했습니다. 이것은 격변설이라고 불리는 이론의 시작이었습니다. 이 이론은 시간이 지남에 따라 발전했고 기본적으로 우리 행성의 지질 구조는 홍수, 지진, 화산과 같은 재앙에 의해 만들어졌다고 말했습니다. 이 이론은 사실 지구가 불과 몇 천 년 밖에 되지 않았다는 우리의 생각과 잘 들어맞기 때문에 오랫동안 유행했습니다. 그러나, 그것에 도전한 또 다른 이론이 나타났습니다. 제가 무엇을 말하려는지 아는 사람 있나요?

S - 전 그것이 균일설이라고 생각합니다.

P - 맞습니다. 유명한 지질학자 제임스 허튼이 그 아이디어를 제안했습니다. 균일설 이론은 지구상의 지질학적 특징들이 재앙적인 사건 대신, 지속적인 지질학적 과정에 의해 만들어졌으며, 수 십억 년 동안 지속되었고 오늘날까지도 계속되고 있다고 말합니다. 이 이론은 격변설을 정면으로 반박합니다. 허튼은 지구의 역사는 현재 지구에서 일어나고 있는 일을 보아야만 이해할 수 있다고 말했습니다. 그는 지구상에서 일어나는 지질학적 과정은 균일하며, 이러한 과정들은 지구의 역사를 통틀어 변하지 않았다고 말했습니다.

S - 하지만 교수님, 지구상에서 재난이 일어나지 않았나요? 사실을 살펴봅시다. 화산은 매년 폭발하고 지진은 항상 지형을 무너뜨립니다. 이러한 사건들은 지속적으로 지구의 표면을 변화시킵니다.

P - 물론입니다, 다시 한 번 맞혔군요. 그리고 학생의 말은 우리를 역사적 지질학의 현대적 관점으로 이끕니다. 지구의 지질학적 역사에서 재난이 발생했다는 것은 부인할 수 없습니다. 화산 폭발, 지진, 그리고 심지어 운석의 충돌도 수 십억 년 동안 일어났고, 오늘날에도 여전히 일어나고 있습니다. 이러한 사건들은 지구의 구조를 변화시킵니다. 그래서 격변설은 실제로 다시 등장했고 이름은 신격변설로 바뀌었습니다. 지질학자들은 신격변설과 균일설 둘 다 우리 행성의 구조에서 중요한 역할을 한다는 것에 동의했습니다.

6) 강의의 핵심은 무엇인가?

    A) 자연 지질학과 역사 지질학의 비교
    B) 지구의 지질학적 역사에 관한 상반된 이론들
    C) Hutton이 어떻게 지구의 지질학적 역사에 기여했는가
    D) 왜 오래 전부터 사람들이 지구의 나이를 결정하는데 어려움을 겪었는가

7) 교수는 왜 규모에 대한 인간의 편견에 대해 말하는가?

    A) 인간이 지질학적 과정에 어떻게 영향을 미칠 수 있는지 입증하기 위해
    B) 인간 이해의 빠른 발전을 보여주기 위해
    C) 현대인의 수명을 옛날과 비교하기 위해
    D) 왜 사람들이 지구의 긴 역사를 이해할 수 없었는지를 지적하기 위해

8) 강의에 따르면, 왜 격변설이 오랫동안 유행했는가?

    A) 해양 화석의 수로 입증하기 용이했다.
    B) 지진 및 화산 기록이 이를 뒷받침했다.
    C) 공통적인 지질학적 과정이 발생하는 이유를 기술했다.
    D) 당시의 지구 나이 추정과 일치했다.

9) 균일설에 대해 유추할 수 있는 것은?

    A) 그리스 철학자들의 이론에 의해 영향을 받았다.
    B) 격변설과 같은 시기에 만들어졌다.
    C) 우리 행성이 수십억 년 된 것으로 추정한다.
    D) 화산이 우리 행성에 영향을 미쳤다는 생각과 정반대되는 것이다.

10) 논의의 일부를 들으시오. 그 후 질문에 답하시오.
    학생은 왜 이렇게 말하는가?

    A) 오늘날에도 재난이 발생한다는 것을 보여주기 위해
    B) 지질학적 사건에 대해 강의를 듣는 학생들이 주변을 관찰하도록 권장하기 위해
    C) 화산과 지진은 매일 발생하는 것이 아니라는 점을 지적하기 위해
    D) 지형 변화에서 주로 재난이 원인이 된다고 주장하기 위해

ANSWERS AND SCRIPT

11) 각 문장은 격변설과 균일성 중 무엇에 대해 설명하고 있는가?
각 구에 대해 올바른 칸을 선택하시오.

	격변설	균일설
A) 지구가 수십억 년이 되었다는 가정		
B) 지구가 인류의 역사 만큼 오래되지 않았다는 추정		
C) 그리스 철학자들이 이 이론에 영향을 주었음		
D) 지질학자 제임스 휴턴에 의해 만들어졌음		

Part 2 - Lecture

ANSWERS – 12(B) 13(D) 14(B) 15(B) 16(B) 17(Preparation theory – B,D / surplus energy theory – A / Flexibility Theory – C)

We will continue our lecture on animal behavior. Let's discuss why animals play. I'm sure all of you have seen baby animals play, maybe at the zoo? For a long time, this behavior was a major topic to be discussed amongst biologists, especially the question of evolutionary adaptability. One has to wonder how playful behavior is an important requirement for the survival of a species. In fact, several different theories have been proposed to answer this question.

The oldest theory given by a greek philosopher for why animals play is called the preparation theory. This is the oldest theory because since ancient times, playful behavior in all animals, including humans, has resembled adult behavior. For example, human children are given toys to play with so they can learn to use tools when they become adults. So playing helps prepare children to be adults. If this logic is applied to animals, the same can be said true. Many animals like lions and dolphins display playful behavior that resembles hunting and fighting.

The problem with this theory is that many of the playful behavior do not actually mirror adult behaviors. For instance, when two lion cubs play, they will often engage in playful behavior by taking on different roles. One will attack the other, while the other plays along, allowing it to win the struggle. However, this gameplay is not applied as adults. When two adult male lions fight, one will not simply play along and let the other win. So back to the question, why do animals play?

During the late 19th century, an English philosopher proposed a new theory. He called it, the surplus energy theory. It states that young animals play out of boredom. Adult animals spend their entire day hunting or foraging for food, while looking out for danger. However, the young do not have to engage in such activities. Because the young need an outlet for their energy, they engage in playful behavior.

우리는 동물 행동에 대한 강의를 계속 하겠습니다. 동물들이 놀이하는 이유에 대해 토론해 봅시다. 여러분 모두는 아마 동물원에서 아기 동물들이 노는 것을 본 적이 있을 거예요. 오랫동안, 이 행동은 생물학자들 사이에서 논의되어야 할 주요한 주제였고, 특히 진화 적응성에 대한 물음이었습니다. 어떤 종이 생존하기 위해 노는 행동이 얼마나 중요한 요건인지에 대해 의문을 품어야 했습니다. 사실, 이 질문에 답하기 위해 몇 가지 다른 이론들이 제안되었습니다.

동물들이 놀이를 하는 이유 중 가장 오래된 이론은 생활 준비 이론이라고 불립니다. 이것은 고대부터 인간을 포함한 모든 동물들의 놀이 행동이 어른들의 행동과 닮았기 때문에 가장 오래된 이론입니다. 예를 들어, 인간 아이들은 어른이 되었을 때 도구를 사용하는 것을 배울 수 있도록, 가지고 놀 장난감을 받습니다. 그래서 놀이는 아이들이 어른이 될 준비를 하는데 도움이 됩니다. 만약 이 논리가 동물들에게 적용된다면, 같은 논리가 사실이라고 말할 수 있습니다. 사자나 돌고래와 같은 많은 동물들은 사냥이나 싸움과 비슷한 놀이 행동을 보입니다.

이 이론이 가지는 문제는 많은 놀이 행동이 실제로 어른들의 행동을 반영하지 않는다는 것입니다. 예를 들어, 두 마리의 사자 새끼가 놀 때, 그들은 종종 다른 역할을 맡아 놀이를 합니다. 한 마리는 상대방을 공격할 것이고, 다른 한 마리는 이에 동조하여 상대가 싸움에서 승리할 수 있게 할 것입니다. 하지만, 이 게임 플레이는 어른에게는 적용되지 않습니다. 두 마리의 성인 수컷 사자가 싸울 때는, 한 마리가 단순히 동조하여 다른 사자가 이기도록 내버려 두지 않을 것입니다. 다시 질문으로 돌아가서, 동물들은 왜 놀이를 할까요?

19세기 후반, 한 영국 철학자가 새로운 이론을 제안했습니다. 그는 그것을 과잉 에너지 이론이라고 불렀습니다. 그 이론은 어린 동물들이 지루함에서 벗어나기 위해 논다고 말합니다. 어른 동물들은 위험에 주의하며 하루 종일 먹이를 찾거나 사냥하는 데 시간을 보냅니다. 하지만, 어린 동물들은 그러한 활동에 참여할 필요가 없습니다. 어린 동물들은 그들의 에너지를 발산할 수단이 필요하기 때문에, 놀이를 합니다.

ANSWERS AND SCRIPT

Although it makes some sense, it still does not provide strong support to show why many animals show playful behavior. After many years, scientists found out that playing satisfies a very important role.

The flexibility theory was proposed. Scientists had observed that playful behavior tended to increase during an animal's early life until the animal reached maturity. At that point, the play greatly decreased or stopped completely. Scientists noticed that this pattern actually coincided with the development of the brain. In other words, the time that animals engaged in playful behavior was the time that their brains were developing. Many other experiments have confirmed and concluded this theory. The most famous one was a study done on rats, where one group was allowed to play while the other was prevented from playing. After the rats matured, the group that played freely had well developed brains, while the group that was neglected of play had significantly less developed brains. This study showed that playing was important to the development of the brain.

In conclusion, biologists can now say that animal play have a few different purposes. **However, there is one more question that needs to be answered: why do adults play? Let me answer that with an observation. Few years ago in Canada, a polar bear and a dog were observed playing with one another. The two adult animals wrestled and softly bit each other, and even lay on the ice together.** <u>Hard to believe right? But it's true.</u> How can two adult animals from different species play like juveniles? Well, a theory was proposed to explain this behavior as well. It's called the motivation theory. Playing is not only necessary for growing and surviving, but it's also fun. It seems pretty obvious that aside from adaptive strategies, animals will also play out of pure entertainment.

비록 어느 정도 말이 되긴 하지만, 그것은 여전히 왜 많은 동물들이 놀이 행동을 하는지를 보여주는 강력한 근거를 제공하지 않습니다. 수 년 후에, 과학자들은 놀이가 매우 중요한 역할을 한다는 것을 발견했습니다.

융통성 이론이 제안되었습니다. 과학자들은 동물이 성숙할 때까지, 어린 시절 동안 놀이 행동이 증가하는 경향이 있다는 것을 관찰했습니다. 그 시점에서 놀이는 크게 줄거나 완전히 중단되었습니다. 과학자들은 이 패턴이 실제로 뇌 발달과 일치한다는 것을 알아냈습니다. 다른 말로 하자면, 동물들이 놀이를 하는 시간은 그들의 뇌가 발달하는 시간이었습니다. 많은 다른 실험들이 이 이론을 확인하고 결론을 내렸습니다. 가장 유명한 것은 쥐를 대상으로 한 연구인데, 한 그룹은 놀 수 있는 반면 다른 그룹은 놀 수 없도록 한 것이었습니다. 쥐들이 성숙한 후, 자유롭게 논 그룹은 두뇌가 잘 발달된 반면, 놀이에 소홀했던 그룹은 두뇌가 현저하게 덜 발달되었습니다. 이 연구는 놀이를 하는 것이 뇌 발달에 중요하다는 것을 보여주었습니다.

결론적으로, 생물학자들은 이제 동물의 놀이에는 몇 가지 다른 목적이 있다고 말할 수 있습니다. 하지만, 대답할 필요가 있는 한 가지 질문이 더 있습니다: 어른들은 왜 놀이를 하는가? 관찰된 것을 통해 답변하겠습니다. 몇 년 전, 캐나다에서는 북극곰과 개가 서로 노는 것이 목격되었습니다. 두 마리의 성인 동물들이 서로 씨름하고 부드럽게 물고, 심지어 함께 얼음 위에 눕기도 했습니다. 믿기 어렵죠? 하지만 사실입니다. 어떻게 다른 종에서 온 두 마리의 성인 동물들이 어린 동물들처럼 놀 수 있을까요? 자, 이 행동을 설명하기 위한 이론도 제안되었습니다. 이것은 동기 이론이라고 불립니다. 놀이는 성장하고 생존하는 데 필요할 뿐만 아니라 재미도 있습니다. 적응 전략 외에도 동물들 역시 순수한 오락을 위해 노는 활동이 필요하다는 점은 꽤 명백해 보입니다.

12) 강의의 핵심은 무엇인가?

    A) 동물의 놀이와 관련된 위험
    B) 동물의 놀이 행동에 대한 몇 가지 설명
    C) 놀이는 종마다 어떻게 다른가
    D) 인간과 동물의 행동 비교

13) 교수에 따르면 사람들은 생활 준비 이론에 반하여 뭐라고 하는가?

    A) 동물은 놀다가 다칠 수 있다.
    B) 놀이 행동은 사냥 능력을 키우지 않는다.
    C) 다른 동물들이 같은 행동을 한다.
    D) 어린 동물들의 행동이 어른 동물들과 같지 않다.

14) 교수는 과잉 에너지 이론에 대해 어떻게 생각하는가?

    A) 그것은 유망하다고 생각하므로 더 탐구되어야 한다.
    B) 놀이 행동을 완전히 설명하지는 못한다고 생각한다.
    C) 많은 사람들이 그것을 지지하지 않는 것에 화가 났다.
    D) 융통성 이론에 통합되어야 한다고 생각한다.

15) 강의 내용에 따르면, 어린 동물의 놀이를 금지한다면

    A) 동물의 체력을 감소시킨다.
    B) 뇌 발달을 방해한다.
    C) 문제 해결 능력 향상시킨다.
    D) 타인과 상호 작용하는 능력을 손상시킨다.

16) 강의의 일부를 들으시오. 그 후 질문에 답하시오.
    교수가 이 말을 할 때 무엇을 시사하는가?

    A) 그 행동이 얼마나 정상적인지를 표현하기 위해
    B) 그 사건이 사실일 것 같지 않다는 것을 말하기 위해
    C) 학생들이 관찰한 사항에 대해 의문을 갖도록 하기 위해
    D) 관찰한 것을 신뢰할 수 없음을 말하기 위해

ANSWERS AND SCRIPT

17) 교수는 동물이 왜 놀이를 하는지 세 가지 이론을 이야기한다.
    각 선택 항목에서 알맞은 이론에 표시하시오.

    각 구에 대해 올바른 칸을 선택하시오. 이 문제는 2점짜리이다.

	생활 준비 이론	과잉 에너지 이론	융통성 이론
A) 지루함을 잊기 위해			
B) 중요한 기술을 익히기 위해			
C) 뇌를 발달시키기 위해			
D) 그리스 철학자에 의해 제안됨			

Actual Test 05

Page.161~166

Part 1 – Conversation

ANSWERS – 1(D) 2(C) 3(B) 4(B) 5(C)

E – Welcome to the residential office! What can I help you with today?
S – Hello, I have a question about my living arrangement. I'm a first year student and as I understand, university rule dictates that first and second year students must live on campus. The thing is… I'm having a hard time getting along with my roommates over at Brendon Hall.
E – I see. Did you try talking to the residence hall monitors? They usually help in these situations.
S – Well, it's actually not anything bad. Let me explain. I'm an only child. And growing up without having any brothers or sisters, I'm just not used to living with a group of people. No one did anything wrong. My parents just happened to move close to the university and I think I would feel more comfortable living with them. I would sleep better, which would also help improve my grades. I would also save a lot of money not living in the dormitory.
E – Ah ha, I see. I can actually relate to what you're talking about. My dorm room life was quite noisy. I was glad to move out and get my own place after I finished school. But I must remind you that the main reason why the university has the first and second years stay on campus is so that students can create good habits and do well on their studies. We wouldn't want the students to live off-campus and become distracted by outside activities. If students lived in the dorms, it would help them to stay focused. But, we do make exceptions for those who want to live at home with their family members. Here is the application for a housing exemption. If your application is approved, you will have to bring a proof of your family's residence, like a deed to their house, a rental contract, or a telephone bill. Basically a piece of paper with their names and an address.

E - 기숙사 사무실에 오신 것을 환영합니다! 무엇을 도와드릴까요?
S - 안녕하세요. 제 거주 계약에 대해 질문이 있습니다. 저는 1학년이고 제가 알기로, 대학 규칙에서 1학년과 2학년 학생들은 반드시 캠퍼스에서 살아야 한다고 정하고 있지요. 중요한 점은… 저는 브렌던 홀에 있는 룸메이트들과 지내는 것이 힘들어요.
E - 그렇군요. 기숙사 관리인과 얘기해 봤어요? 그들은 보통 이런 상황에서 도움을 줘요.
S - 음, 사실 나쁜 건 아니에요. 설명해 드릴게요. 저는 외동이에요. 그리고 형제나 자매가 없이 자라서, 저는 그저 한 무리의 사람들과 함께 사는 것에 익숙하지 않을 뿐이에요. 아무도 잘못한 건 없어요. 저희 부모님께서 우연히 이 대학 근처로 이사하셨고, 전 부모님과 함께 사는 것이 더 편할 것 같아요. 잠을 더 잘 자면 성적 향상에도 도움이 될 거예요. 또 기숙사에 살지 않으면 돈도 많이 절약될 거예요.
E - 아하, 그렇군요. 사실 학생이 무슨 말을 하는지 알겠어요. 제 기숙사 생활은 꽤 시끄러웠어요. 학교를 졸업하고 나가서 내 집을 갖게 돼 기뻤어요. 하지만 전 이 대학이 첫째, 둘째 해를 캠퍼스에 머물도록 하는 주된 이유가 학생들이 좋은 습관을 만들고 공부를 잘 할 수 있도록 하기 위해서라는 것을 학생에게 알려 주어야 해요. 우리는 학생들이 캠퍼스 밖에서 생활하고 외부 활동에 의해 산만해지는 것을 원하지 않아요. 만약 학생들이 기숙사에 산다면, 그들이 집중하는데 도움이 될 거예요. 하지만, 우리는 집에서 가족과 함께 살기를 원하는 사람들을 위해 예외를 두고 있습니다. 이것은 거주 면제를 위한 신청서입니다. 신청서가 승인되면 가족 거주 증명서, 임대 계약서, 전화 요금 명세서 등을 가져와야 합니다. 기본적으로 그들의 이름과 주소가 적힌 종이 한 장입니다.

S – That sounds great! I'm sorry to have bothered you on the matter… but like you said, it's important for students to stay focused in school. I don't want anything to get in the way of my studies.

E – You seem to be focused all right. Just bring back the application after you've filled it out. We should also discuss about your transportation. We have two parking lots on campus. Since first and second years are required to live on campus, the school does not give out parking permits to park in those lots. How do you plan on coming to school?

S – Hmm… I didn't know that parking permits would not be given to first year students. My parents live 30 minutes away and I was actually planning to drive to school.

E – I see…. That's going to be a problem….You know what? I just remembered that the city will be giving away free bus passes to university students! How does that sound?

S – That would be wonderful! Riding the bus would actually help me save money on gas.

E – Alright then! I know I have the application for that somewhere around here…. Here it is. **It says in the paper that you have to bring a copy of your class schedule, as well as your student ID. Do you know where the city's public transportation office is?**

S – **Isn't that the building next to the city hall?**

E – Yup. Ok, so here is the application for the housing exemption and the application for a student bus pass. Also, don't forget that we need the documents to prove where your family lives.

S – Yes. Thank you for your help!

S - 멋진데요! 이 문제로 귀찮게 해드려 죄송합니다… 말씀하신 것처럼 학생들이 학교에 집중하는 것은 중요해요. 전 어떤 것도 제 공부에 방해가 되는 것을 원하지 않습니다.

E - 당신은 잘 집중하고 있는 것 같아요. 신청서를 다 작성하면 다시 가져오세요. 우리는 또한 당신의 교통수단에 대해 논의해야 해요. 캠퍼스에는 주차장이 두 개 있습니다. 1학년과 2학년은 캠퍼스에서 생활해야 하기 때문에, 학교는 그 주차장에 주차할 수 있는 주차 허가증을 내주지 않아요. 당신은 학교에 어떻게 올 계획인가요?

S - 흠… 1학년 학생들에게 주차 허가증이 주어지지 않을 줄 몰랐어요. 우리 부모님은 30분 거리에 사시고, 전 사실 차로 학교에 다닐 계획이었어요.

E - 그렇군요. 그게 문제가 되겠네요… 그거 알고 있나요? 시에서 대학생들에게 무료 버스 승차권을 줄 것이라는 것이 방금 기억났어요! 어때요?

S - 정말 좋을 것 같아요! 버스를 타면 사실 기름값을 절약하는 데 도움이 될 거예요.

E - 그럼 좋습니다! 그 신청서가 이 근처 어딘가에 있어요. 여기 있어요. 신문에 당신이 학생증뿐만 아니라 수업 일정표 사본도 가져와야 한다고 쓰여 있어요. 시의 대중 교통 사무소가 어디 있는지 아세요?

S - 시청 옆에 있는 건물 아닌가요?

E - 네. 좋아요, 여기 거주 면제 신청서와 학생 버스 이용권 신청서가 있어요. 또한, 우리가 학생의 가족이 어디에 사는지 증명할 서류가 필요하다는 것을 잊지 마세요.

S - 예. 도와주셔서 감사합니다!

1) 학생은 왜 기숙사 사무실을 방문하는가?

   A) 요금을 낮추기 위해서
   B) 주차 허가증을 갱신하기 위해
   C) 룸메이트에 대한 불만 사항을 제출하기 위해
   D) 가족과 함께 살 수 있는 허가를 받기 위해

2) 학생은 캠퍼스 생활에 대해 어떻게 생각하는가?

   A) 그는 비싼 비용에 화가 나 있다.
   B) 그는 이것이 학교에 집중하는 데 도움이 된다고 생각한다.
   C) 그는 많은 사람들에게 둘러싸여 불편하다.
   D) 그는 많은 문제를 일으키는 룸메이트 때문에 골치 아파한다.

3) 이사를 가면 학생에게 무슨 문제가 생기는가?

   A) 그는 더 비싼 집세를 내야 할 것이다.
   B) 그는 학교에 차를 몰고 갈 수 없을 것이다.
   C) 그는 버스 정류장에서 멀리 떨어진 곳에 살 것이다.
   D) 그는 캠퍼스에서 친구를 사귀는 데 어려움을 겪을 것이다.

4) 학생은 왜 무료 버스 승차권에 기뻐하는가?

   A) 그의 등교 시간이 줄어들 것이다.
   B) 그는 기름값을 아낄 것이다.
   C) 그는 부모님의 차를 운전할 필요가 없을 것이다.
   D) 그는 주차 공간을 찾지 않아도 된다.

5) 다시 한 번 대화를 들으시오. 그 후 질문에 답하시오.
   직원은 왜 이렇게 말하는가?

   A) 사무실의 소재를 파악하기 위해
   B) 학생이 시청을 찾을 수 있도록 도와주기 위해
   C) 학생에게 위치를 알려주어야 하는지 알아보기 위해
   D) 학생이 어디서 학생증을 얻을 수 있는지 보여주기 위해

ANSWERS AND SCRIPT

Part 2 - Lecture

ANSWERS – 6(B) 7(A) 8(C) 9(D) 10(B) 11(C)

Last time we talked about the fundamentals of airplane design and how these designs are derived from the physique of birds. Specifically, the wings on the airplanes were modeled after the wings on a bird. Today, we will begin our lesson on the airplanes of the future. Nowadays, engineers are getting their influence for future airplane design from an unexpected, yet fascinating creature: bats. I believe that in the future, the airplanes that fly in the sky will be soaring with bat-like movement.

First, let's compare the structure of a bat wing with that of a bird wing. The main difference is that birds have feathers while bats have an elastic membrane, kind of like a stretchy skin. Another difference to note is that bats have more than two dozen joints, all independently moving in their wings. They are similar to the human hand, with five elongated extensions. This feature gives bats extreme flexibility. So they are able to decrease wind resistance by bending their wings backwards or forward after each flap. Birds on the other hand, have a more rigid bone structure in their wings. So birds must account for air resistance by shifting their feathers with each flap of their wings, which will allow air to pass through them.

The flexibility of the wings gives bats another advantage over birds and it involves vortexes. Remember that vortexes are currents of air created by wings that produce the lift needed by birds or bats from falling from the sky. Research has shown that birds can only create a single vortex with each flap of their wings. An experiment was carried out for a bat inside a wind tunnel to better understand their flying abilities. Scientists generated a strong wind inside the tunnel and added some fog so that they can observe how the air moved around the bat. What they uncovered was astounding. The bat was generating two vortexes, one vortex at the end of each wing.

지난 시간에는 비행기 디자인의 기본 원리와 이 디자인이 새의 체형에서 어떻게 유래 되었는지에 대해 이야기했습니다. 특히, 비행기의 날개는 새의 날개를 본떠 만들어졌습니다. 오늘, 우리는 미래의 비행기에 대한 수업을 시작할 것입니다. 오늘날, 엔지니어들은 예상치 못한, 그러나 매혹적인 생물인 박쥐로부터 미래의 비행기 디자인에 대한 영향을 받고 있습니다. 저는 미래에 하늘을 나는 비행기들이 박쥐와 같은 움직임으로 날아오를 것이라고 믿습니다.

먼저 박쥐 날개의 구조와 새 날개의 구조를 비교해 보겠습니다. 주요한 차이점은 새들은 깃털을 가지고 있고 박쥐들은 신축성 있는 피부와 같이 탄력 있는 막을 가지고 있다는 것입니다. 주목해야 할 또 다른 차이점은 박쥐는 24개가 넘는 관절이 있으며, 모두 날개 안에서 독립적으로 움직인다는 것입니다. 그것들은 가늘고 긴 다섯 개의 연장부를 지닌 인간의 손과 비슷합니다. 이 특징은 박쥐들에게 엄청난 유연성을 줍니다. 그래서 그들은 날개를 퍼덕인 후에 날개를 뒤 또는 앞으로 구부림으로써 바람의 저항을 줄일 수 있습니다. 반면에 새들은 날개에 더 단단한 뼈 구조를 가지고 있습니다. 그래서 새들은 날개를 퍼덕일 때마다 깃털을 이동시킴으로써 공기 저항을 이겨내야 하는데, 이것은 공기가 그들을 통과할 수 있게 해줄 것입니다.

날개의 유연성은 박쥐가 새보다 더 유리한 점들을 제공하는데, 여기에는 소용돌이가 포함됩니다. 소용돌이는 하늘에서 떨어지는 새나 박쥐에게 필요한 양력을 만들어내는, 날개에 의해 만들어진 공기의 흐름이라는 것을 기억하세요. 연구는 새들이 날개를 퍼덕일 때마다 하나의 소용돌이를 만들 수 있다는 것을 보여주었습니다. 박쥐의 비행 능력을 더 잘 이해하기 위해 풍동 안에서 박쥐를 위한 실험이 수행되었습니다. 과학자들은 터널 안에서 강한 바람을 일으키고 약간의 안개를 추가하여 박쥐 주위에서 공기가 어떻게 움직이는지를 관찰할 수 있도록 했습니다. 그들이 발견한 것은 큰 충격을 주었습니다. 박쥐는 두 개의 소용돌이, 즉 각 날개의 끝마다 하나의 소용돌이를 만들고 있었습니다.

So how is this relevant to flying? How can two vortexes improve the ability to fly? It turns out that this is crucial to the remarkable feat that bats have in flying. All flying objects… like birds, airplanes, and insects, need some space to turn while flying. However, bats do not need such space and are able to twist 180 degrees and fly instantly in the opposite direction. It appears that the wing's flexibility and the two vortexes allow the bats to perform this action. Engineers are particularly interested in this maneuverability. If they could somehow design an aircraft that can create two vortexes, it would be able to fly through forests and caves without breaking a sweat.

Another useful characteristic of a bat's wing is that bats are able to fly even while carrying a heavy load. For instance, female bats that are pregnant are still able to fly while carrying their babies. Remember that bats are mammals, so they carry their young during the gestation period and care for them even after birth. This is truly remarkable, considering the weight of a newborn bat is half the weight of an adult. If engineers could apply the same techniques in aircraft design, then future airplanes will be able to carry heavier loads.

Finally, the tiny hairs covering bat wings could help improve future planes. Biologists believe that the hairs serve as sensors to gather information from the air. This helps the bat to change its movements in response to changes in air flow. **What if engineers could install tiny sensors across the wings if an aircraft, and they were able to detect the tiniest changes in air pressure, wind pattern, and temperature? And the aircraft would have a computer to make split-second adjustments to the changes.** <u>Now that's the kind of assistant I'd like to fly with.</u>

그러면 이것이 비행과 어떤 관련이 있을까요? 두 개의 소용돌이가 어떻게 비행 능력을 향상시킬 수 있을까요? 이것은 박쥐가 가진 놀라운 비행 능력에서 매우 중요한 것으로 밝혀졌습니다. 새, 비행기, 곤충과 같은 모든 비행 물체는 비행하는 동안 회전할 공간이 필요합니다. 하지만 박쥐는 그러한 공간을 필요로 하지 않으며 180도 비틀어 즉시 반대 방향으로 날아갈 수 있습니다. 박쥐들은 날개의 유연성과 두 개의 소용돌이 덕분에 이 동작을 할 수 있는 것으로 보입니다. 엔지니어들은 특히 이 기동성에 관심이 있습니다. 만약 그들이 두 개의 소용돌이를 만들 수 있는 비행기를 설계할 수 있다면, 그것은 손쉽게 숲과 동굴을 날아갈 수 있을 것입니다.

박쥐 날개의 또 다른 유용한 특징은 박쥐가 무거운 짐을 운반하는 동안에도 날 수 있다는 것입니다. 예를 들어, 임신한 암컷 박쥐는 새끼를 품고도 여전히 날 수 있습니다. 박쥐는 포유동물이기 때문에 임신 기간 동안 새끼를 품고 다니며 태어난 후에도 그들을 돌본다는 것을 기억하세요. 갓 태어난 박쥐의 무게가 어른 박쥐의 절반인 것을 고려하면, 이것은 정말 놀라운 일입니다. 만약 엔지니어들이 항공기 설계에 동일한 기술을 적용할 수 있다면, 미래의 비행기들은 더 무거운 짐을 실을 수 있을 것입니다.

마지막으로, 박쥐의 날개를 덮는 작은 털들은 미래의 비행기를 개선하는 데 도움을 줄 수 있습니다. 생물학자들은 그 털들이 공기에서 정보를 수집하는 센서 역할을 한다고 믿습니다. 이것은 박쥐가 공기 흐름의 변화에 반응하여 움직임을 바꾸는 것을 돕습니다. 비행기의 경우, 만약 엔지니어들이 날개 쪽으로 작은 센서들을 설치하고 기압, 바람 패턴, 그리고 온도에서 생기는 가장 작은 변화들을 감지할 수 있다면 어떨까요? 그리고 항공기는 그 변화에 맞춰 순식간에 조정을 할 수 있는 컴퓨터를 탑재하게 될 것입니다. 이제 저는 그런 조수들과 함께 비행하고 싶습니다.

6) 강의의 핵심은 무엇인가?

A) 다양한 비행 방법
B) 항공기 엔지니어를 위한 새로운 영감
C) 박쥐와 새의 구조 비교
D) 소용돌이가 비행에 미치는 영향

7) 교수는 엔지니어들이 박쥐를 항공기의 모델로 사용하는 것에 대해 어떻게 느끼는가?

A) 그녀는 그들의 결과에 대해 긍정적으로 생각한다.
B) 그녀는 그것이 무의미할 것이라고 주장한다.
C) 그녀는 우리가 박쥐에 대해 최소한의 이해를 하고 있다고 믿는다.
D) 그녀는 새가 비행기 모델이 되는 것을 더 선호한다.

8) 박쥐의 날개는 새의 날개와 비교했을 때

A) 더 단단하다.
B) 사람의 손과 동일하지 않다.
C) 더 독립적인 관절을 보인다.
D) 깃털이 줄지어 있다.

9) 연구자들은 박쥐를 풍동 안에 넣고 무엇을 발견했는가?

A) 안개는 동물의 비행 능력을 방해했다.
B) 박쥐는 바람을 거슬러 날아가는 것에 비해 더 많은 에너지를 소비했다.
C) 박쥐의 날개는 강한 바람을 견딜 수 있다는 것을 보여주었다.
D) 박쥐는 날개에서 두 개의 소용돌이를 만들었다.

10) 교수는 왜 임신한 박쥐에 대해 이야기 하는가?

A) 박쥐의 임신 기간이 얼마나 긴지 보여주기 위해
B) 박쥐가 비행 중에 어느 정도의 무게를 지탱할 수 있는지 강조하기 위해
C) 박쥐가 포유류라는 점을 지적하기 위해
D) 박쥐의 생식률을 나타내기 위해

11) 강의 일부를 다시 들으시오. 그 후 질문에 답하시오.
  교수가 이 말을 할 때 무엇을 시사하는가?

  A) 최신 기내 기술에 대한 만족도를 나타내기 위해
  B) 대기 상태의 영향을 강조하기 위해
  C) 센서 기술이 얼마나 많은 도움을 제공할 것인지를 나타내기 위해
  D) 학생들이 조종사가 되도록 강요하기 위해

ANSWERS AND SCRIPT

Page.167~175

Part 2 – Conversation

ANSWERS – 1(C) 2(B) 3(B) 4(B) 5(C)

P – Hello Janet! How can I help you today?
S – Good morning professor. I wanted to discuss my research paper with you, along with the presentation that is due on Monday.
P – Alright. What did you want to talk about?
S – Well, I finished researching about my topic and managed to write most of the paper. I just started to plan for my presentation, but it seems that I lost my notes. So just out of curiosity, how important is the presentation?
P – You don't remember the importance of the presentation? That was one of the first things we talked about on the first day of class.
S – Well, I think I remember you saying that everyone had to give a presentation. But I think you said that it wouldn't be given a grade. I was wondering if you could make an exception for me. It's just going to be a lot of work to go back and put together the information I wrote on my notes that I lost.
P – Yes, I did mention that the presentation will not be given a grade, with the condition that you present it to class. After all, this is a history class and not public speaking. I wouldn't want anyone to get stressed while preparing for their presentation. So everyone is asked to do the presentation, but it will not be graded. However, if you decide to skip on the presentation, I will take away half of a letter grade from the research paper that you turn in. Do you understand?
S – OK, I guess I didn't focus on the latter part. Well then… can you give me an extension on the presentation? Perhaps I could give my presentation on Wednesday or Friday?
P – Unfortunately I can't do that. Remember that on Wednesday we have a review session, and on Friday we will have the exam. It's almost impossible for me to make any changes during the last week of class.
S – Yikes… I guess I'll just have do with what I have.
P – Well…. Have you been to the student mentoring office?
S – No I haven't. There's an office like that?

P – 안녕하세요 자넷! 오늘 어떻게 도와주면 될까요?
S – 안녕하세요 교수님. 월요일에 있을 발표와 제 연구 논문을 상의하고 싶습니다.
P – 알겠습니다. 무슨 얘기를 하고 싶은가요?
S – 글쎄요, 저는 제 주제에 대한 연구를 끝냈고 논문을 거의 다 쓸 수 있었습니다. 발표 준비를 막 시작했는데, 필기 해둔 것을 잃어버린 것 같아요. 그래서 그냥 궁금해서 여쭤보는 건데, 프레젠테이션이 얼마나 중요할까요?
P – 프레젠테이션의 중요성을 잘 모르나요? 그건 우리가 수업 첫날에 가장 먼저 이야기한 것들 중 하나였어요.
S – 음, 저는 교수님이 모든 사람이 프레젠테이션을 해야 한다고 말씀하셨던 것을 기억합니다. 하지만 교수님께서 그것엔 점수가 주어지지 않을 거라고 말씀하셨던 것 같아요. 저를 예외로 해 주실 수 있는지 궁금합니다. 잃어버렸던 필기에 적었던 정보들을 다시 정리하는 일은 엄청 많을 것 같아요.
P – 예, 강의 시간에 발표한다는 조건 하에 발표에는 점수가 주어지지 않을 것이라고 말씀 드렸습니다. 결국, 이건 역사 수업이고 대중 연설이 아니에요. 난 그 누구도 발표 준비를 하면서 스트레스 받길 원하지 않아요. 그래서 모든 사람이 발표를 해야 하지만, 점수는 매겨지지 않을 거예요. 하지만, 만약 학생이 발표를 건너뛰기로 결정한다면, 저는 학생이 제출한 연구 논문의 점수의 절반을 감점 시킬 겁니다. 이해가 되나요?
S – 네, 제가 후반부에 집중하지 않았던 것 같아요. 그럼 발표를 연장해 주실 수 있나요? 수요일이나 금요일에 발표를 할 수 있을까요?
P – 안타깝게도 그렇게 할 수 없습니다. 수요일에는 복습이 있고 금요일에는 시험이 있다는 것을 기억하세요. 수업 마지막 주 동안에 어떤 변경을 하는 건 거의 불가능해요.
S – 이런… 그냥 제가 가진 걸로 해야 할 것 같네요.
P – 음… 학생은 학생 멘토링 사무실에 가본 적이 있습니까?
S – 아니요. 그런 사무실이 있다고요?

P – It's actually similar to a tutoring service, but student volunteers run the program. When you walk in, you will meet with an upper classman, perhaps a junior or a senior, and they will assist you with whatever homework or assignments that you are having a problem with.
S – That's pretty cool. I think I might stop by sometime. But with this presentation, I'm not sure. I'm not even sure if I will have the time to go there before Monday. I do have to study for my other finals since it's the last week of the semester.
P – Ok then. How about referring to your research paper? Didn't you say you finished writing it?
S – Almost.
P – Well then, I suggest you use your research paper in place of your presentation notes. In fact, you could spend a few minutes writing down the information in the paper onto a new set of notes.
S – I guess I could do that. Oh that reminds me, didn't you mention a while back that the history department will be hosting an essay competition?
P – Yes I did. The department rewards a scholarship to one student every semester based on the essay they turn in.
S – Can I get more information on that? I have to say, this research paper I wrote for you has to be one of the finest essays I have ever written. The scholarship could sure help me with my tuition next semester.
P – Sure. Just go over and talk to the department advisor, Professor Stevens. He is in charge of the program and he will give you an application with more instructions.
S – Umm, I'm sorry professor, but where is the history department building?
P – It's next to the administration office. Aren't you majoring in history?
S – No… I'm actually majoring in biology.
P – Oh.. I'm sorry then. This scholarship can only be applied by history majors and minors.
S – Well, I was thinking about minoring in history.
P – In that case, talk to the department advisor to minor in history.
S – I will. Thank you professor.

P - 그건 실제로 튜터링 서비스와 비슷한데, 학생 자원봉사자들이 프로그램을 운영합니다. 학생이 들어가면, 상급생, 아마도 2학년, 3학년과 만나게 될 것입니다. 그리고 그들은 학생이 골치 아파하는 어떤 숙제나 과제를 도와줄 거예요.
S - 정말 멋지네요. 언젠가 한번 들를 것 같아요. 하지만 이번 발표는, 잘 모르겠네요. 월요일 전에 제가 거기에 갈 시간이 있을지조차 잘 모르겠어요. 학기 마지막 주라서 다른 기말고사 때문에 공부를 해야 해요.
P - 그럼. 학생의 연구 논문을 참조하는 것은 어떻습니까? 다 썼다고 하지 않았나요?
S - 거의요.
P - 그렇다면 발표 노트 대신 연구 논문을 사용할 것을 권합니다. 사실, 학생은 몇 분만에 새롭게 필기를 할 수 있을 거예요.
S - 그렇게 할 수 있을 것 같아요. 아, 그거 생각나네요, 얼마 전에 역사학부에서 에세이 대회를 개최할 거라고 얘기하지 않으셨어요?
P - 네. 그 부서는 매 학기마다 학생들이 제출하는 에세이를 바탕으로 학생 한 명에게 장학금을 지급합니다.
S - 자세한 정보를 얻을 수 있을까요? 제가 교수님을 위해 쓴 이 연구 논문은 제가 지금까지 쓴 것 중 가장 훌륭한 논문 중 하나일 거예요. 장학금은 제가 다음 학기에 등록금을 내는데 도움이 될 거예요.
P - 물론이죠. 학과장인 스티븐스 교수에게 가서 이야기해 보세요. 그는 그 프로그램을 담당하고 있고 학생에게 더 많은 지도와 함께 신청서를 줄 거예요.
S - 음, 교수님, 죄송하지만 역사학과 건물은 어디에 있나요?
P - 행정실 옆에 있습니다. 학생은 역사를 전공하고 있지 않나요?
S - 아니요… 사실 저는 생물학을 전공하고 있어요.
P - 오… 그럼 안됐네요. 이 장학금은 역사 전공자와 부전공자만이 신청할 수 있어요.
S - 음, 저는 역사를 부전공 하려고 생각하고 있었어요.
P - 그런 경우라면, 역사학과 학과장에게 부전공에 대해 상담하세요.
S - 그럴게요. 교수님 감사합니다.

ANSWERS AND SCRIPT

1) 학생은 왜 교수를 방문했는가?

   A) 연구 논문을 제출하기 위해
   B) 그녀가 장학금을 받을 자격이 있는지 확인하기 위해
   C) 발표를 하는 것에 대해 양해를 구하기 위해
   D) 연구 논문의 요건을 확인하기 위해

2) 대화에 따르면, 왜 발표 점수가 매겨지지 않는가?

   A) 학기가 거의 끝났기 때문에
   B) 강좌의 실제 주제와 무관하기 때문에
   C) 완료하는 데 많은 시간이 걸리지 않기 때문에
   D) 추가 학점이 필요한 사람을 위한 것이기 때문에

3) 교수는 학생의 발표와 관련한 문제에 대해 어떤 제안을 하는가?

   A) 그녀의 수업 필기를 살펴본다.
   B) 학생 튜터로부터 도움을 받는다.
   C) 같은 강의를 듣는 학생에게 도움을 요청한다.
   D) 복습 강의에 참여한다.

4) 대화의 일부를 다시 들으시오. 그 후 질문에 답하시오.
   학생이 이렇게 말할 때 이것은 무엇을 의미하는가?

   A) 그녀는 자신의 프로젝트를 위해 무엇을 해야 할지 잘 모르겠다.
   B) 그녀는 튜터링 서비스에 참여하지 않을 것이다.
   C) 그녀는 다른 사람이 자신의 프로젝트를 이해할 수 있을지 의문이다.
   D) 그녀는 아직 발표 주제를 정하지 않았다.

5) 대화에 따르면 이런 경우 역사 장학금은 지급되지 않는다.

   A) 학생이 역사를 단순히 부전공 할 경우
   B) 학생이 학점을 충분히 이수하지 못했을 경우
   C) 학생이 역사학과가 아닌 과를 전공할 경우
   D) 학생에게 추천서가 없는 경우

Part 2 - Lecture

ANSWERS – 6(A) 7(C) 8(A) 9(A) 10(C) 11(B)

P – Shall we get started? Last time in class, we discussed some of the radical movements in modern music. Today we will be talking about the evolution of Western music by focusing on its origins. Can anyone tell me when humans first began to play music?

S – Well, I'm not sure if it is considered music, but I remember reading about early humans and how they used sound-making devices for communication.

P – That's actually worth mentioning. Can anyone tell me what music exactly is? Modern society classifies music as an organization of sound and rhythm. The parts are put together in creative ways so that it is pleasant to listen. So entertainment is one important purpose of music. What about noise makers, like the one you mentioned used by early human? The prehistoric instruments were found in various places all around world and date back several thousand years. Some of these instruments are made of specially carved wood, stone, or bone and had a hole on one end with a cord strung around it. When they spun the instrument in the air, the instrument would make a single, low pitch tone, capable of delivering the sound great distances. Historians probably think that our ancestors back then used these instruments to communicate with one another, but it could have also been used as musical instruments. Can anyone think of another instrument that appeared even earlier?

S – How about the flutes made out of really old bones?

P – There you go! In 2009, archaeologists discovered a flute that was 35,000 years old. It had five holes drilled along the bone, which proved that people were composing music with several tones. So that means even during the Stone Age, our ancestors were already making music inside their caves.

However, historians can safely say that this bone flute was not actually the first musical instrument.

P - 시작할까요? 지난 수업 시간에, 우리는 현대 음악의 급진적 운동에 대해 토론했습니다. 오늘 우리는 서양 음악의 기원에 초점을 맞추어 서양 음악의 진화에 대해 이야기 할 것입니다. 사람들이 언제 처음으로 음악을 연주하기 시작했는지 누가 말해줄 수 있나요?

S - 음, 이것이 음악으로 간주되는지는 잘 모르겠지만, 초기 인류가 의사소통을 위해 소리를 내는 장치를 사용하는 방법에 대해 읽은 기억이 납니다.

P - 그건 실제로 언급할 가치가 있습니다. 누군가 음악이 정확하게 무엇인지 말해줄 수 있나요? 현대 사회는 음악을 소리와 리듬의 구성으로 분류합니다. 각 부분들은 듣기 좋도록 창의적인 방법으로 조합됩니다. 그래서 오락은 음악의 중요한 목적 중 하나입니다. 초기 인류에 의해 사용된 딸랑이 같이 소리를 만드는 물건은 어떨까요? 선사시대의 악기들은 전 세계 여러 곳에서 발견되었고 수 천 년 전으로 거슬러 올라갑니다. 이 악기들 중 일부는 특별하게 조각된 나무, 돌, 또는 뼈로 만들어졌고 한쪽 끝에는 끈이 달려 있는 구멍이 나 있었습니다. 그들이 공중에서 악기를 돌리면, 그 악기는 소리를 아주 멀리 전달할 수 있는, 하나의 낮은 음조를 만들었을 것입니다. 역사가들은 아마도 그 당시 우리 조상들이 서로 의사소통을 하기 위해 이 악기들을 사용했다고 생각할 것입니다. 하지만 그것은 또한 연주를 위한 악기로도 사용될 수 있었을 것입니다. 더 먼저 등장한 또 다른 악기가 생각나는 사람 있나요?

S - 오래된 뼈로 만든 플루트는 어떤가요?

P - 바로 그것입니다! 2009년, 고고학자들은 35,000년 된 피리를 발견했습니다. 그것은 뼈를 따라 다섯 개의 구멍을 뚫었고, 이것은 사람들이 몇 개의 음조로 음악을 작곡했다는 것을 증명했습니다. 그래서 그것은 심지어 석기 시대에도, 우리의 조상들이 이미 동굴 안에서 음악을 만들고 있었다는 것을 의미합니다. 하지만, 역사가들은 이 뼈 피리가 실제로 최초의 악기는 아니라고 확실하게 말할 수 있습니다.

In fact, our body, particularly the hyoid bone is considered as the first musical instrument. The hyoid bone is the structure in your throat which makes it possible for you to talk and sing. The first fossil of a hyoid bone dates back 60,000 years. Of course, we have no idea if humans that long ago sang, but if archaeologists discovered flutes dating back 35,000 years, then we can make a safe assumption that our ancestors had some understanding of music even further down the road. Now, the ancient musical instruments we have discussed so far can all produce different musical tones. However, something is still missing. Can you guess what it is?

S – Oh I know! Rhythm!

P – **Exactly. With these early forms of music, there was no way to add rhythm in a systematic way. Remember that the earliest music were made up of single notes. Later on, people would add changes in pitch. Tonal patterns appeared as people developed their sound, however rhythm was still missing from their music. Rather boring, don't you think?** It was during the baroque period that musicians began to incorporate well-conceived rhythmic patterns into their music. Baroque music truly is different compared to the music before its time. The baroque period introduced a rhythm called common time. Yes, you have a question?

S – Isn't common time similar to the counts in a human heartbeat?

P – You are correct. That's something that you will hear a lot when talking about baroque music. Let me explain. Common time is a steady count of four beats, which also happens to be the same pattern and number of beats in our heart. Interestingly, studies have shown that our heartbeats will increase or decrease to match the rhythm of a music. That's why when you go to a party and listen to some fast tracks, your heart rate increases, but when listen to slow ballad music, your heartrate drops.

사실, 우리의 몸, 특히 목뿔뼈는 최초의 악기로 여겨집니다. 목뿔뼈는 여러분이 말하고 노래하는 것을 가능하게 하는 목의 구조입니다. 목뿔뼈의 첫 화석은 6만년 전으로 거슬러 올라갑니다. 물론, 우리는 오래 전에 인간이 노래를 불렀는지는 알 수 없지만, 만약 고고학자들이 35,000년 전의 플루트를 발견했다면, 우리는 조상들이 훨씬 더 이전에 음악에 대해 어느 정도 이해하고 있었다고 추측할 수 있습니다. 자, 우리가 지금까지 논의한 고대 악기는 모두 다른 음색을 낼 수 있습니다. 하지만, 여전히 뭔가가 빠져 있습니다. 그게 뭔지 추측할 수 있나요?

S – 오 알겠어요! 리듬!

P – 정확합니다. 이러한 초기 형태의 음악 가운데, 체계적인 방법으로 리듬을 더할 수 있는 방법은 없었습니다. 초기의 음악은 하나의 음으로 이루어져 있었다는 것을 기억하세요. 나중에 사람들은 음의 변화를 더했습니다. 발성 패턴은 사람들이 소리를 발달시키면서 나타났지만, 리듬은 여전히 음악에서 빠져 있었습니다. 지루했을 것 같지 않나요? 음악가들이 그들의 음악에 잘 구상된 리듬 패턴을 통합하기 시작한 것은 바로크 시대였습니다. 바로크 음악은 그 시대 이전의 음악과 비교했을 때 정말 다릅니다. 바로크 시대에는 4분의 4박자라고 불리는 리듬을 도입했습니다. 네, 질문 있으세요?

S – 4분의 4박자는 사람의 심장 박동수와 비슷하지 않나요?

P – 맞습니다. 그것은 바로크 음악에 대해 이야기할 때 여러분이 많이 듣게 될 것입니다. 제가 설명해 드릴게요. 4분의 4박자는 네 개의 비트를 일정하게 세고, 이것은 또한 우리 심장과 같은 패턴과 박동 수를 보입니다. 흥미롭게도, 연구들은 우리의 심장 박동이 음악의 리듬에 맞추어 증가하거나 감소할 것이라는 것을 보여주었습니다. 그렇기 때문에 파티에 가서 빠른 곡을 들으면 심박수가 올라가지만 느린 발라드 음악을 들으면 심박수는 떨어집니다.

6) 논의의 핵심은 무엇인가?

   A) 음악의 역사
   B) 초기 음악의 리듬
   C) 다양한 노래 기법
   D) 서양 음악 이론의 기본 요소

7) 연구자들은 여러 곳에서 발견된 선사 시대의 악기가 주로 이것을 위해 사용되었다고 본다.

   A) 사냥 시 동물에게 혼란을 준다.
   B) 뮤지컬 공연
   C) 먼 거리에 있는 다른 사람과 의사소통한다.
   D) 중요한 이벤트

8) 고대 음악에 대한 교수의 의견은 무엇인가?

   A) 오락을 포함한 다른 용도로도 사용됐을 수 있다.
   B) 그것은 아시아에서 시작되었다.
   C) 복잡한 사운드 패턴으로 연주되었다.
   D) 음향 효과가 없는 물체를 사용하였다.

9) 뼈 플루트가 왜 그렇게 중요한가?

   A) 석기 시대에 인간이 의도적으로 음악을 만들었다는 것을 증명했다.
   B) 인간이 처음으로 음악을 연주하기 시작한 때를 보여준다.
   C) 현대 플루트의 디자인 모델이 되었다.
   D) 오래 전에 인간이 오락을 중요하게 여겼다는 것을 나타낸다.

ANSWERS AND SCRIPT

10) 논의의 일부를 들으시오. 그 후 질문에 답하시오.
   교수가 이렇게 말할 때 유추할 수 있는 것은?

   A) 그는 음조보다 리듬이 더 중요하다고 생각한다.
   B) 그는 성악을 좋아하지 않는다.
   C) 그는 좋은 음악에는 리듬이 매우 중요하다고 믿는다.
   D) 그는 오늘날의 음악이 초기 음악의 리듬감 있는 패턴을 잃어가고 있다고 생각한다.

11) 교수는 왜 4분의 4박자에 대해 이야기 하는가?

   A) 바로크와 초기 음악을 비교하기 위해
   B) 음악의 리듬이 어떻게 통합되었는지 보여주기 위해
   C) 바로크 음악이 인기 있는 이유를 설명하기 위해
   D) 음악에서 그것의 중요성을 기술하기 위해

Part 2 – Lecture

ANSWERS – 12(C) 13(B) 14(A) 15(D) 16(C) 17(Chlorophyll: B,D / Carotenoids: A / Anthocyanin: C)

P – So far in class, we have been discussing about the root systems in plants. Remember that they hold the plants in place and are the starting points for their circulatory system. We will be continuing our lesson on plant anatomy by turning out attention to leaves. It is here that food is produced for the plants in a process called photosynthesis. The energy that drives photosynthesis is provided by a cellular structure called chlorophyll, which also happens to give leaves their green hue. Photosynthesis is a complex process that involves carbon dioxide, water, and energy to create sugar and other necessary nutrients.

I'm sure all of you have noticed that leaves lose their green hue and turn brown and orange in the fall. But why do they change color? Here's why. When the temperature starts to fall and the daylight hours shorten, the trees will start to prepare for the coming of winter. Since the leaves eventually fall off, there is no need to continue expending energy in the making of more chlorophyll. So the tree produces less and eventually stops its production completely. When the chlorophyll inside the leaves break down, the green hue produced by it also disappears. Yes, you have a question?

S – I understand why leaves lose their green color, but I don't understand how some plants have red leaves all year long, and not just in the fall.

P – That's a good observation. Let's look at the chemicals that actually cause the pigmentation. People commonly believe that all leaves are green, since most plants are. But as your classmate pointed out, some are red, while others are pink or purple. There are various shades of color in between. These different colors are a result of three different chemicals. The first, I already mentioned, is chlorophyll, which produces the green color and is responsible for photosynthesis. The second chemical is called anthocyanin, which is in charge of the red, purple, and blue coloration. For many years, scientists believed that this chemical was of minimal importance.

P - 지금까지 우리는 식물의 뿌리 시스템에 대해 논의해 왔습니다. 뿌리가 식물들을 제자리에 세우고, 순환 시스템의 시작점이라는 것을 기억하세요. 우리는 나뭇잎으로 주의를 돌려 식물 해부학에 대한 수업을 계속할 것입니다. 여기가 바로 광합성이라고 불리는 과정에서 식물을 위한 식량이 생산되는 지점입니다. 광합성을 촉진하는 에너지는 엽록소라고 불리는 세포 구조에 의해 공급되는데, 엽록소는 또한 잎이 녹색을 띠게 합니다. 광합성은 당과 필요한 다른 영양소를 만들기 위해 이루어지는 이산화탄소, 물, 에너지를 포함하는 복잡한 과정이에요.

여러분은 모두들 나뭇잎이 가을에 녹색을 잃고 갈색과 주황색으로 변한다는 것을 알아챘을 거예요. 하지만 그들은 왜 색을 바꿀까요? 그 이유는 이렇습니다. 기온이 떨어지기 시작하고 낮 시간이 짧아지면, 나무들은 겨울이 올 준비를 시작할 것입니다. 잎들이 결국 떨어지기 때문에, 더 많은 엽록소를 만드는데 에너지를 계속 쓸 필요가 없습니다. 그래서 나무는 엽록소를 덜 생산하고 결국엔 생산을 완전히 중단합니다. 잎 내부의 엽록소가 분해되면, 엽록소가 만들어내는 녹색 빛깔도 사라집니다. 네, 질문 있으세요?

S - 나뭇잎이 왜 녹색을 잃었는지는 이해가 되지만, 몇 식물들이 어떻게 해서 가을뿐만 아니라 일 년 내내 붉은 잎을 가지고 있는지 이해할 수 없어요.

P - 좋은 관찰입니다. 색소 형성을 일으키는 화학 물질에 대해 알아보겠습니다. 대부분의 식물들이 녹색이기 때문에 사람들은 보통 모든 잎들이 녹색이라고 믿습니다. 하지만 여러분의 친구가 지적했듯이, 어떤 것들은 빨간색이고, 다른 것들은 분홍색이나 보라색입니다. 그 사이에는 다양한 색조가 있습니다. 이 다른 색깔들은 세 가지 다른 화학 물질의 결과입니다. 제가 이미 언급했듯이, 첫 번째는 엽록소입니다. 엽록소는 녹색을 생산하고 광합성을 담당합니다. 두 번째 화학 물질은 안토시아닌이라고 불리며, 빨간색, 보라색, 파란색을 담당합니다. 수년 동안 과학자들은 이 화학 물질의 중요성이 아주 작다고 믿었습니다.

ANSWERS AND SCRIPT

Some researchers proposed that the chemical warded off predators of plants, like herbivores and insects. This makes sense because some herbivores are color-blind to the color red. But still, this logic is not strongly supported since others have argued that the color red actually attracts animals to help pollinate and spread seeds. And I must say, I agree with them.

A more reliable research shows that anthocyanin might help protect plants from the sun. During the hot and bright days of summer, ultraviolet radiation and other wavelengths of light cannot be processed by chlorophyll. These wavelengths can actually cause damage to the leaves and can stop photosynthesis. Also, anthocyanin happens to be an antioxidant, so it can block harmful oxidation inside the cells of plants.

The final chemical responsible for coloration is called carotenoids. It includes the chemical carotene, and is responsible for the colors yellow and orange. Carotenoids help chlorophyll by absorbing energy from sunlight to be used in photosynthesis. And like anthocyanin, it creates a protective barrier for chlorophyll and blocks harmful wavelengths of light.

S – Professor, how does a plant not having chlorophyll, but have anthocyanin survive?

P – Well, all plants have varying amounts of these three chemicals. The different amount of chemicals, as well as the acidity in the leaves, produces the colors that we see. So all plants contain chlorophyll because without it, plants would not be able to produce the nutrients they need to live. Likewise, all plants have anthocyanin and carotenoids. These chemicals help absorb sunlight's energy and protect chlorophylls from dangerous wavelengths of sunlight.

일부 연구원들은 이 화학 물질이 초식 동물이나 곤충과 같은 식물의 포식자들을 물리칠 것이라고 제안하였습니다. 일부 초식 동물은 빨간색에 대하여 색맹이기 때문에 이것은 일리 있습니다. 하지만 여전히, 다른 사람들은 빨간색이 실제로 동물들을 유혹하여 수분시키고 씨앗을 퍼뜨리는 것을 돕는다고 주장했기 때문에 이 논리는 강하게 지지 되지 않았습니다. 그리고 저는 분명히 말해, 그들에게 동의합니다.

좀 더 신뢰할 수 있는 연구는 안토시아닌이 태양으로부터 식물을 보호하는데 도움을 줄 수 있다는 것을 보여 줍니다. 여름의 뜨겁고 밝은 날 동안에, 자외선과 다른 파장의 빛은 엽록소에 의해 처리될 수 없습니다. 이 파장들은 실제로 나뭇잎에 손상을 줄 수 있고 광합성을 멈추게 할 수 있습니다. 또한, 안토시아닌은 항산화제여서 식물의 세포 안에서 해로운 산화를 막을 수 있습니다.

색채를 띠게 하는 마지막 화학물질을 카로티노이드라고 부릅니다. 그것은 화학적 카로틴을 포함하고, 노란색과 주황색을 만듭니다. 카로티노이드들은 광합성에 이용되는 햇빛을 흡수함으로써 엽록소를 돕습니다. 그리고 안토시아닌처럼, 그것은 엽록소에 대한 보호 장벽을 만들고 해로운 빛의 파장을 막습니다.

S – 교수님, 엽록소가 없이 안토시아닌만 가진 식물은 어떻게 살아남나요?

P – 음, 모든 식물은 이 세 가지 화학 물질을 서로 다른 양으로 함유하고 있습니다. 나뭇잎의 산성뿐만 아니라 다른 양의 화학 물질도 우리가 보는 색깔을 만들어 냅니다. 모든 식물들은 엽록소를 가지고 있습니다. 왜냐하면 그것이 없이는 식물들이 살아가는 데 필요한 영양분을 생산할 수 없기 때문입니다. 마찬가지로, 모든 식물들은 안토시아닌과 카로티노이드를 가지고 있습니다. 이 화학 물질들은 햇빛의 에너지를 흡수하고 엽록소를 햇빛에서 오는 위험한 파장으로부터 보호하는 데 도움을 줍니다.

12) 강의의 핵심은 무엇인가?

A) 식물의 뿌리 체계
B) 광합성의 과정
C) 잎에서 특정 화학 물질의 중요성
D) 식물의 잎에서 식량을 생산하는 방법

13) 강의에 따르면, 왜 겨울에 나뭇잎이 갈색과 주황색으로 변하는가?

A) 일광 시간의 단축되어서
B) 엽록소가 분해되어서
C) 식물이 에너지를 저장하기 시작해서
D) 저온에서는 광합성이 중단 되어서

14) 교수는 안토시아닌이 초식 동물을 오지 못하게 한다는 이론에 대해 어떻게 생각하는가?

A) 그녀는 그것에 오해의 소지가 있다고 믿는다.
B) 그녀는 더 많은 연구가 필요하다고 생각한다.
C) 그녀는 그것이 인기를 끌 것이라고 확신한다.
D) 그녀는 그 이론이 교과서에 포함되기를 원한다.

15) 광합성에 대해 추론할 수 있는 것은?

A) 엽록소를 만든다.
B) 식물 세포의 유해한 산화를 막는다.
C) 나뭇잎에 화려한 빛깔을 낸다.
D) 특정 파장의 빛을 사용할 수 없다.

16) 강의에 따르면 카로티노이드의 한 가지 목적은 무엇인가?

A) 산화를 중단한다.
B) 안토시아닌을 분해한다.
C) 엽록소의 손상을 방지한다.
D) 종자의 번식을 촉진한다.

ANSWERS AND SCRIPT

17) 다음 중 적절한 화학 물질에 속하는 것은?
각 구에 대해 올바른 칸에 체크하시오.

	엽록소	카로티노이드	안토시아닌
A) 노란색			
B) 초록색			
C) 빨간색			
D) 광합성을 위한 에너지를 공급함